The Critical Situation

The Critical Situation

Vexed Perspectives in Postmodern Literary Studies

Robert T. Tally Jr.

ANTHEM PRESS

Anthem Press
An imprint of Wimbledon Publishing Company
www.anthempress.com

This edition first published in UK and USA 2025
by ANTHEM PRESS
75–76 Blackfriars Road, London SE1 8HA, UK
or PO Box 9779, London SW19 7ZG, UK
and
244 Madison Ave #116, New York, NY 10016, USA

First published in the UK and USA by Anthem Press in 2023

© 2025 Robert T. Tally Jr.

The moral right of the author has been asserted.

All rights reserved. Without limiting the rights under copyright reserved above,
no part of this publication may be reproduced, stored or introduced into
a retrieval system, or transmitted, in any form or by any means
(electronic, mechanical, photocopying, recording or otherwise),
without the prior written permission of both the copyright owner
and the above publisher of this book.

British Library Cataloguing-in-Publication Data
A catalogue record for this book is available from the British Library.

Library of Congress Control Number: 2025935911

ISBN-13: 978-1-83999-616-0 (Pbk)
ISBN-10: 1-83999-616-1 (Pbk)

This title is also available as an e-book.

For Youngmin Kim

CONTENTS

Introduction: The Situation of Criticism — 1

Part I   Critical Positioning Systems — 9

1. Swerve, Trope, Peripety: Turning Points in Cultural Criticism and Theory — 11
2. The Aesthetics of Distance: Space, *Weltliteratur*, and Critique — 25
3. World Literature and Its Discontents — 41
4. Worlding Space: Spatial Literary Studies and the Planetary Turn — 59
5. In the File Drawer Labeled "Science Fiction": Genre after the Age of the Novel — 71

Part II   Post-Americanist Interpolations — 87

6. "Believing in America": The Ideology of American Studies — 89
7. "Some men ride on such space": Charles Olson's *Call Me Ishmael*, the Melville Revival, and the American Baroque — 105
8. The Southern Phoenix Triumphant: The Consequences of Richard Weaver's Ideas — 123
9. Bleeping Mark Twain?: Censorship, *Huckleberry Finn*, and the Functions of Literature — 147
10. I Am the Mainstream Media (and So Can You!): The Hyperreality of "Fake News" — 159

Part III   Errant Trajectories in Postmodern Critical Practice — 179

11. Nomadography: Gilles Deleuze and the History of Philosophy — 181
12. Power to the Educated Imagination!: Northrop Frye and the Utopian Impulse — 195

13. Edward Said and Marxism: Wars of Position in
    Oppositional Criticism   209

14. An American Bakhtin: Jonathan Arac, or, the Vocation
    of the Critic   227

15. Bathsheba's Stomach: *Poiesis* and Criticism in
    Paul A. Bové's *Love's Shadow*   243

Conclusion: An Anagogical Education   251

Acknowledgments   257

Index   259

Introduction

THE SITUATION OF CRITICISM

Among his other prodigious contributions to literature, a great many of Jean-Paul Sartre's writings on literary and cultural criticism were published over the course of thirty years in ten volumes, each bearing the title *Situations*. (We know them as *Situations I–X*, with individual volumes bearing different subtitles, published between 1947 and 1976.) It is telling, but not surprising, that Sartre would use this title, for his philosophy was rooted in what Fredric Jameson has referred to as "the logic of the situation," which entails a thoroughgoing recognition of the fundamental situatedness of the individual subject in relation to others at all times and places. We find ourselves, always and already, in a certain situation, which conditions our sense of self and our comportment toward the world. This a fairly basic, existential reality, but by engaging in critical practice, we find ourselves especially attuned to the ways that the situations in which we find both ourselves and the texts under consideration affect the project in innumerable ways. The situation of criticism is, in this sense, doubly situated, for it entails a persistent consciousness of its own situation while assessing other situations. In describing his attraction to the dialectic, for example, which is also to say his sense of how a properly critical practice would work, Jameson has said that "the emphasis on the logic of the situation, the constant changeability of the situation, its primacy and the way in which it allows certain things to be possible and others not: that would lead to a kind of thinking I would call dialectical."[1] Whether it be explicitly characterized as dialectical or not, criticism is always practiced from and with respect to a given situation, and the awareness and consideration of the situatedness of both the critic's subjective position and the objects of critique are essential aspects of literary and cultural criticism.

The Critical Situation: Vexed Perspectives in Postmodern Literary Studies comprises a selection of essays that register this sense of situatedness amid various intellectual, institutional, and cultural contexts. The title is, in part, a play on words, for the expression "a critical situation" is well known outside of academic literary studies to refer to matters of great urgency, often alarming and dangerous. Such significance makes this title far too grandiose for the present purposes; the essays contained in this volume concern less pressing issues, to be sure. Nor do the selected essays in this book purport to weigh in on "the situation of criticism" today, certainly not in any definitive sense, but not even in the more limited sphere of academic discourse, although I hope they can contribute in some small way to this important discussion.[2] *The Critical Situation* offers a handful of examples of situated criticism, which in turn are concerned with the ways in which literary and cultural criticism are and have been situated in relation to a variety of ideological and institutional structures. These structures continue to influence the ways that criticism is practiced, and due recognition of their continuing effects seems to me to be crucial to the success of any meaningful critical practice in the twenty-first century.

More surprising, for some readers, than the use of the phrase "critical situation" may be the characterizations of these perspectives as "vexed" and of the broader field in which they occur as "postmodern." I will come back to my vexation in a moment, but first, let me explain why I believe the term *postmodern* continues to resonate so many years after its apparent heyday. As several of the essays in this collection discuss, the development of academic literary criticism, of English and of American Studies as disciplinary fields, and of literary theory as its own form of critical practice is a distinctively modern phenomenon. Indeed, these may be parts of a broader panoply of *modernist* phenomena, as historians of criticism from Gerald Graff to Joseph North and others have shown. The transformations of those areas of study after the 1960s may well have indicated, and been part of, the transition to a postmodern condition, which must have been how it felt to many critics during that period.

My own use of "postmodern literary studies" in the subtitle of this volume is probably an unconscious (or, at least, an initially unintended) nod toward Jonathan Arac's in *Critical Genealogies: Historical Situations in Postmodern Literary Studies* (1989),[3] which attempted to delineate some of the trajectories that led from the present back to a number of rich and varied critical traditions, thus making connections between them that ultimately flesh out a more complete picture of criticism in our own time. If the term "postmodern" itself seems dated, now that we are somehow *post-postmodern* (as Jeffrey Nealon's 2012 study of the present would label our moment), it is undoubtedly because of the powers of commodification so prevalent in "late" (or "just-in-time") capitalism all-too-readily turn even the most tentative inklings of thought into "brands" to be marketed, distributed, exploited, and rendered obsolete in a timely manner. But that is also a feature of the postmodern condition itself, so in certain respects, the attempt to "think the present," as Fredric Jameson famously put it in his still essential *Postmodernism, or, the Cultural Logic of Late Capital* (1991), is a distinctively postmodern act.[4]

Needless to say, much has changed since the "postmodernism" of the 1980s, and for literary criticism and the conditions under which it is practiced, much has changed for the worse. Above all, the persistent assault on higher education by both separate and concerted efforts of partisans hoping to "starve the beast" (i.e., cut taxes so government spending would have to be curtailed), neoliberal dogmatists who transformed the very idea of education into a mere investment made on behalf on one's individual (economic) interests, administrators aiming to "run" colleges "like a business" (thus reducing students to customers, faculty to service providers, and entire educational institutions to shopping malls), moralizing crusaders out to punish those needing student loans and bankers eager to profit off them (e.g., the Bankruptcy Abuse Prevention and Consumer Protection Act of 2005, which made it nearly impossible to discharge student debt, effectively declaring war on the poor and on those who aspired to higher education), and the feckless promoters of all manner of educational scams (e.g., "Trump University," which was hardly much different from many other such models), some of whose "pitches" are hardly distinguishable from the supposedly more legitimate recruitment efforts at major universities ... these postmodern phenomena, among many others, have transformed higher education in the United States (and elsewhere, of course) nearly beyond recognition, when compared to what things looked like four or five decades ago. The overreliance on non-tenure track faculty to teach the students mired in this odious system is, in part, a feature built into these policies and practices. In all fields, natural sciences and math just as much as in the arts, humanities, and social sciences, this has proved incredibly detrimental to everyone involved, and in the aggregate, this has had immeasurable, deleterious effects on higher education in general.

As for literary criticism and theory, one cannot even imagine the toll, and yet the efflorescence of truly amazing critical work in our time is remarkable. In many cases, it is produced by critics in the most precarious circumstances, which is not just unfortunate, but well-nigh criminal. Rita Felski in *Hooked: Art and Attachment* (2020) has lamented that, given the "beleaguered condition of the humanities," a "rising class of para-academics" has been forced to "sustain their intellectual passions by writing in online venues"—*quelle horreur!*—a sign that their desire for critique is real but also misdirected. But anyone who reads the work of such critics in such places as the *Los Angeles Review of Books* knows that vital criticism of the highest level is going on there, not to mention that it is often written by those who are not technically "para-academics," whatever that means. As Sheila Liming has noted, it is not these writers or the venues that have made it difficult for literary criticism to thrive, but rather the institutions in which critics and criticism have formerly been situated. Postmodern literary studies cannot help but be part of this system, and undoubtedly the direction criticism takes in the future will be guided by, but perhaps also resist and help to change, the material circumstances in which it is produced.[5]

These conditions are themselves part and parcel of what is meant by "postmodern literary studies" in the current context. To be *vexed* by all this seems to me to be the appropriate attitude. To be annoyed, irritated, frustrated, and worried about the state of affairs as they affect literary criticism and theory today is, one could argue, also simply to be aware of that state of affairs, assuming one is not an apologist for them. But to be vexed is not to be without hope. Far from it, in fact, for a sure sign that one believes that things may be different can be seen in the annoyance one feels with the *status quo*. Those who are without hope can become rather complacent, after all, making themselves "at home" in the place they find themselves, which may be more comfortable but may also tend to involve bad faith.[6] Those who are persistently vexed by the *status quo* cannot help but imagine alternatives.

The essays in this volume were written at different times, in different contexts, and for different purposes over a period of fifteen years or so, and to the extent that they represent any unified project, it is that they embody vexed perspectives on the matters they deal with. This does not make them in any way revolutionary, or even interesting, and still less "correct." It just means that they arise from a kind of annoyed concern with a number of literary critical practices and institutions, and that they constitute somewhat earnest, if also tentative and searching responses to those concerns. As with any collection, the selection and grouping of the essays is somewhat arbitrary. What they all share is an overriding concern for how literary and cultural criticism operates in our time, primarily in the context of academic literary studies, but also with respect to the effects of criticism in society more broadly. They are also largely metacritical, in the sense that they focus on criticism or critics, rather than offering examples of literary critical practice or readings of specific literary texts. As such, the scope of these essays is quite limited, each in its own way and all together; for the most part they represent merely punctual interventions into the broader discourses, and while they might occasionally seem dated when viewed outside of the original contexts, I am confident that most of their insights and provocations are still relevant (one might add, "alas!") to criticism in our present situation.

The fifteen chapters have been grouped into three parts, each reflecting a sort of theme by which the essays included therein might be further related to one another. The title of Part I, "Critical Positioning Systems," is intended as a play on the more familiar "geographical positioning systems" (GPS), but it also registers Hester Blum's sense that "critical turns" operate as "academic positioning systems."[7] Chapter 1 concerns the idea of the critical "turning point" itself, looking at various ways that such turns might affect critical practice. Chapter 2 explores the relationship between the "spatial turn," world literature, and postcritical or antitheoretical approaches, while Chapter 3 looks at the rise of "world literature" as a distinctive field or genre, along with the reactions to its burgeoning influence. Chapter 4 examines the "planetary turn" in relation to spatial literary studies, and Chapter 5 looks at the question of literary genre and the increasing predominance of so-called "genre fiction" in an age of globalization.

Part II, "Post-Americanist Interpolations," includes essays that all, in various ways, speak to the role of American literary studies after "the American Century," as Henry Luce in 1941 famously and provocatively had dubbed the twentieth century. Animating them is a critique, implicit or otherwise, of the nationalist project that pervades American Studies as a disciplinary field, even as scholars operating within its bounds have sought to challenge its foundational myths and symbols. Chapter 6 addresses the rise of the field and its quasi-religious nationalist ideology, which persists in various ways among the "new" Americanists, including some of the most astute critics of that earlier ideological project. In Chapter 7, I examine a specific work, Charles Olson's *Call Me Ishmael*, which preemptively freed Melville's masterpiece from the nationalistic uses to which many canonizing critics put it, and thus Olson's work represents a "postmodern" alternative to that nationalist tradition right at the moment that American Studies was establishing itself. Chapter 8 deals with a different counter-tradition altogether, rooted in the reactionary, racist, agrarian thought of Richard Weaver, an ideologue and apologist for the "old South," whose cultural anti-modernism has come to dominate even mainstream conservative politics in the twenty-first century. In Chapter 9, I look at the fate of another nineteenth-century literary work, *Adventures of Huckleberry Finn*, in the context of its twentieth- and twenty-first century uses, particularly with respect to the ways in which the novel has been wielded in debates over racial justice and liberal values. In viewing the text as preeminently or quintessentially "American," both defenders and detractors of Twain's novel indicate the baleful effects of such a nationalist approach to literature, while also undermining the function of criticism more broadly in their efforts to enlist critical practice in the service a strictly nationalist paradigm. Chapter 10 examines a feature of recent popular culture in the United States, the rise and burgeoning power of satirical "fake news" television programs—in particular, *The Daily Show* and *The Colbert Report*, whose influence carried far beyond the comedy audience for which they were originally intended—that have so transformed journalistic, political, and cultural discourse in the twenty-first century.

Part III, "Errant Trajectories in Postmodern Critical Practice," includes five essays each devoted to an individual critic who has, in one way or another, transgressed the boundaries of the disciplinary field, its customs and traditions, in which the work takes place. *Errancy*, of course, is not the same as *error*, although the opponents of *errant* thought might hold otherwise; errancy refers to movement, wandering (but not purposelessness), and a healthy disrespect for established rules. The critics I discuss in the part—Gilles Deleuze, Northrop Frye, Edward Said, Jonathan Arac, and Paul Bové—have each established errant trajectories within the fields in which they operate. Deleuze, of course, is a philosopher (although he has written a great deal on "literature" as well, including book-length studies of Proust and Kafka), but his approach to the history of philosophy as an institution is instructive for literary and cultural critics engaged with their own critical traditions. The "nomads" Deleuze identifies in, and rescues from, that tradition are not united by nation, language, period, genre, style, or other such characteristic, but by a "subterranean" chain of associations made by Deleuze himself, in the work of creative thinking and reading, as I discuss in Chapter 11. Chapter 12 examines the utopianism of Frye's criticism, linking his perspectives to those of the radical theorist Herbert Marcuse in order to show how, in Frye's view, literary studies empowers the imagination and thereby helps students to resist the forces within a society that are hell bent on constraining the power of the imagination, thus serving those forces' own ends by attacking literary criticism and critique. Chapter 13 examines the curious relationship between Said's work and the Marxist tradition that Said simultaneously disavowed and drew from, making for an oddly ambivalent "oppositional" criticism. In Chapter 14, I survey the career of Jonathan Arac, whose nearly unclassifiable corpus helps to illuminate and transform postmodern literary history, the theory of the novel, and criticism more generally, thereby modelling ways that engaged criticism can operate in our own time. Chapter 15 discusses the work of another postmodern critic, Paul A. Bové, by focusing on his recent, polemical yet celebratory, and altogether vexed exploration of the role of poetics and criticism in our lives today, *Love's Shadow* (2021).

Finally, in a brief conclusion, I argue that the vocation of criticism lies in the service of an anagogical education, invoking the ostensibly religious language of Dante and Max Weber in order to emphasize the urgent, *worldly* project at the heart of the liberal arts. In a moment and a situation in which the liberal arts and higher education seem the be especially imperiled, with both circumstances and powerful forces arrayed against practices of creative interpretation, analysis, evaluation, and speculation, the need for criticism could not be more critical.

Notes

1 Fredric Jameson, "Interview with Xudong Zhang," in *Jameson on Jameson: Conversations on Cultural Marxism*, ed. Ian Buchanan (Durham: Duke University Press), 194.
2 See, e.g., Bruce Robbins, *Criticism and Politics: A Polemical Introduction* (Stanford: Stanford University Press, 2022).
3 See Jonathan Arac, *Critical Genealogies: Historical Situations in Postmodern Literary Studies* (New York: Columbia University Press, 1989).
4 See Jeffrey Nealon, *Post-Postmodernism, or, the Cultural Logic of Just-in-Time Capitalism* (Stanford: Stanford University Press, 2012); Jameson, *Postmodernism, or, the Cultural Logic of Late Capitalism* (Durham: Duke University Press, 1991), ix.
5 See Rita Felski, *Hooked: Art and Attachment* (Chicago: University of Chicago Press, 2020); Sheila Liming, "Fighting Words," *Los Angeles Review of Books*, December 14, 2020: https://lareviewofbooks.org/article/fighting-words/.
6 Hence, the idea that a Felski-supported attitude of "postcritique" could be characterized as "the cultural logic of capitalist realism," as Robert Scott has discussed in *The Los Angeles Review of Books*, September 14, 2022: https://lareviewofbooks.org/article/postcritique-or-the-cultural-logic-of-capitalist-realism/.
7 Hester Blum, "Introduction: Academic Positioning Systems," *Turns of Event: Nineteenth-Century American Literary Studies in Motion*, ed. Hester Blum (Philadelphia: University of Pennsylvania Press, 2016), 1.

Part I

CRITICAL POSITIONING SYSTEMS

Chapter 1

SWERVE, TROPE, PERIPETY: TURNING POINTS IN CULTURAL CRITICISM AND THEORY

In their broadcasts of professional ice hockey games, *The Sports Network* (*TSN* for short), a Canadian cable television network, would identify and feature highlights of what the announcers would refer to as the "TSN Turning Point." That is, in any given hockey game, the turning point in question was some event—often a goal or a great save, but perhaps also an untimely penalty, a key injury, or even a fight—that could in retrospect be marked as the discrete point at which the "game" turned in favor of the eventual victor. Notably, the turning point is not necessarily, or even ever, the game-winning goal, which is to say the particular event that is proven to have assured victory by definition. No, that would be a rather uninspired choice. Instead, it might be the event that swung the momentum, that deflated the eventual losing side or energized the winning side, often well before the actual game-winner is scored. As such, it has a certain ineffable quality in the moment. Players, coaches, commentators, and fans may be able to sense when such a momentous occurrence is taking place, and they can certainly speculate as to whether this or that play might be the point at which things will prove to have turned the winner's way, but it is clear that the true TSN Turning Point cannot be ascertained until the game is over, until all the play has ended, and we are able to look back on the game in its totality to find the moment or moments when everything changed. In the midst of things, those experiencing or witnessing what may later be recognized as the turning point cannot be certain of the meaning of the situation. Only from a perspective made available sometime later can we may look back upon the game to discover the turning point, which is to say the most significant moment in the narrative we must retrospectively produce about the events that were occurring in real time. Although he was not thinking about it with respect to hockey, this is in part what Hegel meant by his evocative line about the Owl of Minerva taking flight at dusk. The turning point, like the narrative in which it functions, cannot be *known* in the moment of its happening, but only afterwards.

In recent years, various discourses in the humanities and social sciences have been subject to, or simply witnessed, a number of *turns*: the linguistic turn, the spatial turn, the hemispheric, transnational, or planetary turns, even the postcritical turn, to name but a few. Such turns are emblematic of what Hester Blum has referred to as "academic positioning systems," ways of orienting or reorienting fields of critical inquiry in order to explore new territories or gain new insights into ever-changing bodies of knowledge. Pointing out that "*turns* in literary history have been at once ideological, conceptual, and material," Blum explains,

> The notion of a turn marks a differentiation between what came before and what is to come, indicating routes plotted if not yet explored, imagined if not yet surveyed. The fact that intellectual reorientations have been predicated on the use of this particular term suggests an orienteering impulse, one that presumes transits that have continuity, linearity, and cartography. To turn is to have followed a path, a line of demarcation that has subsequently been altered; while the terminus of that turn might be unknown or imagined, it bears an established trajectory, a traceable origin. Turns are observable when there has been a change.[1]

Along these lines, we might think of a turning point as being inherently prospective and oriented toward the future. That is, while it may still be that the turning point can only be identified and ascertained after it has happened, and indeed, after its effects have already become cognizable as well, the turning point is nevertheless taken as a sign of future developments. Turns represent a changing situation, from which many corresponding changes of perspective, focus, and attitude necessarily follow.

"All transitions are crisis," notes Goethe in *Wilhelm Meister's Apprenticeship*, and Marshall Brown has observed that "the turning point is a trial," a process by which we try to make sense of our position in history, such that we come to be aware of, if not to *know*, "a turning point in the turbulence of its occurrence."[2] One might argue that registering such a change, as well as analyzing, evaluating, and interpreting it, is a crucial part of the vocation of criticism and theory. If the figure of the turn has been useful for understanding changing ways of understanding the world and, metacritically, the changing ways in which we understand the ways that we understand the world,[3] the "turning point" is one of the more evocative concepts in the critic's arsenal. It is equally well suited to the evaluation and analysis of a given moment in one's day as to those of a more distant historical event, and it indicates directions, topics, and methods of future inquiry.

But how does one recognize a turning point? As we find ourselves always "in the middest," both spatially and temporally, we are constantly occupying spatiotemporal sites or observing others that may be points at which many things can be seen to turn or rather, at some later moment, can have been said to have turned. Indeed, it is usually only possible to identify a turning point, as it were, from a distance, from the remove of space and time which allows for a sense of recognition, based in part on original context and in part of perceived effects. The task of the critic, in part, is to help to locate and to make sense of such significant points.

In this chapter, I argue that the apprehension and interpretation of a turning point involves a fundamentally critical activity. Or, to put it another way, the work of the critic is often bound up with processes of locating and making sense of those turning points in a given narrative, broadly conceived. Examining three distinctive models by which to understand the concept of the turning point—the *swerve*, the *trope*, and *peripety* (also known as *peripeteia* or the dialectical reversal)—I affirm the significance of the turning point as a concept in literary and cultural theory, and I conclude that the identification, analysis, and interpretation of turning points represent significant elements of any critical project today.

Swerve

The *swerve* might be best understood as a point of departure, a jumping-off point, or what Erich Auerbach has referred to as the *Ansatzpunkt* in his influential essay "Philology and *Weltliteratur*." For Auerbach, this point must be concrete and precise, but its most significant feature is its "potential for centrifugal radiation."[4] As Edward Said explains, the *Ansatzpunkt* has two distinct aspects that animate one another:

> One leads to the project being realized: this is the transitive aspect of the beginning—that is, beginning with (or for) an anticipated end, or at least an expected continuity. The other aspect retains for the beginning its identity as *radical* starting point: the intransitive and conceptual aspect, that which has no object but its own constant clarification.[5]

In this way, the point of departure maintains both centrifugal and centripetal forces, as it were, projecting outward in ways that manifest its effects, while also looking inward in order to ceaselessly meditate upon the *point* at which such departures become possible.

Like the point of departure, the swerve is a *beginning*, to be sure, but no beginning can occur *ex nihilo*; hence, it is also very much a turning point, an identifiable moment or site from which the new movement or direction can be seen. In the figure of the swerve, which is defined by a sudden spatiotemporal shift, one can perceive what might be characterized as an *event of difference*, a momentary change from one thing to another which also, in a moment, changes everything.

In speaking of the swerve, I am of course invoking the idea of the *clinamen* from the classic *De Rerum Natura* of Lucretius. Lucretius there attempts to explain an odd feature of Epicurean atomism: the idea that atoms moving in their fixed paths sometimes, very slightly and even rarely, *swerve*, and that this slight and sudden change in motion sets off a sort of chain reaction, with atoms crashing into and bouncing off other atoms. For Epicurean atomism as Lucretius elaborates the theory, this event and its ramifications, in turn, create and sustain the dynamic momentum of the cosmos itself. In Lucretius's words,

> When the atoms are travelling straight down through empty space by their own weight, at quite indeterminate times and places they swerve ever so little from their course, just so much that you can call it a change of direction. If it were not for this swerve, everything would fall downwards like rain-drops through the abyss of space. No collision would take place and no impact of atom on atom would be created. Thus nature would not have created anything.[6]

Notably, the *clinamen* or swerve occurs at "no determinate time or place," and that its occurrence therefore cannot be predicted. Moreover, it cannot even really be observed, except in its effects or as a logical inference. For Lucretius and the Epicureans before him, the *clinamen* helped to explain the existence of free will, since it gave evidence of a deviation from fixed determination or fate. As Lucretius explains, "the fact that the mind itself has no internal necessity to determine its every act and compel it to suffer in helpless passivity—this is due to the slight swerve of the atoms at no determinate time or place."[7] This slight swerve quite literally marked a turning point, insofar as the previously fixed course of all things, even thoughts, is disrupted, allowing all those infinite number of moving billiard balls to suddenly take off in different directions.

Gilles Deleuze, in his consideration of this matter in *The Logic of Sense*, remarks without much further explanation that "the *clinamen* leads thought to false conceptions of freedom," since "the *clinamen* represents neither contingency nor indetermination"; rather, according to Deleuze, "the *clinamen* is the determination of the meaning of the causal series."[8] Deleuze is alluding to an ancient debate between the Epicureans and the Stoics over the nature of fate or destiny, and he wants to suggest that the *clinamen* offers an alternative to the strict "free will-versus-determinism" binary. The function of the *clinamen*, for Deleuze, is to represent something like the "necessity of chance" as he calls it in *Nietzsche and Philosophy*.[9] Or, as he puts it, the *clinamen* represents "causality without destiny."[10] In other words, we might view this "slight swerve" as a motive force for change or dynamism that is both internal to the nature of the atom itself and has ramifications for all atoms in nature. Or, to get back to my main point, it represents a turning point as potential beginning, a mobile, dynamic starting point. From this point of departure, which is itself a turning point, we witness or create the chains of events, the causal links, or the connections between apparently disparate objects, events, or circumstances. It is a site for "leaping off" into an investigation or project.

More recently, this idea of the swerve has garnered widespread attention since Stephen Greenblatt employed it as the title of his popular, entertaining, but surprisingly uncritical narrative of the "rediscovery" of Lucretius during the Renaissance.[11] The premise of the book, revealed in the hyperbolic subtitle ("How the World Became Modern") and to the dismay of many medievalists or historians more generally, is that the rediscovery of Lucretius itself marked a swerve-like turning point, a moment in which Europe emerged from a superstitious and benighted epoch of ignorance into the enlightened, knowledgeable realm of modern science and art. Needless to say, and surely Greenblatt himself knows better, this characterization of pre-sixteenth-century Europe as the Dark Ages has been wholly debunked by modern historiography and research, and in any case, it always seemed rather inaccurate to anyone studying the places and periods in question. I am not going to discuss Greenblatt's overall argument here, but I want to mention a couple of things about his usage of this term *swerve*. First, it is notable that, apart from summarizing the brief section of *De Rerum Natura* from which I quoted Lucretius above as a means of defining the "swerve," Greenblatt does not really discuss the concept ever again. That is, instead of elaborating upon the idea, Greenblatt allows its supple suggestiveness merely to permeate the study, giving tacit authority to his premise that the rediscovery of Lucretius's text inaugurated a Renaissance, thus saving Europe from the seemingly perpetual Dark Age that preceded it. Second, I believe that Greenblatt's misuse of the notion can serve as a cautionary example, which also may be useful in thinking about the idea of the turning point more generally.

Greenblatt sees the rediscovery and dissemination of Lucretius's putatively "lost" book as *the* swerve that set off the chain reaction that made modernity what it was and has been, and Greenblatt's tone, rhetoric, and express conclusions all indicate that this is somehow a definitively beneficent and wholesome outcome. Greenblatt even ends the book by insisting upon Lucretius's influence on Thomas Jefferson, thus crediting the atomist philosopher with helping to spawn the Declaration of Independence, if not modern democracy itself![12] The moral righteousness of the turning point is thus taken for granted by Greenblatt, who suggests that without its salutary effects, the world would have been an immeasurably worse place. Although this moral impetus may make for thrilling storytelling, not to mention permitting the readership to feel simultaneously more reasonable and more ethical than their imagined subalterns of the tenebrous past, thus patting themselves on the back for being "better" people than those who came before them, one may well question the progressive, moralistic teleology of the narrative.

In fact, turning points are never so clear as this, and their ambiguity—a term which, etymologically, suggests "both ways at once"—should be emphasized instead. I believe that the oversimplifications in Greenblatt's version of the swerve can serve as a warning that the "turning point" ought not to be cast in a rhetoric of morality, that is, in terms of good and evil or light and darkness. The turning point is not an indication of a particularly progressive movement, a teleological arc that bends toward justice, or any moral improvement. The dangers of that sort of thinking are amply revealed by any consideration of history that is not already intractably beholden to what many critics and historians have dismissed as "Whiggish thought." But, as I will discuss more below, such thinking is misleading not only in its optimistic sense of infinitely expanding moral or political progress, but also in its blindness to the possibility of reversals or other dynamic processes incapable of being reduced to narratives of ineluctable, linear progress. If nothing else, the very existence of a *swerve* offers a cautionary example of how such linear thinking can and must go awry.

Trope

My second figure or model of the turning point is the trope, which in its etymology quite literally refers to a "turning." From the classical Greek, *tropos* meant "turn," and the verb *tropein* meant "to turn" or "to change." In Latin, *tropus* means "metaphor" or "figure of speech." As the brilliant historian and theorist Hayden White explains in his *Tropics of Discourse*,

> All of these meanings, sedimented in the early English word *trope*, capture the force of the concept that modern English intended by the word *style*, a concept that is especially apt for the consideration of that form of verbal composition which, in order to distinguish it from logical demonstration on the one side and from pure fiction on the other, we call by the name *discourse*.[13]

Tropes are figures of speech, but they also mark turning points in discourses, which is to say, also, in the narratives by which we come to know and make sense of the world and our place in it. Over his career, in such works as *Metahistory* and *The Content of the Form*, White has consistently shown how even the most scientific discourses rely upon figures of speech, metaphors, or tropes, and that a properly tropological analysis of works of both the artist and the scientist is crucial for understanding "all the various dimensions of our specifically *human* being."[14]

The turn that is implied by the trope or figure of speech bodies itself forth in the expression, "turn of phrase," and we might look at the trope as another form of turning point, here, grounded in the materiality of language and thought (as opposed to the more abstract materiality of Epicurean atomic physics, I suppose). Traditionally, the study of tropes belonged to the field of rhetoric, and with special attention paid to various examples or types of trope, such as metaphor, metonymy, allegory, and so forth. That rhetorical background remains crucial for any critical theory today, particularly as the proliferation of languages and media have rendered the social sphere all the more complex and resistant to interpretation, if not downright unintelligible at times. As Fredric Jameson has famously observed, "no society has ever been quite so mystified in quite so many ways as our own, saturated as it is with messages and information, the very vehicles of mystification."[15] The need for interpretation and analysis has perhaps never been greater, and making sense of the ways we make sense of things becomes more critical than ever. As such, the tropological perspective is significant and timely.

Regarding the "turning point," these tropes offer figures for seeing the change from one thing to another, such that alterity or difference is a key component or characteristic of the analysis. For one thing to mean another in language, which is a rather elementary definition of "metaphor," there needs to be an understanding of difference, and difference makes the meaning what it is. "A rose is a flower" is not much of a metaphor, but "my love is like a red, red rose" is (albeit, here, in the form of simile). In making this connection between factually dissimilar things, the one is "turned" into the other. At this point, the poet (as well as the reader) twists the meaning of a word toward that of another, thereby establishing a new or different sense of both terms. Similarly, the three other "master tropes" identified by Kenneth Burke—that is, in addition to metaphor, metonymy, synecdoche, and irony—create meaning by differentiation, torturing the language to make possible alternative representations.[16] Transposing Burke's tropology to historiography and to narrative more generally, White asserts that these tropes "are especially useful for understanding the operations by which the contents of experience which resist description in unambiguous prose representations can be prefiguratively grasped and prepared for conscious apprehension."[17] In other words (no pun intended), the trope helps us to make sense of things while being located amid the ineffable, the inscrutable, or merely the difficult to express, which is all to say, in our historical and geographical *situation*, to invoke a Sartrean term.

The trope or figure of speech is a turning point *in mediis rebus*, in the middle of things. It assumes a basic familiarity with distinctive terms and discourses of which it is a part, thus positioning itself within that system of familiar words and ideas, while also defining itself to some degree as *different*. By definition, in this way, it involves a sort of transgression. As White points out, a trope

> is always not only a deviation *from* one possible, proper meaning, but also a deviation *towards* another meaning, conception, or ideal of what is right and proper *and true* "in reality." Thus considered, troping is both a movement *from* one notion of the way things are related *to* another notion, and a connection between things so that they can be expressed in a language that takes account of the possibility of their being expressed otherwise.[18]

In this turning away from one semantic or interpretive field toward another, the resulting *displacement*, which had at first appeared to cut off or distance one thing from another, reveals itself to be simultaneously a creative *connection*, which establishes links between otherwise apparently unrelated forms and figures. To borrow an expression from Jameson again, "difference relates."[19]

Making connections is what this is all about. And this tropical activity is also, both figuratively and literally (although these terms must now be subjected to enhanced scrutiny in this context), the basic activity of the critic, here understood as a literary critic but also broadly conceived so as to include others. By examining the trope, we become attuned to alterity, a fantastic and speculative activity that is also nonetheless crucial to make sense of the real world, a world that itself is dynamic and protean. The turning point, understood in terms of the trope, is less of an *Ansatzpunkt* or beginning, and more of a way of coming to terms with the inexorable mediation or middleness in which we find ourselves in the present. In the middle of things, difference reigns.

Peripety

My third model, *peripety* (which is perhaps better known via Aristotle, among others, in its Greek form as *peripeteia*) is itself a literary trope. It is also literally a "turning point," referring as it does to a reversal of the situation, or, as Aristotle put it in *The Poetics*, "a change by which the action veers round to its opposite."[20] His apt example, taken from Sophocles's *Oedipus the King*, is the moment when the witness to the murder of Laius arrives to tell Oedipus about the scene of the crime: Oedipus, who had been accused by Tiresias of committing the murder, fully expects to be exonerated by the witness's testimony, which—hence the reversal—in fact definitively proves to Oedipus that he was the murderer; at this point, it becomes clear to Oedipus that the earlier killing at the crossroads was merely the first of many abominations and that he is entangled in a web of horrifying actions and consequences partly of his own making. Everything "turns" on this point, which is where Oedipus at last recognizes what is and has been going on in and around Thebes. (Aristotle says that all of the best tragedies include this reversal, but that tragedies are at their very best when that reversal also leads to a recognition [*anagnoresis*], as it does with Oedipus in this play.) The effect of *peripeteia* is dramatic, and it also provides a lesson about *hubris*, the tragic flaw of Oedipus. One ought not be too proud of one's present achievements or status, since one does not yet know the full story, a lesson paraphrased in the well-known dictum, uttered by the Chorus in the final line of *Oedipus Rex*, "count no man happy till he dies, free of pain at last."[21]

Not that this was Sophocles's point, but the lesson taught by *peripeteia* about hubris stands also as a warning against moralizing more generally. That is, an action, event, or circumstance that might appear to be "good" or "bad" at the moment may well be revealed, in the fullness of time, to be otherwise. This lesson about peripety from Aristotle, Sophocles, or more generally history itself ought to keep us humble, but it also adverts our critical attention to those possible moments of reversal, turning points, at which a new recognition or knowledge becomes possible. The moment of peripety is thus momentous for *criticism* and *theory*, activities that combine the meticulously analytical, cautiously evaluative, and creatively speculative.

The dialectical reversal, a ruse of history, the unforeseen consequences of this or that action or reaction: these are the events that ultimately press a stamp of significance upon the given moment or situation. Peripety, then, is an essential element of theoretical practice or of theory itself, whose speculative vocation in the end can only be successful once the various reversals of fortune are disclosed. Almost like a kind of spatiotemporal *Nachträglichkeit* (to invoke a Freudian term), one does not really "know" the event or its meaning until after it has happened or unless one has some sort of distance from the event in question. More often than not, the import of the event is disclosed only in connection with a later reversal, whether this comes in the form of additional information (as with Oedipus), shifting circumstances, or merely a change in perspective.

Jameson has identified *peripeteia* as perhaps the core element of dialectical thinking, which for him is also crucial for understanding modern (or postmodern) social forms and relations *tout court*. As he puts it,

> The basic story which the dialectic has to tell is no doubt that of the dialectical *reversal*, that paradoxical turning around of a phenomenon into its opposite [...]. It can be described as a kind of leap-frogging affair in time, in which the drawbacks of a given historical situation turn out in reality to be its secret advantages, in which what looked like built-in superiorities suddenly prove to set the most ironclad limits on its future development. It is a matter, indeed, of the reversal of limits, of the transformation from negative to positive and from positive to negative.[22]

This is from 1971's *Marxism and Form*, and Jameson offers a then-timely example of such a dialectical reversal in the contemporary history of the Cold War arms race, as he recounts how the technological superiority of the United States in producing atomic weapons led the Soviet Union to experiment with missiles that could carry their much more cumbersome nuclear bombs, which resulted in a benefit to their space program, where they surpassed the United States technologically; however, the consequent Soviet superiority in rocket technology led the Americans to develop smaller, more efficient, transistorized instruments, leading to better computers, and so on. The point is not just that an apparent disadvantage turns out to have been a clear advantage when judged from a certain point of view, but that the situation is itself reversed. The previous evaluation was not in itself wrong, even when judged from a different spatiotemporal vantage point, but rather the *situation* is changeable, and hence any evaluation must be understood as tentative and subject to revision. Like Oedipus, whose personal perspective had been limited but who discovered that a vast constellation of factors were at play in determining his circumstances, we understand that we exist *in mediis rebus*, and thus we must muddle through as best as we can, without knowing the whole story, as it were. In concluding his Cold War example, tellingly, Jameson notes that his discussion neglects the various events and reversals which came before but which constituted the conditions for the possibility of the technological arms race or space race: "a complete picture of this particular set of dialectical reversals would ultimately have involved a reimmersion in the very element of concrete history itself."[23]

This reimmersion in history is impossible at the level about which Jameson is talking, and it indicates a sort of comportment toward the field of study, one characterized (and, I hope, tempered) equally by audacity and humility. It is audacious in the sense that the critic will, and must, attempt to make sense of the world—or, as Frank Kermode has insisted, to make sense of the way that people (poets, specifically) have tried to make sense of the world—knowing full well the difficulty, if not futility, of ever getting a proper handle on it. It is humble insofar as critics must recognize that we cannot *know* the subjects or objects of our enquiry for certain, that therefore our critiques must be always somehow provisional, tentative, and incomplete. Yet for all that, the critique must still be undertaken.

Conclusion

If the *swerve* represents a point at which we can begin, a point of departure for a critical project, it is because it is also viewed as an inaugural event; it is the beginning of a causal chain or set of reactions. It is not a natural beginning—what could be?—but a choice based on the critic's identification of something interesting, something new, a sense that something has changed. It is noteworthy. The *trope* as turning point strikes me as a site for continuous and sustained inquiry, or the place at which various enquiries come together and proliferate. It is a critical middle ground in which different projects may take shape at once, immersed as we are in the fundamental spaces of linguistic and semantic difference. Finally, *peripety* seems to be a turning point to be visited and revisited in a more retrospective way, even if one cannot really wait for the End of History, or rather to assert that it has already happened, before checking in. This turning point, like the others, can only be identified as such from a distance, in space as well as in time, but it is especially clear that the idea of peripety requires caution. Like Oedipus, we might find our own absolute certainty to be a hindrance to the truth, which becomes all the more horrific when ultimately disclosed.

In all of these cases, with each of these models, it is assumed that the critic's tasks include the identification, analysis, evaluation, and theorization of turning points, for these are the sites of novelty, difference, force, and significance in cultural work. These also serve as turning points—that is, points of departure, points of shifting meaning, and points of dramatic reversals—in our own work, which can only benefit from our awareness of its scarcely manageable dynamism.

Among other things, critics are constitutionally oriented toward the turning point, to that site in which something meaningful, or perhaps something that can afterwards be said to be or have been meaningful, has happened. In examining such points, the critic registers changes, makes connections, and develops theories, all while remaining careful readers or observers of the texts in question. The peripety or "ruse of history" disclosed by critical and theoretical practice makes possible the recognition or understanding of the world, and only through such a process does one begin to imagine alternatives. Hence, a utopian or fantastic project also subtends the vocations of criticism and theory, which allows critics to project an imaginary map in order to navigate the real spaces more effectively and, perhaps, to gain a vista into other potential spaces beyond. Literature has always served as a site for representing the world and, at the same time, for depicting radically alternative visions. Criticism, in turn, must do its part.

Notes

1 Blum, Hester. "Introduction: Academic Positioning Systems," *Turns of Event: Nineteenth-Century American Literary Studies in Motion*, ed. Hester Blum (Philadelphia: University of Pennsylvania Press, 2016), 1, 3.
2 Marshall Brown, *Turning Points: Essays in the History of Cultural Expressions* (Stanford: Stanford University Press, 1997), 3–4.
3 See Frank Kermode, *The Sense of an Ending: Studies on the Theory of Fiction* (Oxford: Oxford University Press, 1967), 3: "It is not expected of critics as it is of poets that they should help us to make sense of our lives; they are bound only to attempt the lesser feat of making sense of the ways we try to make sense of our lives."
4 Erich Auerbach, "Philology and *Weltliteratur*," trans. M. and E. W. Said, *Centennial Review* 13 (Winter 1969): 15.
5 Edward W. Said, *Beginnings: Intention and Method* (New York: Columbia University Press, 1985), 72–73.
6 Lucretius, *On the Nature of the Universe*, trans. Ronald Latham (New York: Penguin, 1951), 66.
7 Ibid., 68.
8 Gilles Deleuze, *The Logic of Sense*, trans. Mark Lester with Charles Stivale, ed. Constantin Boundas (New York: Columbia University Press, 1990), 277, 269–270.
9 See Deleuze, *Nietzsche and Philosophy*, trans. Hugh Tomlinson (New York: Columbia University Press, 1983), 25–29, 197.
10 Deleuze, *The Logic of Sense*, 6.
11 See Stephen Greenblatt, *The Swerve: How the World Became Modern* (New York: W.W. Norton, 2011).
12 Greenblatt, *The Swerve*, 263.
13 Hayden White, *Tropics of Discourse: Essays in Cultural Criticism* (Baltimore: Johns Hopkins University Press, 1978), 2.
14 White, *Tropics of Discourse*, 23.
15 Fredric Jameson, *The Political Unconscious: Narrative as a Socially Symbolic Act* (Ithaca: Cornell University Press, 1981), 60–61.
16 See Kenneth Burke, "The Four Master Tropes," *The Kenyon Review* 3.4 (Autumn 1941): 431–438; a version of this essay appears as Appendix D in Burke's monumental study, *A Grammar of Motives* (Berkeley: University of California Press, 1970 [1945]), 503–517.
17 White, *Metahistory: The Historical Imagination in Nineteenth-Century Europe* (Baltimore: Johns Hopkins University Press, 1973), 31.

18 White, *Tropics of Discourse*, 2.
19 See Jameson, *Postmodernism, or, the Cultural Logic of Late Capitalism* (Durham: Duke University Press, 1991), 31.
20 Aristotle, *The Poetics*, trans. S. H. Butcher (New York: Hill & Wang, 1961), 72.
21 Sophocles, *Oedipus the King*, in *Three Theban Plays*, trans. Robert Fagles (New York: Penguin, 1982), 251.
22 Jameson, *Marxism and Form: Twentieth-Century Dialectic Theories of Literature* (Princeton: Princeton University Press, 1971), 309.
23 Ibid., 310.

Chapter 2

THE AESTHETICS OF DISTANCE: SPACE, *WELTLITERATUR*, AND CRITIQUE

Although there is no precise date on which the spatial turn in the humanities could be said to have occurred, a combination of forces and events over the past few decades has ensured that spatiality has become a key concept, and as a consequence, this has effectively transformed many approaches to literary and cultural texts. Geocriticism and spatial literary studies, among others, have focused attention on matters of space, place, and mapping. More generally, critics inspired by such practices have made important connections between literature and geography, architecture, urban planning, and environmental studies, along with other spatially oriented arts and sciences. The spatial turn in the humanities and social sciences has been occasioned by a number of factors, practical and theoretical, but perhaps the most urgent are those associated with the processes and ramifications of globalization. With the advent of globalization, here understood mainly as the extension and expansion of the capitalist mode of production across national boundaries and to a worldwide scale, many of the previously settled social and spatial arrangements—including such formerly crucial distinctions as core and periphery, urban and rural, domestic and foreign, or even near and far, to name a few—have been unsettled and subject to revisionary thinking. In Fredric Jameson's revolutionary formulation, postmodernism itself emerged as the cultural logic of late capitalism, which is also to say that postmodernity may be associated with the age of globalization, and postmodern thought in its various respects a response to the radically transformed social, political, economic, and cultural terrain of this epoch.[1] As Edward Soja has made clear in such works as *Postmodern Geographies* and *Thirdspace*, the postmodern era and postmodernism are both characterized by a new spatiality and a renewed emphasis in critical social theory on space, place, and mapping.[2]

During roughly the same period, world literature has gone from a minor concept, little discussed even in academic criticism and theory, to a major force within both academic literary studies and the wider realms of literary journalism, not to mention the sudden prominence of the concept for anthologists, booksellers, prize committees, and consumers in general. World literature has not only become a distinctive academic subject, rivalling and influencing the study of various national literatures, but it has also become something of a brand, a commodified and marketed genre offering carefully measured amounts of the unfamiliar, the exotic, and locally colorful while also appealing to mainstream audiences in metropolitan centers.[3] Perhaps coincidentally, though likely not only so, the moment of world literature's ascension has also witnessed the rise and extension of new forms of literary criticism expressly defining themselves as opposed to older forms of interpretation, analysis, and especially critique. In what has been termed the *postcritical turn*, a number of prominent critics, theorists, and scholars have advocated for approaches to literary and cultural studies that eschew "critique" in favor of more descriptive, affective, and even celebratory forms of reading.[4]

These phenomena are more closely interrelated than has been hitherto observed. Connecting the spatial turn in the humanities to this age of world literature by looking at the multiple ways that globalization has shaped literary and cultural studies, I assert that the postcritical turn is largely an effect of the same processes, while I counter that any meaningful assessment of the current situation will require a renewed and reinvigorated critical theory, drawing upon the insights of a Marxist critical tradition now adjusted to the spatio-political realities of a world system in the age of globalization. Fittingly, perhaps, the era of globalization is the age of world literature, notwithstanding the august prehistory of *Weltliteratur* in Goethe, Marx, and early twentieth-century critics.[5] World literature, both as a disciplinary force and as a literary phenomenon, has arguably required the unfolding of the various features of globalization, which may be figured forth in the abstract ideas of an interconnected or "borderless" world or which may be grounded in more material analyses of institutional conditions for the possibility of the rise of world literature, such as the formation of international literary events, multinational publishers, and internationally attuned consumers, as in Sarah Brouillette's superb study, *UNESCO and the Fate of the Literary*.[6] The embrace of a world literature by academic and cultural arbiters of literary taste is arguably also tied to a turn away from critical theory, and in particular a turn away from Marxism, as the formerly incisive critical interventions of earlier forms of postcolonial theory and cultural studies gave way, in the 1990s and more recently, to an anemic, easily marketable discourse of transnational diversity. Not surprisingly, though it may have been a largely unintended consequence, these processes have aligned themselves neatly with those of neoliberalism in the spheres of higher education and in society at large. In response to the rise of postcritical approaches to literary study, along with the commodification of world literature and its effects, the present situation calls for a return to a Marxist critical theory suited to our time and place in today's world system.

This spatially oriented and highly critical perspective reflects a kind of aesthetic of distance at the heart of criticism and theory in the present age, manifested in part by what Jameson has referred to as "that new spatiality implicit in the postmodern" and by the exigencies of the globalization of capitalism.[7] "Aesthetic" here refers to artistic theory and practice, on the one hand, and to "ways of seeing" the world on the other, and a more complete discussion would have to engage with the ideological content of the term as well, whose long history has been traced by Terry Eagleton in *The Ideology of the Aesthetic*, for example.[8] "Distance" refers to various levels of spatial and temporal remove, drawing in part from Friedrich Nietzsche's idea of the "pathos of distance," from *On the Genealogy of Morals*, and also from the sense of the critical separation needed to apprehend larger systems, the latter of which can be seen both in Moretti's somewhat flawed notion of distant reading or in Edward Said's insistence on the critical perspective made possible by an exilic point of view.[9] This aesthetic of distance must be viewed dialectically, recognizing the advantages and disadvantages that accompany it. Distance alone cannot save us, after all, and proximity, including that to be found in a methodology of close reading, is also necessary. An aesthetic of distance would be bound up in a number of interconnected cultural relations, not least of which might be a certain politics of proximity that simultaneously resists and informs the aesthetic. As such, due attention to the ideology of distance in contemporary criticism and theory is crucial. Marxism, as a politically engaged critical practice attuned to both the logic of the situation and to the need for making connections between a wide variety of historical and social sites, ultimately squaring the circle of the subjective and objective registers in the attempt to map a totality, is perhaps the most suitable discourse for dealing with the unique problems of literary and cultural critique in an era of globalization.

The Politics of Spatiality

When Foucault famously named ours at the "epoch of space," he was above all thinking of the shift away from nineteenth-century historicisms with their powerful sense that the unfolding of events over time revealed the meaning of our lives, experiences, and perceptions.[10] The "spatial turn," as it has been called, is not so much a rejection of the temporal or historical in favor of the spatial and geographical as it is a sort of rebalancing of the scales. Henceforth, as spatially oriented critics might assert, matters of space, place, mapping, and so forth must be given their due, and we must emphasize the degree to which all things are conditioned by spatiotemporality, and not just by spatiality or temporality alone. If the emphasis has recently been placed on spatiality, that is in part because of the persistent feeling that temporality has previously been privileged, and hence matters of space must be reckoned with more directly.[11]

Among the most significant features of the spatial turn in the humanities is the recognition that space be seen as more than an empty container, a mere setting for the characters and events to establish their more meaningful effects over time.[12] To be sure, a poem's or story's setting has itself always been a significant element for literary discussion, but there was still a general sense that the spatial configurations were mostly seen as a backdrop or stage upon which the "real" story takes place. The renewed attention to the ways that space and spatial relations actively shape characters and events typifies the geocritical or spatial approach to literature.

To a certain extent, writers have always been well attuned to this, in a way that critics or readers may not have been. As I have argued elsewhere, nearly all creative writing may be taken as a form of literary cartography, a sort of figurative mapmaking by which the writer helps to give form to, and make sense of, the world.[13] By engaging in such literary cartographic practice, the writer could be said to employ a poetics of the boundary, demarcating territories, establishing borders, drawing lines, making connections, and projecting spaces beyond. The aesthetic program associated with this mapmaking can involve any number of techniques, aims, and effects, of course, but the delineation of spaces and places within a narrative, say, will not only establish the setting for the other actions, but actively determines the actions as well as the conditions for their possibility. In not only depicting the world, but also affirmatively shaping it, the literary cartographic process discloses its implicit political project.

The geocritical approach to literature must take into account the real significance of space and place, much the way most writers already do, but in so doing it must also recognize the political impetus and effects. The spaces that we inhabit and represent are not merely given, outside of any social context, but are actively formed and contoured by an array of practices that affect their organization and their effects. This is especially obvious when it comes to matters of land use planning, zoning, or the like, but equally political, if not always so visible, are the forces that in different ways constitute the organization of spaces in everyday life, from the ways that students' classrooms are arranged to the geopolitical system writ large. Spatially oriented-literary or cultural studies would have to take such power relations into account. However, recent trends in literary criticism and, perhaps especially, in the spatial humanities have obscured if not actively repressed the political or ideological aspects of criticism, in part by favoring mere description over interpretation and critique. Since space itself is inherently ideological, a spatially oriented approach to literature necessarily involves some kinds of ideology critique, which of course means both acknowledging the ideological content and context of the various texts under consideration and affirming the value of critique itself.

Critical practices in the humanities have often been connected to political values, movements, and theories, some more overtly than others. Ecocriticism, for instance, with its close ties with the environmental movement and Green social policies, announces itself as a participant in real world politics, taking sides and making a stand in significant matters of public controversy. Similarly, feminist criticism not only describes the ways in which gender roles are constructed or represented in a given work, but also more or less explicitly takes up arms against misogynistic practices or patriarchal structures in society as a whole. By contrast, geocriticism would appear to be somewhat neutral in its politics. "*Vive l'Espace!*" does not appear to be a very effective or meaningful slogan, and urging readers to pay more attention to matters of space, place, and mapping in literary and cultural studies hardly seems like a politically motivated program. And yet, many of the leading theorists and critics associated with the spatial turn in the humanities have emerged from the political Left, with a strong tradition of Marxist or revolutionary critical theory underlying much of what is recognized as geocritical practice today. Key thinkers whose work has informed and shaped geocritical practice include such Marxists as Antonio Gramsci, Walter Benjamin, Henri Lefebvre, Raymond Williams, David Harvey, Soja, Jameson, and Moretti, among many others. And such influential non-Marxists as Foucault, Deleuze, Said, or Westphal can hardly be considered apolitical, after all. Indeed, part of the point of a geocritical approach is to disclose and call attention to the politics of spatiality.

This is no coincidence, even if there are many different spatially oriented approaches to literature, culture, and society that do not align themselves with Marxist or otherwise radical politics. Contrary to first appearances, perhaps, matters of space and spatial relations are intensely political, infused with ideology, and subject to extensive debate. Space, place, and mapping are fundamentally bound up with ideology, such that any geocritical approach must be, among other things, a form of ideology critique. At a time when so-called surface reading, thin description, or other ostensibly postcritical approaches to literature have been increasingly championed by prominent scholars and critics, this sort of ideology critique is needed more than ever, and that the spatially oriented critique made possible by geocriticism is particularly well suited to the crises and mystifications facing us in the twenty-first century.[14]

Distance as Method

To take one of the more interesting of such approaches as a cautionary example, we might look at Moretti's fascinating and yet problematic project of "distant reading," which arose in part from Moretti's interests in literary geography and spatial criticism, and which was developed as a way of apprehending and studying world literature more effectively. The challenge of world literature, combined with his sense that mapping could yield important insights into literary history and criticism, led Moretti to explore a approach to literary historical research that employed distance as a method, as he would put it, and he pursued this project with zeal for the past twenty years. This much heralded project came to a sort of close in 2015, at least from Moretti's own perspective, so we are in an advantageous position to assess its strengths and weaknesses.

The publication of *Distant Reading*, which collects many of his key essays, along with *Canon/Archive*, a collection of studies conducted by his Literary Lab at Stanford, appears to mark the end of Moretti's direct engagement with computational criticism, and Moretti recently retired from teaching. Moretti famously introduced the idea of distant reading in his 2000 essay "Conjectures on World Literature," in part to deal with a problem he posed in "The Slaughterhouse of Literature," published that same year (both essays appear as chapters in his *Distant Reading*). That is, because the field of literature includes far more texts that anyone could possibly read, literary critics and historians had of necessity limited their investigations to a tiny fraction of the work actually published, making literary history little more than a commentary upon various monuments of literature rather than of literature itself. Moretti argued that other means would be required to assess the field as a whole. "Distant reading"—the very name is a provocation aimed at proponents of textual analysis, from the New Critics to advocates for deconstruction, who cherish "close reading"—would offer a new way of seeing literature made possible by looking only at data, and thus eschewing the literary text entirely.

Distant reading is not, therefore, an innovative means of interpreting texts, but a wholesale abandonment of textual interpretation. As Moretti puts it,

"A larger literary history requires other skills: sampling; statistics; work with series, titles, concordances, incipits."[15] As such, the gathering, organizing, and analyzing of data is essential, and Moretti takes advantage of large archives or Google Books to provide the data, while assiduously avoiding any reading of the individual texts themselves. In his words, "literary history will quickly become very different from what it is now: it will become 'second hand': a patchwork of other people's research, *without a single direct textual reading*."[16] The distant reader examines other units, "much smaller or much larger than the text: devices, themes, tropes—or genres and systems" (48–49), which means that distant reading does not supplement close reading, but abandons it in favor of empirical research, data collection, and data analysis.[17] This is also a spatialization of the field of literary history, such that it can be surveyed more broadly and effectively, at least from Moretti's point of view.

One of the key dichotomies I discuss in examining literary cartography involves the distinction between the itinerary and the map, which has been explored by such diverse theorists as Jameson, Michel de Certeau, and the linguists Charlotte Linde and William Labov, among others. The itinerary and the map yield two different visions of, and experiences with space, which might be understood in the older philosophical idiom as subjective and objective, but which are inextricably intertwined in practice. That is, the subject's perspective in moving about space on the street level, as it were, is informed by the speculative overview of a map-like representation, a figurative bird's-eye-view that enables a provisional sense of spatial totality while also allowing one to navigate the space along discrete, mobile trajectories. To put it more simply, as individual subjects move about, they cannot but project a mental overview or map, which in turn helps to make possible their own trajectories as well as alternate itineraries.

In an evocative play on such practices, Moretti's project of distant reading, it seems to me, attempted to engage this distinction at the level of literary history, with unexpected results. One of the more provocative literary programs to emerge in the last twenty-five years or so, Moretti's controversial approach to world literature attempted to redefine literary history according to a grand mapping or panoptic overview, moving readers farther and farther away from the "street-level" of literature. Those who know Moretti's work will already be aware of how much space and spatial practices inform his thinking, and his distant reading project grew out of a large "mapping" project to which he had been devoted for years.[18] This project of distant reading demonstrates some of the excitement, as well as the problems, with spatial criticism.

A 2017 issue of *PMLA* (i.e., *Publications of the Modern Language Association*) contained a special section devoted to Moretti's *Distant Reading*. The section included a number of interesting essays on the work, followed by Moretti's own brief response. There Moretti offers an interesting analogy, drawn from Goethe, to explain his preference for viewing things at a distance:

> When you arrive in a new town, writes Goethe in his *Italian Journey*, you should first of all climb to the top of the bell tower, to get a sense of the city as a whole. Someone else could have said: go straight to the cathedral, and see what's inside. They are both good ideas; it all depends on what you are interested in. I'm more interested in designs and layout than in brushstrokes and cathedrals. Whence *Distant Reading*.[19]

Moretti adds that "it's not just a matter of liking it better—it's that I *understand* it better if I am far away," although he concedes that both design and details may be equally important, depending on what the scholar is interested in studying.[20]

Moretti's preference for the grand overview comports well with my own sense of literary cartography. After all, the figure of the map is itself, in a sense, a means by which a clarifying overview might be achieved through a distant perspective. Yet a map is also a document to be closely read, and the dialectical relationship between minute detail and a broader representational expanse typifies the ways that maps are more-or-less useful. Moreover, the cult of "big data" to which Moretti allies himself with in this project has led not only to a movement away from close reading, but away from literature in general, and the effect, perhaps even the aim, is detrimental to the literary humanities as a whole.[21] It has also had the effect of derailing what was a more effective train of thought within spatial literary studies, while hopping aboard a trolley bound for a *cul-de-sac*, as Moretti's own retrospective comments suggest, as I discuss below.

By relying on data, the distant reader can forgo not only close reading, but any *reading* at all. In *Graphs, Maps, Trees*, Moretti provides the "abstract models" for such an approach. Using quantitative research from various sources, graphs can be made that will offer a distant reader a broad overview of the rise and fall of various genres; by plotting elements of a text on a diagram, maps provide a new look at the way literary spaces are represented and experienced; and, by graphically showing the dead ends and the continuing lines of literary conventions, trees provide a model for the "evolution" of literary forms. Each model allows the distant reader to examine different facets of the literary field, and each involves a form of explanation that minimizes the process of interpretation. As Moretti points out, the models "share a clear preference for explanation over interpretation; or perhaps, better, for the explanation of general structures over the interpretation of individual texts."[22] Here, what is interpreted are data, not texts. Unstated in Moretti's account is the degree to which collecting such data itself requires a form of reading, not unlike another kind of mapping, which depends upon ways of seeing (or aesthetics), literary conventions, principles of selection, and so on.

In a *New York Times* article, published on October 30, 2017, Moretti concedes that his aspirations in dabbling with these dark arts were not realized, but he remains largely unapologetic. "I'd rather be a failed revolutionary," he affirmed, "than someone who never tried to do a revolution in the first place."[23] However, Moretti also identified an area in which his own research and writing have suffered since he allowed himself to engage in "computational criticism." Specifically, he mentions that his work has suffered from a lack of theory, and in an understated aside admits "and, to be frank, I think it's true of the digital humanities as a whole." A certain glibness takes over in these practices, Moretti says, and knowledge itself is the ultimate victim:

> Time after time, I have felt myself (and others?) slip into micro explanations; ad hoc, often improvised reactions to the pressure of this or that finding, which I couldn't connect with any broader horizon. Knowledge seemed to shrink into half-knowledge; a false modesty, bordering on intellectual hide-and-seek; or the coarse anti-intellectualism exemplified by *Wired*'s proclamation that "correlation is enough" and that "the scientific method" is "obsolete."[24]

This general antipathy toward critical theory, so prevalent in recent years, has found both allies and champions among enthusiasts for "postcritical" approaches to literature as well. Different as their aims and methods are, Moretti's project of distant reading, perhaps unwittingly, contributed to this anti-critical and anti-theoretical tendency in contemporary literary studies.

In fairness, Moretti's own claims for this work have been somewhat more reserved, and he has not allowed himself to become so besotted with big data that he has turned his back on theory. As he has admitted, the "[f]act is, big data has produced a decline in theoretical interest, which, it its turn, has made our results often mediocre. 'More' data is not the solution here; we have enough data already. Only a resolute return to theory may change the way we work."[25]

I would argue that a "resolute return to theory" is precisely what is needed for any meaningful approach to world literature as well. Theory can provide that desirable critical distance with respect to both the texts under consideration and the resources made available by computers and databases, and it may do so without succumbing to the Silicon Valley's mania for tech-enabled "disruption." Moretti's analogy taken from Goethe offers other possibilities as well. Climbing to the top of the highest building and looking around *versus* going straight to the town's cathedral and inspecting the interior inside? These do not simply approximate the methods of distant *versus* close reading. They represent two ways of approaching the territory to be mapped, or, to put it differently, two levels of scale or frames of reference upon which to build the representation in process. Notably, Moretti also mentions Northrop Frye, who differentiates the close-up view of brush strokes in a painting versus a more distant perspective that discloses designs, and Moretti says that he finds both worthy, yet prefers "design and layout" to the details and brushstrokes. Mere preferences aside, it is clear that designs and brushstrokes are *both* necessary to the work of art, and criticism ought to pay attention to both.

Moretti's metaphor is telling. He calls for something like an "aesthetic of distance," a perspective from far away (and above), a bird's-eye view, or, in a more idealistic model, a God's-eye view that could somehow take in everything at once and allow us to see shapes, patterns, and interconnections that would be hard to discern from a more pedestrian vantage. This idea is arguably similar to that of *cognitive mapping*, whereby one attempts to create a sense of place for oneself in an otherwise unrepresentable system, but in Jameson's grander vision, becomes another example of that "desire called Marx," which is ultimately the "desire for *narrative*."[26] And yet, the map is not the territory, and it seems that many of the proponents of computational criticism or of a program of distant reading have mistaken *data* itself—or even mere *data-collection* itself—for the work to be done.

An aesthetic of distance holds merit as an attempt to map the unmappable, yet it also risks the dangers of bloodless abstraction and inhuman techno-utopianism, at which point it becomes another part of the proliferating ideologies of distance, which like those of "disruption" have become so prevalent in the era of neoliberalism. Moretti's call for a return to theory is a sign of his remorse, it could be. In any event, the approach to world literature that would use the models of distant reading should also be supported by theoretical practices that can help to make sense of this work.

The overview from the bell tower and the detailed view inside the cathedral *each* provide valuable information about the town, to continue employing Moretti's *Italian Journey* metaphor, but neither is definitive. One does not "know" the town better—whatever that would mean—by favoring one method over the other. The artist, in practice, tends to engage both registers, paying careful attention at all times both to individual brushstrokes and to more expansive designs, or to use a more literary idiom, to narrative details and to broadly descriptive overviews in a novel. Similarly, the critic ought to be able to focus on both aspects of the artist's work as well.

In literature, texts operate along the boundaries of these perspectives, combining empirical experience or personal experiences with broader social, cultural, and historical themes and concepts. Spatial literary studies would need to keep these in mind as well, making punctual interventions into the vast literary history and geography of world literature while also attempting to maintain some sort of big picture, even if that picture is constantly modified and updated. This imaginary space in between the subject's perception and the global totality, the boundary between close and distant reading, offers a promising zone for critical and theoretical practices today. Moving from methods of literary criticism or literary history back out into the broader social sphere, we can see how these alternative but interrelated frames of reference shape not only our perception of social space, but the spaces themselves.

Theory at the Limits

When Foucault sought to illustrate the operations and effects of power as a means of discipline and control in modern societies, he famously used an architectural model, Jeremy Bentham's proposed prison design for "The Panopticon." It is a memorable figure, as we may envision captive bodies are distributed within a fixed, carefully regulated space, bodies subjected to continuous, automatic surveillance. However, the chapter begins, not with a description of the prison structure, but with another analogy, namely the way in which late-seventeenth-century authorities responded to a health crisis (in this case, the outbreak of the plague) in their cities: "First, a strict spatial partitioning," in order to situate in different places those who may be classified as normal or abnormal. "Inspection functions ceaselessly" to monitor these spaces and subjects, and this "surveillance is based on a system of permanent registration," in order to record and render knowable the subjects in their spatial ensemble.[27] The organization of space and the localization, surveillance, and registration of individuals and groups within this spatial array are essential to the formation of the modern society as a whole, in Foucault's reckoning. An unidentified voice tells us: You are here, we are watching you, and we know who you are, where you are from, what you have been up to, and ultimately, where you do and do not belong. Unsurprisingly, as a number of his critics have noted, Foucault's vision thus resembles George Orwell's in *Nineteen Eighty-Four*; nor is it surprising that Orwell seems so timely today, in a moment when discussions of borders and walls, surveillance, and social distancing proliferate across the media. Unlike that of Orwell's Big Brother or Party, however, the disembodied voice sounds eerily like our own.

The establishment of *de facto* or *de jure* borders is, in some senses, an essential aspect of power and its functioning. The lines are almost always imaginary, like the parallels and meridians on the globe, but their effects are all too real. Even informal or casual borderlines, such as those separating so-called "good" from "bad" neighborhoods, for example, often function as rigid boundaries, which for some might as well be as impenetrable as walls, while for others they demarcate zones of contact or passage. Of all the real and imaginary lines that appear on our physical or mental maps, lines that we cross and lines that we dare not cross, surely none is so salient as the national border, a fact that forms itself into being over a very long history of various collective fantasies.

If a nation is an "imagined community," after all, then its borders are merely abstract, artificial, and utterly contingent; just how contingent, indeed, history itself reveals, as we see the lines drawn, erased, and redrawn all the time. Nationalism has never really respected borders, in fact, for its ideological power rests in identifying nations both within and beyond a given national space's figured limits on the map. (This is why many residents of the United States do not count as "real Americans" to those who think in terms of nationalism; this is also why nationalisms frequently embrace territorial expansion, to bring those "real" people out there into the imaginary space of the nation-state. But despite this, nationalists almost always do insist that we draw those lines somewhere.) The national border is thus itself a powerful symbol and a symbol of power; symbolic, yes, but with all too real effects and consequences.

For all the talk of a global community or a borderless world, one need only be stopped at the border—by customs officials, the police, the military, "Homeland Security" (and just think of the ideological resonances of that term!), and so on—to know just how effective and resilient those supposedly blurred lines between countries remain. And yet it is also the case that, with increased mobility and sometimes unavoidable displacement, these national borders *must be* transgressed. The global economy demands it, and this is essential to the very world market that is the foundation of all economic and political relations affecting the United States today, much to "the chagrin of the reactionaries," as Marx and Engels famously put it.[28] Indeed, the very *raison d'etre* of the border involves not merely separation but connection, for a line that marks different sides is also a line to be crossed. Transgressivity is a fundamental feature of its space.

In Latin, the idea was indicated by the term *limes* (plural, *limites*), which could be used to designate any number of limits, but which also stood for the frontier or boundary of the Roman Empire itself. The *limes* represents an end, the outer boundary, or the mark of enclosure. However, what we think of as liminality is far from the closed space of a delimited territory, but itself an in-between space of potentiality. In a ruse of etymology, one of those philological phantasms that trick the mind with false similitude or homophony, the *limes* does not necessarily share a root with the *limen*, the latter designating a "threshold." To be sure, a boundary or border might become a threshold, but only when it is transgressed. The *limen* suggests a space more explicitly understood as a site of transgressivity, a point of entry into another zone. Unlike the closed space or place given form by its perceived limits (*limites*), the liminal space or site of the *limen* is one of opening, unfolding, or becoming. Indeed, one could say that a political program of liminality, if there were any, would have to involve the transformation of the *limes* into a *limen*, the boundary becoming the threshold.

As we reflect on the restrictive or limiting power of borders, we do well to recall, to acknowledge, and to embrace the potential joy that comes with overcoming them. Indeed, to return to the Foucault and his theory of power, the forces shaping our social spaces and our selves are themselves subject to constant resistance, reversal, and redirection. To apprehend the limits as mere walls is to fail to see what lies beyond, along with what they are made of and what they represent. World literature must be quite literally beyond the bounds of any national space, and in its very worldliness, ought to be imagined as thoroughly transgressive.

Geocriticism as Critique

To the extent that spatial literary studies or geocriticism can be fruitfully brought to be on the question of world literature, therefore, these practices must also be sustained by critical theory and maintain themselves as means of critique. I would thus oppose them to those now-fashionable "postcritical" approaches, championed by Rita Felski, Toril Moi, and others.[29] Indeed, to use an older expression redolent of the Marxisms of yore, there is a fundamental element of *Ideologiekritik* in the geocritical program, which takes space, place, and mapping as concepts, phenomena, and practices wholly bound up in the mystifications, but also potential demystifications, of modern social existence.

This partly means a return to interpretation itself, as opposed to allowing literary criticism to be satisfied with mere description or summary. In a memorable paragraph from *The Political Unconscious*, Jameson observes that "Interpretation [...] always presupposes, if not a conception of the unconscious itself, then at least some mechanism of mystification or repression in terms of which it would make sense to seek a latent meaning behind a manifest one." Jameson acknowledges "the objection of the ordinary reader, when confronted with elaborate or ingenious interpretations, that the text means just what it says," but adds,

> Unfortunately, no society has ever been quite so mystified in quite so many ways as our own, saturated as it is with messages and information, the very vehicles of mystification (language, as Talleyrand put it, having

been given us in order to conceal our thoughts). If everything were transparent, then no ideology would be possible, and no domination either: evidently that is not our case.[30]

Not surprisingly, Jameson's sense of narrative as a socially symbolic act is connected to a project of ideology-critique, but of course he also insists that the critique of ideology also always includes the registering of the "positive" or utopian elements of a work.

In recent years, this sort of approach to narrative and to social criticism has come under increasing fire. *Ideologiekritik* is not only viewed as old-fashioned, but objectionable in the very worldview of its practitioners, operating as they do through a "hermeneutics of suspicion" that seeks ever to uncover hidden—sometimes intentionally hidden—meanings. And yet it seems like awfully bad timing to abandon critique. If Jameson in 1981 was thinking of a society of the spectacle, of consumer capitalism, and of what he was just beginning to refer to as *postmodernism*, then how much more suspicious ought we to be in our time of the internet's World Wide Web of "fake news," social media scandals, and complex yet stark ideological divides? We live in a time in which it has been famously remarked that it is easier to imagine the end of the world than the end of capitalism, but indeed, in which our popular culture and even our criticism seem to embrace such apocalyptic visions, as Peter Y. Paik has noted.[31] Much as critics may disdain the unnecessarily complicated, the overly simplified seems far more dangerous.

Even more than the deliberate attempts to mislead with the "fake news" and bald-faced lies that permeate public discourse today, the honest belief, held by many, that there is little beyond the ordinary appearance of things is pernicious. If anything, the boundless mystifications of our era call for more hermeneutics and more suspicion, such that appeals to the plain, the simple, and the ordinary cannot help but serve the forces of mystification and hence, the status quo, if only as an unintended consequence.

By way of conclusion, I would merely add that the achievement of a sense of place in a rapidly changing, vicissitudinous social, spatial, and spatiotemporal ensemble is not to be taken for granted, and is itself a worthy goal. This was the pedagogical and political impetus behind Jameson's conception of "cognitive mapping," and the practice of cognitive mapping (or whatever else we may want to call it) is ongoing, as the ways we make sense of the world, like the world itself, are constantly changing. But this is also why doing so can be so rewarding, a fact rarely acknowledged by the enemies of critique. As Jameson has said, "inasmuch as ideological analysis is so frequently associated with querulous and irritable negativism, it may be appropriate to stress the interest and delight all the topics, dilemmas and contradictions as well as jests and positions still have for me."³² That is, ideology critique is not only necessary and effective, but also enjoyable.

This seemingly trivial aside is actually rather important, as the critics of critique have frequently claimed that they are helping students return to or embrace the affective pleasures of literature, and yet in their disdain for critique, this pleasure sometimes resembles the hollow, consumerist ethos of mere fandom, which can hardly compare to the delights of criticism.³³ The true lovers of literature do not simply fawn over the uncritically appreciated texts. Rather, they engage with it, and in so doing, it becomes part of them. There is thus a powerful politics of proximity animating the love of literature, which can only be possible through a kind of critical aesthetic of distance. In the case of world literature, the very alterity of which is part of its appeal as it transgresses borders and transports readers from the familiar to the alien and back again, this aesthetic of distance brings foreign spaces and experiences into renewed focus, allowing us to map them even as we explore, moving effortlessly from the clocktower's expansive overview to the cathedral's intimate nooks of fine detail. As a result, world literature makes possible a greater love for the world and its multifarious spaces.

Notes

1 See Fredric Jameson, *Postmodernism, or, the Cultural Logic of Late Capitalism* (Durham: Duke University Press, 1991).
2 See Edward J. Soja, *Postmodern Geographies: The Reassertion of Space in Critical Social Theory* (London: Verso, 1989); and *Thirdspace: Journeys through Los Angeles and Other Real-and-Imagined Places* (Oxford: Blackwell, 1996).
3 See, e.g., David Damrosch, *What Is World Literature?* (Princeton: Princeton University Press, 2003); Emily Apter, *Against World Literature: On the Politics of Untranslatability* (London: Verso, 2013); and Pheng Cheah, *What Is a World? On Postcolonial Literature as World Literature* (Durham: Duke University Press, 2016).
4 See Elizabeth S. Anker and Rita Felski, eds. *Critique and Postcritique* (Durham: Duke University Press, 2017).
5 See, e.g., Youngmin Kim, "Scale, Untranslatability, Cultural Translation, and World Literature," *Journal of English Language and Literature* 64.3 (2018): 469–482.
6 See Sarah Brouillette, *UNESCO and the Fate of the Literary* (Palo Alto: Stanford University Press, 2019). On the idea of a "borderless world," see Kenichi Ohmae, *The Borderless World: Power and Strategy in the Interlinked Economy*, rev. ed. (New York: HarperCollins, 1999).
7 Jameson, *Postmodernism*, 418.
8 See Terry Eagleton, *The Ideology of the Aesthetic* (Oxford: Blackwell, 1990).
9 See Friedrich Nietzsche, *On the Genealogy of Morals*, ed. and trans. Walter Kaufmann (New York: Vintage, 1967); Edward W. Said, "Reflections on Exile," *Reflections on Exile and Other Essays* (Cambridge: Harvard University Press, 2000), 173–186.

10 Michel Foucault, "Of Other Spaces," trans. Jay Miskowiec, *Diacritics* 16 (Spring 1986): 22.
11 See Nigel Thrift, "Space," *Theory, Culture, and Society* 23.2–3 (2006): 139–146.
12 Bertrand Westphal, *Geocriticism: Real and Fiction Spaces*, trans. Robert T. Tally Jr. (New York: Palgrave Macmillan, 2011), 9–10.
13 See, e.g., my *Topophrenia: Place, Narrative, and the Spatial Imagination* (Bloomington: Indiana University Press, 2019), 40.
14 See., e.g., my *For a Ruthless Critique of All That Exists: Literature in an Age of Capitalist Realism* (Winchester: Zer0 Books, 2022); see also Bruce Robbins, *Criticism and Politics: A Polemical Introduction* (Palo Alto: Stanford University Press, 2022).
15 Franco Moretti, *Distant Reading* (London: Verso, 2013), 67.
16 Ibid., 48.
17 Ibid., 48–49. For an example of the sort of quantitative research undertaken by Moretti, see his "'Operationalizing,'" in Moretti, ed., *Canon/Archive: Studies in Quantitative Formalism from the Stanford Literary Lab* (New York: n+1 Books, 2017).
18 See Moretti, *Graphs, Maps, Trees: Abstract Models for a Literary History* (London: Verso, 2005). Spatially oriented literary criticism and history featured prominently in his earlier books as well, in particular *Atlas of the European Novel, 1800–1900* (London: Verso, 1998) and *Modern Epic: The World System from Goethe to García-Márquez* (London; Verso, 1994).
19 Moretti, "Franco Moretti: A Response," *PMLA* 132.3 (May 2017): 686.
20 Ibid.
21 For a contrary view, see Ted Underwood, *Distant Horizons: Digital Evidence and Literary Change* (Chicago: University of Chicago Press, 2019), which argues for the use of digital archives, statistical tools, and computational criticism in literary studies.
22 Moretti, *Graphs, Maps, Trees*, 9.
23 Quoted in Jennifer Schuessler, "Reading by the Numbers: When Big Data Meets Literature," *New York Times,* October 30, 2017, https://www.nytimes.com/2017/10/30/arts/franco-moretti-stanford-literary-lab-big-data.html.
24 Moretti, "A Response," 687.
25 Ibid.
26 Jameson, "Introduction," *The Ideologies of Theory, Volume 1: Situations of Theory* (Minneapolis: University of Minnesota Press, 1988), xxxviii.
27 Foucault, *Discipline and Punish: The Birth of the Prison*, trans. Alan Sheridan (New York: Random House, 1977), 195–196.
28 Karl Marx and Friedrich Engels, *The Communist Manifesto*, trans. anon. (New York: Signet, 1998), 54.
29 See Rita Felski, *The Limits of Critique* (Chicago: University of Chicago Press, 2015); and Toril Moi, *Revolution of the Ordinary: Literary Studies after Wittgenstein, Austin, and Cavell* (Chicago: University of Chicago Press, 2018).
30 Jameson, *The Political Unconscious: Narrative as a Socially Symbolic Act* (Ithaca: Cornell University Press, 1981), 60–61.
31 See Peter. Y. Paik, "Extinction and Judgment: Misanthropy in the Anthropocene," *Journal of English Language and Literature* 65.2 (2019): 203–223.
32 Jameson, *The Ideologies of Theory* (London: Verso, 2008), xi.
33 See Robbins, "Critical Correctness," in *The Chronicle of Higher Education,* March 12, 2019, http://www.chronicle.com/article/The-Neoliberal-Looting-of/245874.

Chapter 3

WORLD LITERATURE AND ITS DISCONTENTS

Any discussion of world literature today is apt to lead critics into a garden of forking paths, a grand narrative that is also an elaborate labyrinth, where each step simultaneously reveals or forecloses apparently infinite possibilities. Or, perhaps, to cite another tale by Jorge Luis Borges from the same period, it is more like the library of Babel, a hauntingly vast bibliographic phantasmagoria in which every imaginable work of literature confronts the bewildered reader, from sheer nonsense to supreme masterpiece, although part of the unending *Angst* of such an approach to the whole "world" of literature is the awareness that such distinctions cannot be easily made.

The question of world literature, its functions and effects, as well as its value as a formal object of literary study, is deceptively complex. On the one hand, the widespread availability of and interest in literary works produced in various countries, languages, and cultures from around the globe would seem to be wholly beneficial; these texts educate readers about foreign experiences and social forms, while making possible transnational and cross-cultural literary relations. On the other hand, such seemingly cosmopolitan practices have participated in processes of globalization which have frequently elided cultural specificity, either reducing or fetishizing the differences among societies, and at the same time creating a marketplace for a certain type of "world literature," often at the expense of the variety and wealth of literature written, read, and studied throughout the world. During an era of multinational capitalism or of the globalization of culture, these questions have gained greater urgency and complexity, and it is perhaps not surprising that *world literature*—as a concept, a field of study, or even a genre—has emerged as a major topic in literary studies in these opening years of the twenty-first century, and it has become a key element of contemporary criticism and theory.

World Literature in the Twenty-First Century

Exemplary of this sense of urgency, Emily Apter's provocative book, *Against World Literature: On the Politics of Untranslatability*, raises troubling questions about the study of world literature as a disciplinary or subdisciplinary field.[1] To be clear, Apter is for the most part an advocate of expanding the study of literature beyond national borders and linguistic traditions, and she certainly does not argue that literary studies ought to return to a more narrowly circumscribed social, national, or linguistic domain. However, she is justly concerned that "World Literature" as a field of study and as a marketing genre has for several decades functioned as a cultural adjunct to those processes of globalization which have masked, undermined, or even destroyed cultural differences in the name of the of a single world market and a global consumerist or neoliberal economic system. "World Literature," which Apter capitalizes in order to distinguish it from the literature or literatures of the world, has also established a star-system of transnational writers or texts whose ready-made translatability at once fetishizes cultural differences and makes them easily consumable commodities for a largely Western (if not strictly American) book-buying public. This, in turn, displaces and disavows those social customs, experiences, and even words that are fundamentally untranslatable. Apter argues that, by focusing precisely on untranslatability, critics will be better able to understand and celebrate the importance of world literature for comparative literary studies in the twenty-first century, while also being better prepared to battle the influence of the crudely commodified "World Literature" foisted upon us by the forces of cultural globalization.

Apter's fascinating book joins a panoply of studies whose general theme might be characterized, with apologies to Nietzsche, as "the use and disadvantages of world literature for life." In the past twenty-five or thirty years especially, the subject of world literature has received increasing consideration both from scholars of comparative literature and those who have traditionally operated within fields such as English, along with those hybrid disciplines that may be circumscribed by a single, discernibly national language and literature or focused on a slightly broader domain, such as linguistic grouping (say, Romance languages) or area studies (e.g., Asian Studies).

During this period, for example, major works by Franco Moretti, including *Modern Epic: The World-System from Goethe to García Márquez*, *Graphs, Maps, Trees: Abstract Models for a Literary History*, his massive five-volume project on *The Novel* (in English, two volumes), and, most recently, *Distant Reading*, a compendium of ten of his more controversial articles over the past two decades, have invigorated and transformed the older discussions of world literature, while also inciting lively debates about the subject.[2] Pascale Casanova's celebrated study, *The World Republic of Letters*, outlined a novel view of world literature using world-systems theory and the sociological theory of Pierre Bourdieu; her approach rejected claims of universality, but it also drew criticism for its apparent Eurocentrism. One ought not to discount the role played by the enhanced attention to what used to be called "Third World literature" in helping to generate renewed interest in world literature, and leading postcolonial theorist Gayatri Chakravorty Spivak, in *Death of a Discipline*, introduced the concept of planetarity in arguing for a comparative literature more attuned to the geopolitical inquiry of area studies. Additionally, several important collections of essays—for example, Christopher Prendergast's *Debating World Literature*, Haun Saussy's *Comparative Literature in an Age of Globalization*, and Wai Chee Dimock and Lawrence's Buell's *Shades of the Planet*—chronicled and contributed to ongoing critical controversies over the phenomenon of world literature.[3] Operating as an author (*What Is World Literature?*; *How to Read World Literature*), as the editor of significant essay collections (*World Literature in Theory*; *Teaching World Literature*), and as general editor of a widely used textbook (*The Longman Anthology of World Literature*), David Damrosch has tirelessly promoted world literature, while remaining astutely aware of its challenges and limitations.[4] Alexander Beecroft's *An Ecology of World Literature: From Antiquity to the Present Day* has drawn connections between ancient and modern literature, as well as between western and non-western texts, in developing new ways of looking at both small- and large-scale bodies of literature.[5] This is only to name a few of the key works of the past few decades, and the list is far from comprehensive.[6] But to shift from a Nietzschean to a Freudian idiom, it does give some indication of the wealth of recent criticism devoted to world literature and its discontents.

My own interest in world literature derived, initially, from an aversion to what I took to be artificial and unhelpful limits placed on the study of literature, particularly in the form of literary nationalism and more particularly in what I took to be the parochial nationalism of American literary studies. Coming from a rather Eurocentric, but decidedly transnational, theoretical background in twentieth-century literature and philosophy, in which texts originally written in English, French, German, Danish, Russian, Spanish, and Italian might be considered in the same course of study, I felt "irked, cramped, and fettered" (to use Herman Melville's words) by the profoundly national organization and project of literary studies in the United States and of American Studies in particular. Working on a dissertation devoted to Melville, a powerfully postnational writer in his own time who was nevertheless subjected to an intensive critical project of hypercanonization and presented as a typically "American" writer in the twentieth century, I rediscovered Goethe's concept of *Weltliteratur* through the quite different perspectives of

Erich Auerbach, Edward Said, and Franco Moretti, among others. Philology, *Weltliteratur*, world-systems theory, and geocriticism, broadly conceived, enabled me to grasp both the postnational project of *Moby-Dick* (as I argued for it) and the critique of the institutions of literary criticism that served to occlude the international or transnational elements of American literature as a disciplinary field. For me, then, world literature was a critical weapon to be wieldy against a narrow-minded, arrogant, and largely isolationist field of study.

This chapter revisits this sense of world literature by focusing on a few moments in the trajectory of the concept, that is, on key points in the development of the idea of *Weltliteratur*, from Goethe through Marx, thence to Auerbach, Said, and Moretti, to name a few of the most famous figures. Obviously, there is nothing remotely exhaustive or even representative about this particular narrative. But, in focusing on world literature as a critique of the nationalist organization of culture in the form of literary studies circumscribed by, and limited to, a nationalist politico-historiographic project, I want to register its value for rethinking the study of literature more broadly. This is particularly relevant in an era when, in the United States, literary studies in general is under fire, but most endangered are programs in comparative literature, ancient and modern languages, and classics. The reasons for such attacks are manifold, but one element of them which recurs in political discourse is the need to train Americans in skills and knowledge they are supposed to need as citizens and workers. Hence, the nationalism of an earlier form of American Studies (see *infra* Chapter 6) is causing lasting, possibly irreversible damage to literary studies in the present.

A Cosmopolitan Character

Although the word *Weltliteratur* predates Goethe's usage of it and although we could undoubtedly cite earlier visions of what today is understood to be "world literature," Goethe is almost universally credited as the originator of the concept.[7] The word is used in conversation with Eckermann from 1827, in the context of having recently read a Chinese novel. Surprisingly, perhaps, at a moment when many national literatures (including, of course, German literature) were only beginning to achieve the sort of status and recognition that the most fiercely nationalist proponents might have hoped for, Goethe asserts that "national literature does not have much to say."[8] Goethe advises that writers must look to foreign examples for an aesthetic education that will be truly worthy of the modern world. Ironically, perhaps, it is the works of "the ancient Greeks, in whose works the beauty of mankind is constantly represented," who provide the model for Goethe, but in the clearly prenational cultures of classical antiquity, Goethe seems to discover a smaller-scale "world literature" that is of incomparable value to producers of *Weltliteratur* in the present age. *Nationalliteratur* is not a very useful concept, according to Goethe, who declares "the epoch of world literature is at hand, and all must strive to hasten its approach."[9]

The more zealous readers might descry in that imperative a rallying cry of "Writers of the World, Unite!" In any case, one proponent of a sort of literary international and admirer of Goethe appeared to endorse the project of a *Weltliteratur*. Unfortunately, Karl Marx never wrote a work of literary criticism, although according to Paul Lafargue, he planned to write a book on Balzac's *La Comédie Humaine* "as soon as he had finished his book on economics,"[10] but that proved to be a rather demanding project. Nevertheless, a meditation on literature pervades Marx's thought, even when it is presented in the sometimes arid economic writings, and Marx's influence on the study of literature has been tremendous. S. S. Prawer, in his magnificent study *Karl Marx and World Literature*, has demonstrated how Marx used the works of various poets and creative writers to make his points about politics, economics, and social theory. Indeed, whether one wishes to view him as a particularly "literary" writer or not, as the initiator of a certain *discursive practice* (to use the Foucauldian formulation),[11] Marx is one of the most important figures in the history and study of world literature. And for Marx, it is a "world" literature, for he will assert that the developments of capitalism, and in particular the emergence of the world market in which may be glimpsed the initial vistas of our own era of globalization, render local and national literatures obsolete. Like Goethe before him, Marx affirms that the time has come for world literature.

Marx's re-conception of Goethe's somewhat untimely notion of *Weltliteratur* must be understood in terms of the revolutionary social and spatial transformations associated with the rise and spread of capitalist relations of production. In *The Communist Manifesto*, Marx and Engels explicitly link the emergence of a world literature to the world market and to the incipient, but also ineluctable processes of globalization within the capitalist mode of production. The *national*, upon their view, is essentially reactionary or retrogressive. In the famous passage, they write:

> The bourgeoisie has through its exploitation of the world market given *a cosmopolitan character* to production and consumption in every country. To the great chagrin of Reactionists, it has drawn from under the feet of industry the national ground on which it stood. All old-established national industries have been destroyed or are daily being destroyed. They are dislodged by new industries, whose introduction becomes

a life and death question for all civilized nations, by industries that no longer work up indigenous raw material, but raw material drawn from the remotest zones; industries whose products are consumed, not only at home, but in every quarter of the globe. In place of the old wants, satisfied by the production of the country, we find new wants, requiring for their satisfaction the products of distant lands and climes. In place of the old local and national seclusion and self-sufficiency, we have intercourse in every direction, universal inter-dependence of nations. And as in material, so also in intellectual production. The intellectual creations of individual nations become common property. National one-sidedness and narrow-mindedness become more and more impossible, and from the numerous national and local literatures, there arises a world literature.[12]

Weltliteratur is thus part of the dynamic processes of the establishment and spread of the *Weltmarkt*. The resistance to this emergent form of globalization was, in Marx's view, largely driven by reactionary politics and by a socially retrogressive view of culture, history, and economics. Nationalism, which in its cultural forms must include the celebration of a national literature, is from this perspective a reactionary force, one which Marx could recognize as already *residual*—in the sense of Raymond Williams's famous tripartite scheme of residual, dominant, emergent forms—in 1848.[13]

Even earlier, in *The German Ideology*, Marx and Engels had suggested that the world market actively conditioned the mental or intellectual productions of individuals. There they write that "separate individuals have, with the broadening of their activity into world-historical activity, become more and more enslaved under […] a power which has become more and more enormous and, in the last instance, turns out to be the world market." And, Marx and Engels go on,

> the real intellectual wealth of the individual depends entirely on the wealth of his real connections. Only then will the separate individuals be liberated from the various national and local barriers, be brought into practical connection with the material and intellectual production of the whole world and be put in a position to acquire the capacity to enjoy this all-sided production of the whole earth (the creations of man).[14]

For Marx, in the struggles of the 1830s and 1840s and in the heady moments of the revolutions of 1848, the promise of the overthrow of capitalism was also tied to the overthrow of national and local "narrow-mindedness."

Literature, like other "intellectual productions" and the "creations of man," must therefore strive to be world literature.

As Marx and Engels maintained in 1848, the development of the world market had begun to accomplish something like the cultural work of globalization, lending to any work of "high" culture (art, literature, music, and so on) a "cosmopolitan character," and definitively casting asunder those local and national prejudices which, like the "idiocy of rural life," limited the human potential ultimately to be achieved only upon "the world stage." As Prawer notes, even at this early phase of Marx's career, world literature forms an indispensable element of Marx's own thought. "Above all: the economic development with which, in Marx's view, the fate of literature was inevitably bound up, was working toward the creation of *world* literature," Prawer writes. "On the evidence of Marx's literary allusions in *The Communist Manifesto* and the *Neue Rheinische Zeitung* one might say that in one important sense the era of world literature had already arrived. It already existed in Marx's mind, that store-house of literary experiences and reminiscences from many centuries and many lands."[15]

The Rise of English Literature

In what is perhaps best viewed as one of those Hegelian ruses of history, the dramatic expansion of the world market in the late nineteenth and early twentieth centuries was arguably accompanied by a much more intensive form of cultural nationalism, which manifested itself in a variety of ways. Most relevant to my purposes, here is the rise of a self-consciously national literature, which was reinforced if not created by new institutions designed, at least in part, to shape a peculiarly national culture. Among these developments, the rise of modern literature departments organized by language or linguistic groups, but frequently operating as custodians of a distinctively national literary tradition, is one of the more influential. For example, an aspiring writer in Nathaniel Hawthorne's day would not have had the opportunity to study English literature (i.e., literature written in the English language, regardless of its author's country of origin) at college or university. But a century later, English as an academic discipline was well established as part of the curriculum of postsecondary education, and in many cases, the Anglophone tradition established by and in this disciplinary field could serve nationalist ideological ends.

Harvard University dates the birth of its English Department to 1876, the year that the long-standing Harvard professor of rhetoric Francis James Child was officially appointed as "Professor of English." This movement from rhetoric to literature (via language, presumably), and thence toward national literatures, was fairly typical of the development of the discipline. As Robert Scholes notes in *The Rise and Fall of English*, Yale University first listed a Professorship in Rhetoric and English Literature only in 1863, and it was the same position that had been previously established as a Professorship in Rhetoric and Oratory in 1817.[16] Hence, even with the term "English literature" in the title, the office was still essentially that of a rhetor, and the literature studied was fundamentally exemplary, offering models for oratorical or rhetorical style. The study of literature was secondary at best, until perhaps the end of the nineteenth century, for most professors of English.

For Scholes, the "fall of English" is a result of the discipline's conscious decision to make literary studies the primary area of instruction and scholarly focus, thus adopting the hermeneutic approach from philology, among other things. But the turn toward literature was also very much part of a nationalist cultural movement, both in Great Britain and in the United States. One can see this clearly in Terry Eagleton's brief sketch of "The Rise of English" in *Literary Theory: An Introduction*, which focuses primarily on the rise of that field within the United Kingdom, and David Shumway, in *Creating American Civilization*, has traced a much more detailed genealogy of the rise of American literature as an academic discipline in the United States.[17] Once the British Empire required an "innate" literary and cultural heritage on par with that of the Roman Empire, such a tradition was found to have been there all along, and thus could be made ready for dissemination among the burgeoning ranks of formally educable citizenry. Once the American Empire (or whatever its advocates prefer to call it) began to rival and overlap with the British, it too needed such a treasury of distinctively "American" culture, and unsurprisingly the artifacts that would constitute something like a canon could be easily found and promoted. The rise of modern literature as a field of study goes hand in hand with, and tacitly undergirds, a nationalist cultural and political program.

Additionally, the turn toward modern languages and toward the national literature coincided, not necessarily coincidentally, with the marked demotion of ancient languages, especially Greek and Latin, in the curriculum. The preference for work and tongues *à la mode contemporaine* is not surprising, but turning away from ancient languages is also part of a broader and long-developing nationalist movement. As Benedict Anderson put it in *Imagines Communities*, "the old sacred languages—Latin, Greek, and Hebrew—were forced to mingle on equal ontological footing with a motley plebeian crowd of vernacular rivals, in a movement which complimented their earlier demotion in the market-place by print capitalism."[18] The rise of the vernacular in Europe is associated in the Renaissance with the chrysalid emergence of the modern nation-state. As the older "universal" languages disappear, the modern languages mark their distinctiveness and express an increasingly national character.

Similarly, but also operating at a rather different institutional level, the late-nineteenth-century development of English and other disciplines in the modern languages served essentially nationalistic purposes. For instance, Shumway has shown that American literature's "most significant achievement was to secure for Americans a belief in their success as a culture. [...] The discipline, in other words, produced a widely accepted representation of American civilization that not only defined its character but 'verified' its existence."[19] From its early stirring at the turn of the century and increasing momentum after World War I, this idea became during the Cold War a way of establishing the United States as "not merely a civilization, but the savior of civilization itself," since the unique tradition of American literature placed it slightly outside and above the rest world literature.[20] At its most obvious, we see this in the revelations about the CIA's involvement with literary journals such as *The Paris Review*, which became part of a concerted effort to show that American culture (to be found in, say, an Ernest Hemingway) was superior to the communist cultures (seen in the work of a Jean-Paul Sartre, e.g.), thus fighting the Cold War on an aesthetic and literary front.[21]

However, in another ruse of history—at this early moment of intensive cultural nationalism in the run up to, waging of, and ensuing aftermath of World War I, with institutions of literature being established on largely national grounds and serving discernibly national ends—many of the leading practitioners of literature (i.e., poets, novelists, and other creative writers) were quite self-consciously transgressing these conceptual borders by attempting to produce works that, in a sense, could be global in their frames of reference and effects. The great works of high modernism, as Moretti discovered in his study of the subject, *Modern Epic*, tended to exceed the boundaries of the nation-state, becoming what he refers to as "world-texts." Works like T. S. Eliot's "The Waste Land" or Joyce's *Ulysses* figure forth "worlds" well beyond the English or Irish national imaginary, just as Goethe's *Faust* or Melville's *Moby-Dick* had attempted in various ways to represent the whole world in their pages. The "modern epic," the modernist work of art that breaks the generic limits of the novel-form, is the "symbolic form" for this new, multinational or postnational world system, according to Moretti.[22] Ironically, perhaps, many of these same "world-texts" have become almost sacred national texts within their countries of origin, where they are viewed as particularly evocative of a uniquely national character (e.g., seeing *Moby-Dick* as "the great American novel"), and yet the scope of their geopolitical frame of reference transcends the national entirely. As with Marx's *Weltliteratur*, whose development was tied to the *Weltmarkt*, the imperialist and commercial expansions of the late nineteenth and early twentieth centuries created the conditions for a world literature, even as the (cultural) reactionaries were seeking ever more fervently to impose a narrow-minded nationalism on literary cultures domestically.

The Perspective of Exile

Along these lines, it is worth noting how international so-called national literatures really are. Eagleton's early study of "English" modernism, *Exiles and Émigrés*, begins by observing that "the seven most significant writers of twentieth-century English literature have been a Pole, three Americans, two Irishmen, and an Englishman. [...] With the exception of D. H. Lawrence, the heights of modern English literature have been dominated by foreigners and émigrés: Conrad, James, Eliot, Pound, Yeats, Joyce."[23] Eagleton argues that the tumultuous experiences of the early twentieth century made it impossible for the traditional English novelist to achieve a sense of totality that would have seemed more feasible in previous eras; rather, the perspective of the outsider, with its "originality of vision," was required. Or, to mention another modernist critic, George Steiner has asserted that much of the great twentieth-century literature was produced by writers—such as Conrad, Beckett, or Nabokov—who were using a foreign language, distinct from their native tongues. Amid the horrors of the first half of the last century, as Steiner observes in *Extraterritorial*, "[i]t seems proper that those who create art in a civilization of quasi-barbarism which has made so many homeless, which has torn up tongues and peoples by the root, should themselves be poets unhoused and wanderers across language."[24]

Ironies abound. While the rise in the formal study of literature, which presumably would include the works that constitute the putative field of world literature, served nationalist ideological purposes, the aims and substance of the texts studied in such departments were often far from nationalist. Modernism's tense relationship with national cultures accounts for this, in some ways. In his sequel to his earlier study, *English After the Fall*, Scholes asserts that the movement from rhetoric to literature, which made possible the formation of English as the discipline it became, was abetted if not caused by the prevalence of modernist texts. "Because modernist works like *Ulysses* or *The Waste Land* needed explaining, the whole new discipline of English became oriented to explication, with texts difficult enough to require academic interpretation becoming privileged in our classrooms, including complex older works, like the metaphysical poems of John Donne."[25] Scholes's observation helps to account for the emergence of literary critical expertise, of the need to train students in a sort of exegetical method by which the texts under considered could disclose hidden or at least difficult to discern meanings. But this does not explain why practitioners within the linguistically determined field of English literature (or French, German, Spanish, Italian, Chinese, Japanese, etc.) became custodians of more strictly national literary heritages. The rise of comparative literature, a disciplinary field which partakes of this movement while also resisting it, highlights the dilemma faced by literary scholars who found themselves trapped within the institutional parameters of national languages and cultures.

One of the most important figures in both the emergence of comparative literature as a disciple and in the reassertion of world literature into critical discussions is Auerbach, whose "Philologie der Weltliteratur" (translated by Miriam and Edward Said as "Philology and *Weltliteratur*") provided a theoretical rationale for the sort of comparative literary practice he envisioned, and whose *Mimesis: The Representation of Reality in Western Literature* stands as the exemplar of this type of work. Famously, the philologist undertook and completed the project while in exile in Turkey, in flight from the Nazis, before coming to the United States after the war.[26] Said, in his "Reflections on Exile," has suggested that Auerbach's own work, as well as that of the great many "exiled" writers, benefits mightily from an "originality of vision": "Most people are principally aware of one culture, one setting, one home; exiles are aware of at least two, and this plurality of vision gives rise to an awareness of simultaneous dimension, an awareness that—to borrow a phrase from music—is *contrapuntal*."[27] Of course, Said himself is a kind of exile, a Palestinian-born, secular Christian living in New York City, and his own "contrapuntal" analysis animates his most influential works.

For Auerbach, as for Marx but in very different circumstances, the prospect of a world literature is celebrated precisely in its contrast to the baleful effects, and perhaps even baleful aims, of national literature. Given then-recent events, Auerbach's desire to transcend the nationalisms of the day is completely understandable. In "Philology and *Weltliteratur*," Auerbach concludes that "our philological home is the earth: it can no longer be the nation. [...] We must return, in admittedly altered circumstances, to the knowledge that prenational medieval culture already possessed: the knowledge that the spirit [*Geist*] is not national."[28] Auerbach then quotes the *Didascalion* of the twelfth-century theologian Hugh of Saint Vincent (or Hugo of Saint Victor) in the original Latin, which would have been the "universal" language in the monk's day; in English, it reads:

> It is, therefore, a great source of virtue for the practiced mind to learn, bit by bit, first to change about in visible and transitory things, so that afterwards it may be able to leave them behind altogether. The man who finds his homeland sweet is still the tender beginner; he to

whom every soil is as his native one is already strong; but he is perfect to whom the entire world is as a foreign land.[29]

Summing up his discussion of the philology of world literature, Auerbach insists that such a worldview, transposed and adapted to our own era, "is a good way also for one who wishes to earn a proper love for the world."[30]

World literature thus becomes a sort of literature of exile, by which even non-exiles might perceive the "entire world as a foreign land," thereby avoiding and combatting the "national narrow-mindedness" so opposed by Marx. From this perspective, as Apter discusses at some length,[31] world literature is almost a theology, a practice by which humanity may be redeemed.

A New World Order

Near the end of his magisterial *Mimesis*, Auerbach observes that "[t]he strata of societies and their different ways of life have become inextricably mingled. [...] Beneath the conflicts, and also through them, an economic and cultural leveling process is taking place."[32] This "economic and cultural leveling process" is akin to the forces of bourgeois capitalism that had "given the world a cosmopolitan character," in Marx's view. In Auerbach, the recognition is bittersweet, for it simultaneously registers an elegiac sense of the loss of local specificity, distinctive cultures, and literary diversity while also highlighting a sort of utopian humanism, in as much as these national differences had motivated their partisans to engage in war, genocide, racism, and terror. The "approaching unification and simplification" of culture and society might alleviate the "dangers and catastrophes" of the present era, Auerbach asserts, but it may not please those who "admire and love our epoch for the sake of its abundance of life and the incomparable historical vantage point which it affords."[33]

Auerbach's assessment of the "economic and cultural leveling process" is perfectly in line with then-contemporary critiques, whether formulated by critics on the left (such as Max Horkheimer and Theodor W. Adorno in *The Dialectic of Enlightenment*) or launched from a much more conservative position (as in Richard Weaver's analysis of "the dissolution of the West" in *Ideas Have Consequences*).[34] Yet, in the discontinuous expansions of capital and culture in the decades that followed these postwar works, the proteiform processes that by the late 1980s had been given a single, rather expansive name, *globalization*, made possible new ways of imagining both national literatures and world literature, among which the aforementioned rise in mainstream awareness of Third World literature is perhaps the most easily recognizable development.[35] In the intervening years, Said and other Auerbach-inspired scholars kept the flame alive for a world literature that could be the true ground for a comparative literary studies, a *Weltliteratur* that neither simply effaced national differences nor produced a World's Fair exhibition of cultural stereotypes. However, on the curricular level and in literary scholarship, at least in the United States, world literature remained a marginal area of inquiry.

Not surprisingly, perhaps, it was around the moment of the now risible "End of History"—not Hegel's, but Francis Fukuyama's epigonic formulation of Hegel's notion, which was supposed to have heralded the fall of the Berlin Wall, the break-up of the Soviet Union and of the Eastern Bloc, and the anti-climactic conclusion to the Cold War—when there seems to have opened up conceptual space for considering world literature anew.[36] In any event, the explosion of journal articles and books on the subject in the 1990s suggests a *Zeitgeist* favorable for *Weltliteratur*, and the tendency shows no signs of slowing in the opening decades of the twenty-first century. For example, according to a recent search of the *MLA Bibliography*, the number of articles and books in English whose titles included the term "World Literature" or "Weltliteratur" doubled from the 1980s to the 1990s; from 2000 to 2015, over three hundred such publications have appeared, which is nearly twice the total published in the entire twentieth century. Some 180 years after Goethe's famous pronouncement, it appears that, at least in the domain of literary scholarship, the epoch of world literature is at hand.

At the same time, the late rise of world literature has drawn criticism. For one thing, as Apter and others have noted, world literature has become a marketing genre, a commodified and easily consumed product for which "exotic" is merely an advertising label, and whose consumers are likely no more worldly than consumers of other products manufactured in the far-flung regions of the planet but available at retail chains like Walmart, Amazon, and so on. As a subdiscipline within English, world literature (sometimes called "World Literature in English") has emerged from the spectacular aftermath of what Salmon Rushdie called "The Empire Writes Back," in which poets from former British colonies like India, Nigeria, or Jamaica begin to be recognized as leading figures in contemporary English literature. And yet the generally welcome inclusion of new authors into a canon of English literature has, in many cases, established only a new elite, which in turn has the (possibly unintended) effect of sometimes ignoring, if not proscribing, authors and texts deemed too different for inclusion. Apter's "untranslatables" offer a telling example. The parallels between *this* form of world literature and a triumphalist embrace of commercial globalization are discomfiting, and Apter remains uneasy with "the entrepreneurial, bulimic drive to anthologize and curricularize the world's cultural resources."[37] World literature, in this sense, becomes little more than the well-stocked market in which exotic fruits are sold alongside local produce. This may not a bad thing, in and of itself, but it hardly constitutes a revolutionary rethinking of literary practice, criticism, or theory. Moreover, in fetishizing and commodified cultural difference along national lines, "world literature" so conceived might in effect reify the very nationalistic ideological characters that were to have been overcome by adopting a more worldly, perhaps postnational perspective.

Another objection has to do with what lies within these worldly texts. That is, to what extent are they part of a "world" literature? Are they not merely local, regional, or national texts originating in various parts of the planet? Or are certain texts somehow more worldly than others, hence better suited for inclusion in a world literature? As Christian Thorne notes in "The Sea is Not a Place; or, Putting the World Back in World Literature," "*world literature* is the name for a certain tendency within the global literary system, the propensity for works aiming for an international audience to make themselves frictionless."[38] In effect, then, the basic model of national literatures persists, only now they might include various settings outside of a particular nation state. The fundamental alterity to have been made available for readers' experience by world literature goes by the wayside.

Leviathan in an Era of Multinational Capitalism

Thorne argues that the novel form itself likely cannot operate with the world, as opposed to the nation, the region, or some smaller geographical and conceptual unit, as its effective frame of reference. Interestingly enough, Thorne concedes in a note that *Moby-Dick* might serve a valid counterexample. *Moby-Dick* does seem to exceed the bounds of not only national literary and cultural reference, but of all boundaries, including those of good taste and propriety. (This is part of its delights, as many fans would argue.) Said has proposed that Melville's text is "about" the whole world, although he confesses that "it seems silly to say it this way."[39] In *Modern Epic*, Moretti identified it by name as a "world-text," one whose "frame of reference is no longer that of the nation state," but that of the world-system in Immanuel Wallerstein's sense.[40] I have argued in *Melville, Mapping, and Globalization* that Melville's uncategorizable novel can be seen as proleptically sketching a literary cartography of the world system in its emergence, a world system that, in the words of Fredric Jameson, has become "the true ground of Being" and the "untranscendable horizon" of thinking today.[41] And yet, if *Moby-Dick* somehow represents an emblematic text for our own age of globalization, it is curious to find its memorable, multicultural *dramatis personae* jostling alongside the cosmopolitan characters of Marx and Engels in the mid-nineteenth century. The great "world-text" produced in an epoch of *Weltliteratur*, a deviously cruising, zig-zagging, and circumnavigating whale which refuses to become a Hobbesian leviathan or nation-state, *Moby-Dick* is a perfect example of a text to be included in a course on world literature. But it is hardly a model for world literature today, is it?

Perhaps. In his marvelous study of "Herman Melville and the World We Live In," the subtitle to *Mariners, Renegades, and Castaways*, C. L. R. James—like Marx, Auerbach, and Said, an exile—argues that the 1851 novel does not belong to its own times so much as it does to "ours," in the postwar generation that had witnessed the slaughterhouse produced by rampant nationalism, industrial capitalism, bureaucratic statecraft, psychological malaise, and the ineffectuality of the intellectuals, all elements which (according to James) are analyzed and criticized with spectacular acumen and insight by Melville in his writings. Famously, James wrote this book while being detained at Ellis Island (he was eventually deported), and under such circumstances, it abounds with historical ironies. In the early 1950s, *Moby-Dick* was becoming thoroughly absorbed within the newly established field of academic American Studies as perhaps the quintessentially "American" novel. This is also right around the time of Auerbach's panegyric to a certain understanding of *Weltliteratur* as an escape from the national. In the original edition of *Mariners, Renegades, and Castaways*, James includes an impassioned and telling dedication to his son, who, he adds "will be 21 years old in 1970, by which time I hope he and his generation will have left behind them forever all the problems of nationality."[42] For the very worldly James, *Moby-Dick* offered a glimpse into the prospects of a world and a literature worthy of a postnational epoch.

Now I have gone and named a text, a "hypercanonical" one at that, which is somehow supposed to represent the world of world literature, while clearly maintaining its own limited position within a global literary history. An eccentric choice, maybe? But then *Moby-Dick* is a rather eccentric text. We began this chapter by traversing the grounds of a garden of forking paths and exploring a library of Babel, only to stumble upon another Borgesian figure, the Aleph, an impossible spatiotemporal being containing all points in time and space, everywhere and all at once.[43] At one point in the novel, the narrator hyperbolically laments the sheer outrageousness of his ambition, and implores his friends to hold his arms,

> For in the mere act of penning my thoughts of this Leviathan, they weary me, and make me faint with their outreaching comprehensiveness of sweep, as if to include the whole circle of the sciences, and all the generations of whales, and men, and mastodons, past, present, and

to come, with all the revolving panoramas of empire on earth, and throughout the whole universe, not excluding its suburbs.[44]

It is a lot to take in. A text that contains the whole world would indeed be well suited to world literature, should such a thing be possible or even conceivable!

As a practical matter, the identification and study of certain "masterpieces" is a fairly standard approach to world literature. In his introduction to *Teaching World Literature*, Damrosch mentions three basic models—classics, masterpieces, and windows to the world—which have their advantages and disadvantages in the classroom. A text like *Moby-Dick* could neatly fit into each category, while also blurring the lines between them. "World literature surveys can never hope to cover the world," notes Damrosch. "We do better if we seek to *uncover* a variety of compelling works from distinctive traditions, through creative combinations and juxtapositions guided by whatever specific themes and issues we wish to raise in a particular course."[45] This is probably a good way to think about the theory and practice of world literature as well. In any case, the mere impossibility of a project ought not prevent one from undertaking it, a lesson taught so often and so well by literature from around the world.

Notes

1 See Emily Apter, *Against World Literature: On the Politics of Untranslatability* (London: Verso, 2013).
2 See Franco Moretti, *Modern Epic: The World System from Goethe to García Márquez*, trans. Quentin Hoare (London: Verso, 1994); *Atlas of the European Novel, 1800–1900* (London: Verso, 1998); *Graphs, Maps, Trees: Abstract Models for a Literary History* (London: Verso, 2005); *Distant Reading* (London: Verso, 2013); and, as editor, *The Novel*, 2 volumes (Princeton: Princeton University Press, 2006).
3 See Pascale Casanova, *The World Republic of Letters*, trans. M. B. Debevoise (Cambridge: Harvard University Press, 2004); Gayatri Chakravorty Spivak, *Death of a Discipline* (New York: Columbia University Press, 2003); Christopher Prendergast, ed., *Debating World Literature* (London: Verso, 2004); Haun Saussy, ed., *Comparative Literature in an Age of Globalization* (Baltimore: Johns Hopkins University Press, 2006); and Wai Chee Dimock and Lawrence Buell, eds., *Shades of the Planet: American Literature as World Literature* (Princeton: Princeton University Press, 2007).
4 See David Damrosch, *What Is World Literature?* (Princeton: Princeton University Press, 2003); *How to Read World Literature* (Oxford: Wiley-Blackwell, 2009); and, as editor, *Teaching World Literature* (New York: MLA Press, 2009) and *World Literature in Theory* (Oxford: Wiley-Blackwell, 2014).
5 See Alexander Beecroft, *An Ecology of World Literature: From Antiquity to the Present Day* (London: Verso, 2015).
6 See also Theo D'Haen, *World Literature in an Age of Geopolitics* (Boston: Brill, 2021); Marko Juvan, *Worlding a Peripheral Literature* (New York: Palgrave, 2019); and Longxi Zhang, *From Comparison to World Literature* (Albany: SUNY Press, 2015).

7 For an excellent explication and analysis of Goethe's "invention" of *Weltliteratur*, see Damrosch, *What Is World Literature?*, 1–36.
8 Johann Wolfgang von Goethe, *Conversations with Eckermann*, ed. J. K. Morehead, trans. John Oxenford (London: Everyman, 1930), 132, translation modified. See Johann Peter Eckermann, *Gespräche mit Goethe*, ed. Hans Timotheus Kroeber (Weimar: Ripenheuer, 1918).
9 Goethe, *Conversations*, 132.
10 Paul Lafargue, "Reminiscences of Marx," in *Marx and Engels Through the Eyes of Their Contemporaries* (Moscow: Progress Publishers, 1972), 26.
11 See Michel Foucault, "What Is an Author?" *Language, Counter-Memory, Practice*, eds. and trans. Donald F. Bouchard, trans. Boucahrd and Sherry Simon (Ithaca: Cornell UP, 1977), 131–132.
12 Karl Marx and Friedrich Engels. *The Communist Manifesto*, trans. anon. (New York: Signet, 1998), 54–55.
13 Raymond Williams, *Marxism and Literature* (Oxford: Oxford University Press, 1977), 121–127.
14 Marx and Engels, *The German Ideology*, ed. C. J. Arthur (London: International Publishers, 1970), 55.
15 S. S. Prawer, *Karl Marx and World Literature* (Oxford: Oxford University Press, 1976), 165.
16 Robert Scholes, *The Rise and Fall of English: Reconstructing English as a Discipline* (New Haven: Yale University Press, 1999), 3–4.
17 See Terry Eagleton, *Literary Theory: An Introduction*, 2nd ed. (Minneapolis: University of Minnesota Press, 1996); and David Shumway, *Creating American Civilization: A Genealogy of American Literature as an Academic Discipline* (Minneapolis: University of Minnesota Press, 1994).
18 Benedict Anderson, *Imaginary Communities: Reflections on the Origin and Spread of Nationalism* (London: Verso, 1991), 70–71.
19 Shumway, *Creating American Civilization*, 7.
20 Ibid., 339.
21 See Joel Whitney "*The Paris Review*, the Cold War, and the CIA," *Salon*, May 27, 2012, http://www.salon.com/2012/05/27/exclusive_the_paris_review_the_cold_war_and_the_cia/; see also Sarah Brouillette, *UNESCO and the Fate of the Literary* (Palo Alto: Stanford University Press, 2019).
22 Moretti, *Modern Epic*, 51.
23 Eagleton, *Exiles and Émigrés: Studies in Modern Literature* (New York: Schocken Books, 1970), 9.
24 George Steiner, *Extraterritorial: Papers on Literature and the Language of Revolution* (New York: Atheneum, 1976), 11.
25 Scholes, *English after the Fall: From Literature to Textuality* (Iowa City: University of Iowa, 2011), xvi.
26 See Kader Konuk, *East West Mimesis: Auerbach in Turkey* (Stanford: Stanford University Press, 2010).
27 Edward W. Said, "Reflections on Exile," *Reflections on Exile and Other Essays* (Cambridge: Harvard University Press, 2000), 186.
28 Erich Auerbach "Philology and *Weltliteratur*," trans. M. and E. W. Said, *Centennial Review* 13.1 (1969), 17.

29 Jerome Taylor, ed. *The* Didascalion *of Hugh of Saint Victor: A Medieval Guide to the Arts*, trans. Jerome Taylor (New York: Columbia University Press, 1991), 101.
30 Auerbach, "Philology and *Weltliteratur*," 17.
31 See Apter, *Against World Literature*, 193–210.
32 Auerbach, *Mimesis: The Representation of Reality in Western Literature*, trans. Willard R. Trask. (Princeton: Princeton University Press, 1953), 552.
33 Ibid., 553.
34 See Max Horkheimer and Theodor W. Adorno, *Dialectic of Enlightenment: Philosophical Fragments*, ed. Gunzelin Schmid Noerr, trans. Edmund Jephcott. (Stanford: Stanford University Press, 2002); and Richard M. Weaver, *Ideas Have Consequences* (Chicago: University of Chicago Press, 1948).
35 See, e.g., Michael Valdez Moses, *The Novel and the Globalization of Culture* (Oxford: Oxford University Press, 1995).
36 See Francis Fukuyama, *The End of History and the Last Man* (New York: Avon Books, 1992).
37 Apter, *Against World Literature*, 3.
38 Christian Thorne, "The Sea Is Not a Place; or, Putting the World Back in World Literature," *boundary 2* 40.2 (2013), 60–61.
39 Said, "Introduction to *Moby-Dick*," *Reflections on Exile and Other Essays* (Cambridge: Harvard University Press, 2000), 369.
40 Moretti, *Modern Epic*, 51.
41 Fredric Jameson, *The Geopolitical Aesthetic: Cinema and Space in the World System* (Bloomington and London: Indiana University Press and the British Film Institute, 1992), 82. See also my *Melville, Mapping, and Globalization: Literary Cartography in the American Baroque Writer* (New York: Bloomsbury, 2009).
42 See C. L. R. James, *Mariners, Renegades, and Castaways: The Story of Herman Melville and the World We Live In* (Hanover: University Press of New England, 2001).
43 See Jorge Luis Borges, *Ficciones*, trans. anon. (New York: Grove, 1962).
44 Herman Melville, *Moby-Dick, or, the Whale* (New York: Penguin, 1992), 497.
45 Damrosch, *Teaching World Literature*, 9.

Chapter 4

WORLDING SPACE: SPATIAL LITERARY STUDIES AND THE PLANETARY TURN

In the past few decades, what has been called "the spatial turn" in the arts, humanities, and social sciences has been marked by an enhanced awareness of the significance of space, place, mapping, spatial relations, and so on, in those fields. According to the research influenced by this turn, space has been revealed to maintain an active and productive presence in society and culture, as well as in various art forms, rather than functioning as mere setting, an empty container, or a backdrop in front of which the matters of "real" significance unfold. More recently, but perhaps relatedly, a planetary turn in many of these disciplinary fields has reoriented spatial critical theory and practice toward a more global frame of reference, owing much to the imperatives of the worldwide ecological crisis and the prospects of apparently inevitable climate change, as well as to the realities of multinational capitalism and globalization, along with the diffuse, specific, and often local effects of all of this. The conception of the "world," which can be closely related to both spatiality and planetarity, profoundly influences the ways we imagine space and place.[1] Worlds may be either vaster or more limited than other spatial frameworks, and the negotiation of worldly spaces presents challenges to traditional means of mapping or making sense of one's place. In this chapter, I discuss the effects of worlding on spatiality studies, beginning with a discussion of the spatial and planetary turns, then focusing on the crises of representation and of lived experience connected with a global frame of reference.

The Spatial Turn

Although such spatial or geographical considerations have no doubt always been a part of literary and critical practice, the recent resurgence of spatiality and the explosion in the number of spatially oriented books and articles in literary studies follows what has been referred to as the "spatial turn" in the humanities and social sciences.[2] The spatial turn has no particular date of inception, but one may perceive more and more critical attention being paid to matters of space in the 1970s and 1980s. For example, Denis Cosgrove has explicitly connected the spatial turn to poststructuralist theory, and so it is not surprising that Michel Foucault, Gilles Deleuze, and other theorist of their time have been closely associated with the spatial turn. As Cosgrove put it,

> A widely acknowledged 'spatial turn' across arts and sciences corresponds to post-structuralist agnosticism about both naturalistic and universal explanations and about single-voiced historical narratives, and to the concomitant recognition that position and context are centrally and inescapably implicated in all constructions of knowledge.[3]

In what has become a famous lecture from 1967, Foucault declared our age to be the "epoch of space."[4] Tellingly, the lecture was only published as "Des espaces autres" shortly before Foucault's death in 1984, and appeared in English as "Of Other Spaces" only in 1986. Foucault's research into the birth of the prison and other matters in the 1970s led to some of the already spatially oriented thinker's most overtly spatial work, which has in turn influenced spatiality studies across numerous disciplinary fields in recent years.

Another major contribution that was also somewhat belatedly recognized outside of France was Henri Lefebvre's monumental study *The Production of Space*, published in 1974 but translated into English only in 1991. Remaining within a French intellection tradition, one could note that Deleuze, especially in his collaborations with Félix Guattari, increasingly couched his arguments in spatial and geographical terms, and the two thinkers advocated for a "geophilosophy" in their *What Is Philosophy?*[5] These thinkers, among others, were both part of and influential upon the spatial turn as it developed in other areas over the past few decades. At the same time, transformative research in the social sciences, such as that of Anthony Giddens, David Harvey, and Edward Soja, emphasized and insisted upon the need to consider spatial relations and planning in order to comprehend facts and trends in social theory.

Although not all would embrace the terms *postmodern* or *postmodernism*, which have been used to characterize both a historical period and an aesthetic style, among other things, the advent of the postmodern is closely tied to what has been understood as the spatial turn. Art and architecture, always attuned to matters of spatiality and relations of space, appear to have become more emphatically interested in spatiality in the postmodern condition. For instance, Fredric Jameson's analysis of postmodernity memorably employed the figure of a work of postmodern architecture, the Bonaventure Hotel in Los Angeles, as his point of departure for discussing the advent of postmodern hyperspace and its bewildering effects on human perception and subjective experience. Jameson later referred to this in terms of "that new spatiality implicit in the postmodern."[6] The subtitle of Soja's magnificent 1989 study *Postmodern Geographies* announced "the reassertion of space in critical social theory," and Harvey's *The Condition of Postmodernity* from the same year connected the postmodern with the time-space compression associated with global capitalism. In this way, the confluence—not to say, conflation—of poststructuralist theory and postmodern theorizing helped to characterize key aspects of the spatial turn more broadly.

Interestingly enough, amid all this spatially oriented critical theory and practice, the concept of space remained largely on the margins of most discourse in cultural studies. Sometimes a trope only becomes noticeable *after* the turn, one might say. For example, a significant collection of essays designed to register the field-altering changes to literary studies in the aftermath of "theory," *Critical Terms for Literary Study* (1990), edited by Frank Lentricchia and Thomas McLaughlin, contained no entries for space, place, mapping, or geography. Raymond Williams's influential *Keywords* (1976)—notwithstanding the fact that it arose from *The Country and the City*, perhaps Williams's most overtly spatial or literary geographical work—also contained no entry for space or place; the second edition, published in 1983, included twenty-one additional entries, but *space* and *place* remained absent. Harvey himself felt the need to redress this omission in an essay titled "Space as a Key Word," which began by stating that "If Raymond Williams were contemplating the entries for his celebrated text on *Keywords* today, he would have surely have included the word 'space'."[7] Nigel Thrift, in a 2006 essay with the deceptively simple, keyword-like title of "Space," uses the rough span of "the last 20 years or so) to cover the "spatial turn in the humanities and social sciences," and he predicts that the relatively recent critical phenomenon will have lasting results on how we think about ourselves and the world.[8] Nevertheless, to cite an important recent contribution to the subject, the University of Pittsburgh's Keywords Project, which is intended to update Williams's work and which has resulted in the publication *Keywords for Today: A 21st Century Vocabulary*, edited by Colin MacCabe and Hannah Yanacek, still contains no entries for space, place, or mapping.[9]

Needless to say, perhaps, prior to the spatial turn, there were many critical practices that were, in one way or another, already attuned to matters of space, place, and geography. For example, urban studies, regionalism, genre studies based on geography (pastoral poetry, for instance), landscape studies, postcolonial theory, investigations of spatial form, and so forth, have registered space as a key element of their field. Many of these subfields or practices continue to produce valuable scholarship for students and critics interested in spatial studies today. Literature as a disciplinary field of study has a long history of examining such geographically based questions as the relation of an author or a text to its city, region, or nation. Partially as a result of the spatial turn, these older practices have themselves recently become reinvigorated with in assertion of new models or frames of reference. The fundamentally spatial or geographical question of mobile populations and border-crossing has opened up new areas for transnational perspectives, which has not only created different categories for understanding formerly homogenous literatures and cultures (say, diaspora studies, *mestiza* cultures, or the Black Atlantic), but also fashioned new lenses through which to view older fields, as may be seen in recent versions of hemispheric, transnational, or postcolonial American Studies.[10] In the aftermath of the spatial turn, a "planetary turn" has caused many of the traditional discourses within modern language and literary studies to make fascinating connections among the local, regional, national, and global circuits of cultural production.[11]

Planet, Globe, World

In her provocative call for a new comparative literature, *Death of a Discipline*, Gayatri Chakravorty Spivak proposed *planetarity* as the transnational figure around which to organize the study of world literatures and languages. In naming this figure, she hoped to "overwrite" another, more pervasive one—namely, the global—which in an era of globalization had come to dominate critical social and cultural theory. As Spivak put it,

> Globalization is the imposition of the same system of exchange everywhere. In the gridwork of electronic capital, we achieve that abstract ball covered in latitudes and longitudes, cut by virtual lines, once the equator and the tropics and so on, now drawn by the requirements of Geographical Positioning Systems. To talk planet-talk by way of an unexamined environmentalism, referring to an undivided "natural" space rather than a differentiated political space, can work in the interest of this globalization in the mode of the abstract as such. [...] The globe is on our computers. No one lives there. It allows us to think that we can aim to control it. The planet is in the species of alterity, belonging to another system; and yet we inhabit it, on loan.[12]

Planetarity would therefore go beyond the merely transnational, regional, or continental frames of reference which have been used in traditional comparative literature and area studies. As in Wai-Chee Dimock's invocation of a "Literature for the Planet," the planet as a unit of analysis would necessarily require both temporal and spatial coordinates, as a global readership necessarily involves a scope extended beyond the borders of a national language or political organization.[13]

Spivak's sense of the planet or the planetary as a site of otherness that is somehow also a home resonates especially well in a moment in which the dramatic transformations of culture and society caused, or at least occasioned, by the forces of globalization have generated considerable existential anxiety, not to mention a pessimism of the intellect accompanied by an apparent paralysis of the will. Such a moment calls for new ways of imagining the world, new methods of analysis, interpretation, and evaluation, and new forms of collective action. *The Planetary Turn: Relationality and Geoaesthetics in the Twenty-First Century*, edited by Amy J. Elias and Christian Moraru, attempts to elaborate the potential effectiveness of planetary criticism for the present spatiotemporal situation. *The Planetary Turn* simultaneously develops an argument in favor of a planetary criticism and, through its diversity of contributors and essay topics, demonstrates the range and flexibility of a planetary approach to the arts, literature, and culture. The collection offers an incisive and expansive perspective on the ways in which a "planetary imaginary" has emerged in the twenty-first century and on the prospects for an effective planetary criticism that can grapple with the challenges of the age.

In their lengthy, lucid introduction to *The Planetary Turn*, Elias and Moraru elaborate the terms of our present "planetary condition" and argue for a planetary criticism appropriate to it. They begin by distinguishing the planetary from two other seemingly similar paradigms of cultural and critical theory today, globalization and cosmopolitanism. Following Spivak, among others, Elias and Moraru see globalization as a homogenizing system, understood primarily in terms of finance, economics, or technology, whereas the planetarity operates in a more open field, a commons in which ethics and relationality define the parameters of the discussion, with meaningful connections to posthumanism environmentalism or ecologies.[14] Against the cosmopolitan model, which establishes a mindset of enlightened border-crossing, travel, and contact, planetarity instantiates the basic commonality of planetary space as a shared resource. Envisioning a "world commons," the proponents of planetarity imagine "a complex planetary network including nested but nonhierarchical cultural and material ecosystems—communal constellations, sites, and forms of life ranging in scale but acknowledging, serving, and honoring a shared, affectively and materially interrelated, inhabited world space."[15] Hence, while a planetary criticism must grapple with the same or similar conditions that critical discourses around globalization or cosmopolitanism have countenanced, the movement away from homogenizing or potentially Western-centered models might make possible new ways of dealing with the spatiotemporal situation in which we find ourselves.

If this all sounds "cautiously exploratory," as the Elias and Moraru concede, then that is because the discursive and disciplinary field in question is as yet still emergent. Cosmopolitanism, whether connected to globalization or not, has a much longer history, even as its theorization and practices continue to develop in new directions. Cosmopolitanism, as a concept or a *Weltanschauung*, has always also involved a spatial element, which is not merely geographical but also more theoretical. With respect to physical geography and social spaces, cosmopolitanism finds its proper place in the great worldly cities, as the very word suggests. That is, the term derives from the combination of the Greek *kosmos* ("world") and *politês* ("citizen"), the latter understood as one with full standing as a resident of a *polis* ("city"). To a certain extent, then, the cosmopolitan is not merely the *citoyen du monde* of early nineteenth-century social ideals, but also the inhabitant of a "world-city," more frequently understood as a metropolis than as a cosmopolis. The rise of the "global city," as Saskia Sassen dubbed it,[16] emphasizes the cosmopolitan character further, as these cities—Sassen named New York, London, and Tokyo, but surely Hong Kong, Shanghai, and Beijing, could be added to the list today, and that is only in China—become crucial nodes in a worldwide system of production, circulation, distribution, and communication. Such world-cities or cosmopolises very much determine the shape and meaning of the experience of life on this planet in the twenty-first century.[17]

Hence, one might say that cosmopolitanism is implicated within a distinctively urban space, even if this "city" is imaginary. This may be frequently understood only negatively, for example, by imagining those spaces and places that are *not* cosmopolitan: rustic locales or small towns, often, along with provinces (and provinciality), regions, and especially nation-states, the most salient of the modern spatio-political formations, which so frequently entangles with it notions of race, identity, and so on. These social and spatial formations are, if not antithetical to cosmopolitanism, then at least at odds with it. The city is marked by a certain cosmopolitanism. This is especially the case in the very large city, the metropolis, or if smaller, the city that is strategically located as a nexus of trade, transportation, or communication, such as the port city. Sites of contact between cultures, heterotopias that engender different ways of seeing social space, such cities effect the very fabric of the global economy, while also contributing to the manner in which our world is understood. In these spaces, difference arises and relates.

Along these lines, cosmopolitan space, it seems, must also imply a utopian space. It is a space that is at once a *non-place* and a *good-place*, to cite the well-known homophonic pun of Thomas More's initial coining of the term, that is, a word combining *ou*-topos with *eu*-topos. Utopias are famous for not actually existing, of course; they are viewed as being aspirational, critical, satirical, or fanciful, but they are also understood to be *unreal*. In some respects, the cosmopolitan is equally unreal, insofar as the ideals of the world-city and its global-citizen never fully match up to the reality of life in the metropolitan center or in the far-flung periphery. In the world as we know it, there really is no truly cosmopolitan *place*, although any number of places and spaces may partake of some kind of cosmopolitanism or other. One might say that the desire for cosmopolitan space is a feature of our contemporary apprehension of space and place in the era of globalization.

Hence, Marx's insistence on the cosmopolitan character of capitalism, which certainly begins and flourishes in a largely national (and nationalistic) social context, but which, in the hands of the bourgeoisie, increasingly supersedes its national boundaries in pushing production and consumptions ever into the world. In their brief consideration of the world market in *The Communist Manifesto*, Marx and Engels praise the revolutionary and dominant bourgeoisie of the nineteenth century for giving society its "cosmopolitan character," by which they mean, suppressing if not eliminating the distinctively national and thus reactionary character. As they write, "[t]he intellectual creations of individual nations become common property. National one-sidedness and narrow-mindedness become more and more impossible, and from the numerous national and local literatures, there arises a world literature."[18] Marx and Engels' rhetoric in this section of the *Manifesto* reveals the extent to which the authors themselves not only value cosmopolitanism but also view it as essential to the development of a revolutionary proletarian movement. Here the better known imaginary space of the nation must give way to the perplexities and convolutions of a more global space, such that even languages and literatures are affected by the permutations of the world market.

The study of world literature, which perhaps coincidentally has also become a more dominant discourse in the humanities after or alongside the spatial turn, would seem to require a sense of cosmopolitanism, and yet the national does not yield its ground quite so easily as Marx or others may imagine. It is perhaps noteworthy that Christian Thorne, in an essay on the ways in which the novel has remained tied to the conceptual space of the nation-state and cannot seem to adequately represent a supranational or global sphere, titles his exploration of this subject, "The Sea is Not a Place." Thorne does not really mention maritime literature *per se*, and by using the phrase "the sea is not a place" for his title, he seems to suggest that literature "of the sea" may not be localized in space.[19] In any event, such literature will not suffice to represent "world literature," even if it operated in international or transnational spaces.

In a way, this brings us back to the planet as the material embodiment of the globe or the world. In his essay titled "Decompressing Culture: Three Steps toward a Geomethodology," Moraru briefly sketches the outlines of his conception of "planetary reading."[20] Noting that "the planet serves, increasingly and with historically unrivaled force, as a level, matrix, or condition of possibility for a *forma mentis* whose purview covers the conceptual (philosophical), the referential (scientific), as well as the aesthetic (imaginative)," Moraru suggests three provisional steps toward a methodology suited to the present planetary condition. In brief, they are *topological*, connecting the planet itself to the spatialization of the world; *structural* or relational, linking the parts both to each other and to the whole; and *ethical*, inasmuch as a geomethodological approach would not only read the "symptoms of planetarity" in a given text or territory, but would also read "on behalf of" the planet, such that criticism can coincide with a form of stewardship.[21]

Whether ours is an age of planetarity or something else, a spatially-oriented planetary criticism can bring together the disparate, yet clearly interrelated, theories and methods of world-systems theory, area studies, comparative and world literature, geocriticism or spatiality studies, ecocriticism or environmentalism, cosmopolitanism, and globalization. As Spivak observed, the planet is simultaneously otherworldly ("a species of alterity") and our home, and any literary or cultural criticism in an age of globalization, with its persistently postnational forces, hybrid forms, and situations of transgressivity, may well need to take into account the current condition of the planet, not to mention its historical formations and potential future.

Is the World a Place?

As noted above, part of the problem with imagining the entire globe or planet as the frame of reference for cultural analysis is the sheer vastness of the space, along with the indescribably complex relations of power that make it a world. Thorne's observation that "the sea is not a place" corresponds to the planet whose surface is more than two-thirds water. Traditionally, in both the geographic and the political imagination, the sea is not really a "place" in and of itself. Looking at a physical map or nautical chart, the vast blue watery space is largely a backdrop upon which the terrestrial features or *places*—islands, coastlines, reefs, or even shallows—are figured or marked. The sea, somewhat like the inky night sky for the stargazer, represents so much space between and among various places, but does not quite appear as a place, and yet, it is also absolutely crucial to human experience.

The ocean represents what Siobhan Carroll has referred to as an "atopia," a "non-place" far more hostile and resistant to cartographic representation and to homely experience than those that Marc Augé had examined in *Non-Places: An Introduction to Supermodernity*. As Carroll observes,

> Natural atopias, like the North Pole, the ocean, the atmosphere, the desert or the subterranean, are unusual forms of space that, because of their physical features or environmental conditions, resist being converted into the sites of affective habitation we call "place." [...] Of these spaces, the paradigmatic atopia, and the one that continues to influence our conceptualization of unfamiliar spaces, is the ocean. It plays this role in part because of its significant role in legal and political history. On one hand, the ocean has always been essential to travel, global trade and imperial conquest. On the other, its fluidity has posed substantial challenges to states seeking to extend land-based power across its surface.[22]

In an obvious but also odd way, the ocean lacks *territoriality*, and yet it is also a space subjected to ever more complicated and nuanced forms of territorialization over human history. For example, where Stuart Elden's *The Birth of Territory* reveals the long processes by which the earth's terrestrial spaces were transformed into "territories" in the full sense of that term, Philip E. Steinberg, in *The Social Construction of the Ocean*, has demonstrated the manner by which oceanic spaces have been produced over time and across social orders in accordance with different modes of production.[23]

So much of the world's surface is covered by this oceanic space, where so little can be seen or mapped, that it really ought to be central to any discussions of social and natural spaces, and yet it has frequently been relegated to the margins as land-based places, inhabitable and uninhabitable alike, take precedence in spatiality studies, for the most part. In her call for a more materialist approach to oceanic studies, Hester Blum has rightly pointed out that "[t]he sea is not a metaphor. Figurative language has its place in analyses of the maritime world, certainly, but oceanic studies could be more invested in the uses, and problems, of what is literal in the face of the sea's abyss of representation."[24] And yet, even with the historicist and materialist perspective, one that focuses on the actual lives and records of sailors, for instance, the sense of placelessness in oceanic spaces has its real topophrenic consequences, which are related to the challenges to literary or graphic representation in the form of mapping. Take the English expression *to be "at sea,"* which is fundamentally synonymous with being lost or bewildered; one's sense of being dangerously "out of place" is intensified in the vast, abyssal zones associated with the ocean, which in turn may be transcoded onto a larger world system in need of cognitive mapping, to cite Jameson's well-known formulation.

Ultimately, a form of global cognitive mapping would be necessary to make sense of this vast world system and our place within it, which in turn are crucial questions for spatially oriented cultural criticism in the twenty-first century. That is because, even at the more local level, the global system operates and affects us. Jameson's older example, which was based on an earlier stage of globalization, one far less complex and extensive than our own, nevertheless provides some indication of the underlying problem. Jameson has argued that the age of imperialism or of monopoly capitalism brought about a schism between "truth" and "experience," where the material conditions for the possibility of an individual's lived experience in a metropolitan center, for instance, are actually to be found in the far-flung colonial elsewhere. As Jameson puts it,

> the phenomenological experience of the individual subject—traditionally, the supreme raw material for the work of art—becomes limited to a tiny corner of the social world, a fixed-camera view of a certain section of London or the countryside or wherever. But the truth of that experience no longer coincides with the place in which it takes place. The truth of that limited daily experience of London lies, rather, in India or Jamaica or Hong Kong; it is bound up with the whole colonial system of the British Empire that determines the very quality of the individual's subjective life. Yet those structural coordinates are no longer accessible to immediate lived experience and are not even conceptualizable for most people.[25]

For Jameson, the stylistic innovations of literary modernism were attempts to deal with this existential condition, effectively operating as strategies of containment which repressed the historical and political content of the novels. How much more intricate and complicated is today's world system, when not only many raw materials but virtually everything on encounters is bound up within this global network?

As Jameson discusses in *Allegory and Ideology*, the real and conceptual vastness of a global system is not just spatial but social. "Today, in an era of full globalization, the distance between the life of concrete social networks and population size is so great as to be virtually unconceptualizable."[26] Any project of cognitive mapping would have to account for the space of the world system as we attempt to know it, which is to say a global and perhaps even supra-planetary or cosmic space. Given the importance of satellites along with underwater, transoceanic fiber optic cables to our day-to-day activities to the most ordinary experiences imaginable, like placing phone calls or purchasing goods, one might say that the terrestrial globe, though vast, is still too limited a space by which to understand or map our present, postmodern condition. But such a project would also have to deal with the social and political aspects of that system, which move beyond the geographical register, forcing us to confront weirder questions entirely. For example, as Jameson asks in his back-cover endorsement of Alberto Toscano and Jeff Kinkle's *Cartographies of the Absolute* (2015), "How much of capitalism can we see from the moon?" Such is the stuff of science fiction or fantasy, and yet it is also very much part of the "world" that spatiality studies must analyze and theorize in the years to come.

Notes

1 In a fascinating argument to the contrary, Pheng Cheah urges that "world" must be understood as a fundamentally *temporal*, rather than spatial, category. See his *What Is a World?: On Postcolonial Literature as World Literature* (Durham: Duke University Press, 2016).
2 The term has been widely used for some time, but for an important collection that helped to characterize the "turn," see Barney Warf and Santa Arias, eds., *The Spatial Turn: Interdisciplinary Perspectives* (New York: Routledge, 2009). See also Michael Dear, Jim Ketchum, Sarah Luria, and Doug Richardson, eds., *GeoHumanities: Art, History, and Text at the Edge of Place* (New York: Routledge, 2011); David J. Bodenhamer, John Corrigan, Trevor M. Harris, eds., *The Spatial Humanities: GIS and the Future of Humanities Scholarship* (Bloomington: Indiana University Press, 2010). For a quick overview, see Jo Guldi's introductory essays for the Scholar's Lab site, Spatial Humanities: A Project of the Institute for Enabling Geospatial Scholarship: http://spatial.scholarslab.org/spatial-turn/.
3 Denis Cosgrove, "Introduction: Mapping Meaning," in Denis Cosgrove, ed., *Mappings* (London: Reaktion Books, 1999), 7.
4 Michel Foucault, "Of Other Spaces," trans. Jan Miskowiec, *Diacritics* 16.1 (Spring 1986), 22.
5 See Gilles Deleuze and Félix Guattari, *What Is Philosophy?* trans. Hugh Tomlinson and Graham Burchell (New York: Columbia University Press, 1994), 85–113; see also Mark Bonta and John Ptrotevi, *Deleuze and Geophilosophy: A Guide and Glossary* (Edinburgh: Edinburgh University Press, 2004).
6 Fredric Jameson, *Postmodernism, or, the Cultural Logic of Late Capitalism* (Durham: Duke University Press, 1991), 418.
7 Harvey, *Spaces of Global Capitalism: Towards a Theory of Uneven Geographical Development* (London: Verso, 2006), 119.
8 Nigel Thrift, "Space," *Theory, Culture, and Society* 23.2–3 (2006), 139.

9 See Colin MacCabe and Hannah Yanacek, eds., *Keywords for Today: A 21st Century Vocabulary* (Oxford: Oxford University Press, 2018).
10 See, e.g., Jeffrey R. Di Leo, ed., *American Literature as World Literature* (New York: Bloomsbury, 2017).
11 See Amy J. Elias and Christian Moraru, *The Planetary Turn: Relationality and Geoaesthetics in the Twenty-First Century* (Evanston, IL: Northwestern University Press, 2015).
12 Gayatri Chakravorty Spivak, *Death of a Discipline* (New York: Columbia University Press, 2003), 92.
13 Wai-Chee Dimock, "Literature for the Planet," *PMLA* 116.1, special topic: Globalizing Literary Studies (Jan. 2001), 175.
14 Elias and Moraru, *The Planetary Turn*, xvii–xix.
15 Ibid., xxiv.
16 See Saskia Sassen, *The Global City: New York, London, Tokyo*, 2nd ed. (Princeton: Princeton University Press, 2001).
17 Of course, insofar as all cities participate in the cosmopolitanism that is part and parcel of the twenty-first century world system, each with local distinctiveness *and* with innumerable interconnections with globalized networks, nearly all cities have become, in some respects, "world cities." See, e.g., Ato Quayson, *Oxford Street, Accra: City Life and the Itineraries of Transnationalism* (Durham: Duke University Press, 2014).
18 Karl Marx and Friedrich Engels, *The Communist Manifesto*, trans. Samuel Moore (Signet Classics, 1998), 54–55.
19 See Christian Thorne, "The Sea Is Not a Place; or, Putting the World Back into World Literature," *boundary* 2 40.2 (2013), 53–79.
20 See Elias and Moraru, *The Planetary Turn*, 216; Moraru developed this argument at greater length in his *Reading for the Planet: Toward a Geomethodology* (Ann Arbor: University of Michigan Press, 2015).
21 Elias and Moraru, *The Planetary Turn*, 216–217.
22 Siobhan Carroll, "Atopia/Non-place," *The Routledge Handbook of Literature and Space*, ed. Robert T. Tally Jr. (London: Routledge, 2017), 159–160.
23 See Stuart Elden, *The Birth of Territory* (Chicago: University of Chicago Press, 2013); see also Philip E. Steinberg, *The Social Construction of the Ocean* (Cambridge: Cambridge University Press, 2001).
24 Hester Blum, "The Prospect of Oceanic Studies," *PMLA* 125.3 (2010), 670.
25 Jameson, *Postmodernism*, 411.
26 Jameson, *Allegory and Ideology* (London: Verso, 2019), 197.

Chapter 5

IN THE FILE DRAWER LABELED "SCIENCE FICTION": GENRE AFTER THE AGE OF THE NOVEL

In "Science Fiction," a 1965 essay later included in his *Wampeters, Foma, and Granfalloons*, Kurt Vonnegut complained of having been unjustly labeled a science-fiction writer.[1] He said that reviewers had placed his work in that generic category primarily because machines featured so prominently in his first book, *Player Piano*, although Vonnegut himself insisted that the novel was based loosely on the real persons, places, and events he witnessed while working at a General Electric plant in Schenectady, New York, in the early 1950s. True, *Player Piano* included some extrapolations from then-current technology, and it was set in the near future; as noted in the foreword, it was "not a book about what is, but about what could be."[2] That distinction itself might be enough to move one's writings from the genre of literary realism to that of science fiction, but then the postwar period in which *Player Piano* appeared was time when, in the United States especially, people were very much concerned with the nation's possibilities, not merely its quotidian realities. Hence, one might argue that the theme of the book was quite timely indeed. But the question is not so much whether a sort of realism or a more speculative form was better suited to capture the spirit of the age; rather, for Vonnegut, the question was whether one form of writing could be taken seriously at all. In his essay, Vonnegut lamented that, by referring to his work as *science fiction*, literary critics had consigned it to a category which would assure that it could not be viewed or valued *as* literature. "I have been a soreheaded occupant of a file drawer label 'science fiction' ever since," Vonnegut declared, "and I would like out, particularly since so many serious critics regularly mistake the drawer for a urinal."[3]

The humorous, thoroughly Vonnegutian comment reveals his anxieties about being pigeon-holed as a genre writer, and he goes on to concede that, in most science fiction he knows, the actual writing is pretty bad. However, in the same essay, he predicted that so-called science fiction would become increasingly part of the mainstream as more writers incorporated the effects of technology into their literary fiction. Vonnegut in 1965 was making a plea for the wider acceptance of "serious" literature, like his own novels, that could incorporate elements of genre fiction without being restricted to limited space of the generic form. He may have already been thinking of his auspicious work in progress, *Slaughterhouse-Five*, which somehow blended the all-too-real, traumatic, personal wartime experience of the author with a "telegraphic-schizophrenic" narrative of time-travel, intergalactic flying saucers, and space aliens, even though, upon a certain closer reading, all of these fantastic elements could be argued to exist only in the protagonist's mind. When *Slaughterhouse-Five* was published in 1969, it became a bestselling and critically acclaimed novel, despite—or some might say, because of—its use of these science-fiction conventions. Indeed, in the remaining years of his long career, Vonnegut continued to blend science-fictional or fantastic elements with his more straightforwardly realistic stories and gently satirical morality tales, thus establishing a recognizably Vonnegutian style. After the publication of *Slaughterhouse-Five*, his sales, popular appeal, and even critical respectability remained steadily high throughout his life and beyond.

By the time of Vonnegut's death in 2007, the "subliterary" genres of science fiction, fantasy, and horror, as well as some combination of the three presented under the banner of children's or young adult literature, had come to dominate the literary marketplace. The overwhelming sales numbers of the Harry Potter series, for example, led the *New York Times* in 2000 to create a distinct "Children's Best Seller List," partly in anticipation of the fourth installment (*Harry Potter and the Goblet of Fire*), which was expected to give J. K. Rowling the top four spots in the coveted bestseller list; understandably, other publishers began to complain, and the editor, Charles McGrath, even confessed, "we need to clear some room,"[4] which clearly indicated that the genre of children's literature was occupying space *intended* for some other form. (It also indicated that children were not the only readers of these books, of course.) Today, however, many of those recognized as "serious" writers today feel empowered, if not compelled, to create literary works that fit within well-known generic frameworks, such that Thomas Pynchon can write detective novels (see *Inherent Vice*), Kazuo Ishiguro can write fantasy fiction (*The Buried Giant*), or Cormac McCarthy can produce apocalyptic dystopias (*The Road*). In a mere fifty years since Vonnegut's "urinal" lament, therefore, the relationship between literary fiction and genre fiction has changed rather dramatically. Although the distinction still remains, the significance and value of the terms have been fundamentally altered.

What happened to literary fiction? Why has so-called genre fiction displaced it? Or has the line between to two blurred? Have they even merged? What does it say about literature in the twenty-first century that genre fiction so dominates the literary marketplace? What is the value of the literary in the present moment? Or is this even a valid distinction? What is the point of distinguishing literary from genre fiction? What is it that the readership desires or values about these texts, regardless of category?

I want to suggest that these questions can be tied to a more general set of phenomena associated with postmodernity, particularly in connection to the cultural effects of globalization. (Here I follow the basic gist of Fredric Jameson's influential assessment of postmodernism as "the cultural logic of late capitalism.") The continuing expansion of capital into the furthest and minutest recesses of social space have, perhaps indirectly, affected the literary marketplace by demanding greater and greater levels of commodification. Genres are, in many respects, marketing labels, after all, and the need to slot various works of fiction into recognizable market niches undoubtedly drives much of the publishing industry, such that even works intended for large, variegated audiences must somehow be classifiable and "targeted." However, at the formal level as well, the commodification of forms has tended to uproot the "literary" in the literary marketplace. As that market has become more global, genre fiction, including the strangely generic "world literature," has begun to predominate.

Using Vonnegut's example as a point of departure, I would say that the ambitions of "literary" writers of postwar American fiction increasingly turned to generic forms and conventions in the 1970s and in the decades since then. The celebrated hybrid genres, such as literary fantasy, today might be considered as textual versions of financial derivatives, drawing their "value" from other commodities. I propose that such fiction reflects the conditions of the postnational world market after the "age of the novel." In an era of globalization, genre offers a kind of map, enabling both writers and readers to orient themselves in relation to an unrepresentable world system that comes to be rendered knowable in literature of this or that genre, where genre is understood as a frame of reference for ascertaining the proper contours of the world. And yet, I believe, the allure of alterity—that is, the desire for other worlds, strange scenes, unreal characters, and so on—might disclose a utopian aspect of this condition, such that the rise of genre fiction or putatively generic modes in twenty-first century literature may be connected to an incipient longing for radical transformations of the present world system.

The Literary Moment, or, the Age of the Novel

In what must be understood as a literary historical provocation, Jonathan Arac has argued in recent years that the "age of the novel" has definitively ended, for that "age" might be said to encompass roughly the period between the early nineteenth century and the mid-twentieth.[5] Obviously, the novel form antedates this period, and novels continue to be written and read, perhaps more now than ever before. What Arac has in mind is something akin to Raymond Williams's famous conception of *emergent, dominant*, and *residual* cultural forms.[6] The novel, in Arac's view, can be properly considered the dominant form for only those hundred-or-so years. Prior to that epoch, poetry as well as philosophy, religious sermons, political discourses, histories, and other written works would have occupied the central place in the intellectual and literary culture of Europe and North America, at least, while the novel could be seen as still emergent. More recently, with the advent of mass media—first film and radio, then television, video, the internet, and so on—along with other developments in consumer capitalism and a society of the spectacle, one might say that the novel maintains its power (a not inconsiderable power, in truth) but now as *residual* form in a cultural arena in which it can no longer be considered central or preeminent.

In his earlier study of nineteenth-century narrative forms in U.S. literature, Arac had pointed out that the very term *literature* only gained its modern, current meaning sometime during the first half of that century. "In the late eighteenth century, 'literature' meant all culturally valued writing, including what would now be distinguished as 'nonfiction,' such as history, travel, philosophy, and science."[7] The more restrictive understanding of *literature* or the *literary* first developed out of a Romantic tradition but continued to evolve throughout the nineteenth century. That definition saw literature as exemplary of *belles lettres*, but it also depicted literature as a particular type of fine writing characterized by creativity, originality, and the imagination, often understood also to emanate from a gifted or talented author, a person of genius or craft whose work is the result of his or her own creativity, originality, and imagination. The poet and poetry, above all, best represented this new definition of literature, and indeed, the novel form, tainted by its very associations with bourgeois tastes and middle-brow values, likely would not have even been highly valued as "literary," a point made by Terry Eagleton, who has observed that "the eighteenth century was in grave doubt about whether the new upstart form of the novel was literature at all."[8] However, as Arac points out elsewhere, the novel form rapidly overtook poetry in establishing what would count, or not count, as literature: "Hardly had *literature* come to replace *poetry* as the key operative term than literature came to mean novels."[9]

This development in the history of literature is related to other, more materialist transformations. Notably, the emergence of an ideology centered upon individuality or individualism, as Ian Watt famously argued in *The Rise of the Novel*, established the conditions for the possibility of the novel to flourish, particularly as the novel form both reflected and reinforced the ideology. Along those lines, the emergence of print capitalism, as described by Benedict Anderson and taken up by others, placed novels and newspapers in the hands of a populace who, partly through the media of novels, could come to recognize themselves as a "imagined community." Thus the rise of the novel form in Europe has frequently been considered a factor in, not merely coincidental to, the development of the nation-state form and of nationalism more generally. As a matter of cultural hegemony, the rise of the novel in the nineteenth century helped to shape not only the bourgeois household, on the smaller scale, but entire communities or larger social entities. Franco Moretti has pointed out that, in nineteenth-century homes that contained only one book, you would find the bible; in homes containing a bookcase, there would be a "canon," but if there were an actual library, it would contain mostly novels.[10]

Literature in the form of the novel, which had become by the mid-nineteenth century the exemplary literary form in Europe and elsewhere, is tied to the self-conscious development of the nation in a time when certain forms of nationalism become dominant social and economic forces. If we agree with the standard (if contested) literary history that has connected the rise and flourishing of the novel with the emergence and hegemony of the nation-state, then—to move far too quickly, of course—it makes some sense that the postnational condition heralded by postmodernity, globalization, or transnational capitalism would necessarily register a break or disruption in the history of the novel as well. The novel's role as the cultural form best suited to represent a national imaginary community has perhaps been usurped by others. As Arac explains, "In that age of the novel in the United States, say from about the time of *Moby-Dick* and *Uncle Tom's Cabin* to that of *Invisible Man* and *Lolita*, the novel had a special relationship to what we call the national imaginary, and that special relationship has now passed from print, in particular the novel, to other media forms."[11] But it is also the case that the national imaginary itself in an age of globalization is no longer always the spatiopolitical framework by which a given collectivity most readily identifies itself. More importantly, considering the degree to which nationalism remains a powerful force in the hearts and minds of populations around the world, the geopolitical and economic system of late capitalism has displaced national industries and cultures, regardless of one's own personal experience with patriotism or national identity.

From Arac's perspective, then, the end of the age of the novel must also be understood as the end of literature, here understood in the special sense of *literary* writing, in a manner of speaking. Not that what has traditionally been thought of as literature, of writing serious fiction and reading it, has ended, but that its centrality can no longer be taken for granted. As Arac puts it, making reference to Pascale Casanova's provocative argument in her *World Republic of Letters*,

> The global age dares us to write literary history as if the history of *literature* were over. Of course, it is not. The quest for recognition continues in Casanova's world autonomy sweepstakes. Some wonderful works will be produced and reach readers, perhaps even more people than ever before, since so many more people now can read. Yet the place of literature within culture and of culture within the world has changed. We love to write histories that cheer on the emergent and challenge the dominant, but have we yet explored how to write histories of the residual?[12]

Literature, much like the nation-state itself in some respects, may be seen as a residual form in the age of globalization, but then we must also examine the force of its persistence, particularly in light of the apparently unquenchable thirst for other narrative forms, whether in print or in other media. If the *literary* has evanesced or is in the process of disappearing, which is itself not certain, then the outsized influence of supposedly non- or sub-literary genres still needs to be examined.

Literature *versus* Genre-Fiction

Notoriously difficult to define in the best of times, *literature* has come to mean something like writing, mostly fictional and mostly prose, that does not easily fit into any recognizable marketing category.[13] Arac observed that novels replaced poetry as the dominant literary form in the nineteenth century, such that, when people said "literature," they meant *novels*. The word has undergone another transformation in mass culture. As Arac explains,

> Now in American bookstores, the shelves labeled "literature" contain the market niche known as serious fiction, and there are separate sections labeled with what used to be parts of literature—"poetry," "drama," "essays"—as well as sections naming what used to be parts of the novel: "romance," "gothic," "western," "detective," "science fiction." ("Literary History," 757)

(Of course, the bookstore itself may well be a residual cultural form.) Implied but not taken up in Arac's observations is the degree to which literature, now understood to refer to something like serious fiction in the novel form, has become a sort of subgenre within the broader sphere of "novels" in general. The "age of the novel," which Arac asserts had for the most part ended by the 1960s, has a curious afterlife in the persistence of that form in its disparate subliterary generic permutations.[14]

Literature understood as "serious fiction" is thus a genre without a genre. It is not necessarily a default setting or catch-all, for the *literary* still carries a connotation of prestige or elitism. That is, not just any old novel can get classified as "literature," and some novels that were once deemed unworthy may, in the fullness of time and with the right turn of critical events, accede to the level of the great works of literature. Some works previously written, marketed, or received as genre fiction—Vonnegut's early novels, for example, or Octavia Butler's *Kindred*, which went from the otherworldly science fiction straight to Oprah's Book Club (and, in the process, gaining some rather classy looking cover art as well as a new generation of readers)—might become "literature," particularly if the author later achieves critical recognition and acclaim. Unfortunately, however, and rather confusingly for historians of the form, the bookstore category into which many of these newly treasured works will be placed is not so much "literature" as "classics," a terminology that, as with "classic rock" on the radio, strikes one as paradoxical if not absurd. For classicists, whose disciplinary field encompasses "classic" works of ancient antiquity, the idea that George Orwell's *Nineteen-Eighty-Four*, Jack Kerouac's *On the Road*, or E. L. Doctorow's *Ragtime* might be labelled "classics" must seem eccentric, to say the least. But then, I only partly jokingly suppose that, if we live long enough, we all eventually become "medievalists."

Still, "serious fiction" (I will dispense with the scare-quotes hereafter) is highly valued by many readers and, more importantly, by such institutions as anthology publishers, metropolitan book reviewers, university professors, amateur connoisseurs, and so on. Part of its appeal is that it operates without distinguishing generic markers; it can stand apart and on its own from the tokens and signs of lesser genres, establishing its worth upon quality alone, or so it would seem. So-called genre fiction, by contrast, is presumed to have a set of widely recognized characteristics—e.g., themes, settings, and characters—that define the genre, allowing both readers and writers to know in advance how to approach the text. Here the appeal, particularly among those fanatics who define their reading tastes in relation to their beloved genres, lies in a recognizable set of coordinates, offering something like a map of the literary territory that will unfold in its pages. Although the specific details of each world are protean, changing from one text to the next, the overall world is, if not the same, then at least subject to its own internal laws which help to define the genre as such. For example, as Terry Pratchett once put it, somewhat jokingly, in the aftermath of Tolkien and his ilk, there is "consensus fantasy universe," in which "Elves are tall and fair and use bows, dwarves are small and dark and vote Labour."[15] This "consensus" explains both the allure and the disdain of different audiences, depending on perspective; for some, the familiar forms help to shape the pleasurable reading experience, while others find the tropes formulaic or derivative.

Pratchett's own novels represent loving send-ups of the fantasy genre, somewhat in the way that Douglas Adams's *Hitchhiker's Guide to the Galaxy* series affectionately parodied science fiction. It would not be wrong to refer to Pratchett or Adams as fantasists or SF writers, technically, but nor would it be incorrect to see them as satirists whose decision to use these genres is akin to Swift's decision to use the narrative of exploration as the basis for *Gulliver's Travels* or, say, Mel Brooks's tongue-in-cheek homage to the horse operas and oaters of his youth in *Blazing Saddles*. Yet, in exploiting the familiar characteristics of these popular genres, the satirists avail themselves of the power of genre fiction.

Jameson has suggested that genre functions as a way of helpfully limiting interpretative possibilities, thus preventing misreadings and offering a useful frame of reference for readers and the author. As he put it in *The Political Unconscious*,

> Genres are essentially literary *institutions*, or social contracts between a writer and a specific public, whose function is to specify the proper use of a particular cultural artifact. The speech acts of daily life are themselves marked with indications and signals (intonation, gesturality, contextual deictics and pragmatics) which ensure their appropriate reception. In the mediated situations of a more complicated social life—and the emergence of writing has often been taken as paradigmatic of such situations—perceptual signals must be replaced by conventions if the text in question is not to be abandoned to a drifting multiplicity of uses (as *meanings* must, according to Wittgenstein, be described). Still, as texts free themselves more and more from an immediate performance situation, it becomes ever more difficult to enforce a given generic rule on their readers. No small part of the art of writing, indeed, is absorbed by this (impossible) attempt to devise a foolproof mechanism for the automatic exclusion of undesirable responses to a given literary utterance.[16]

To use another figure close to Jameson's heart, we might say that genre offers the reader a "map." Genre helps to orientate the reader, to guide the reader's through novel yet somewhat familiar territory, using conventional forms or elements as landmarks or points of reference for interpretation.

All this is to say, the generic form itself *makes sense*, such that the *meaning* of the novel written to fit such a form is already, at least partially, made visible or cognizable to the reader. Bearing this in mind, then, one might conjecture that the prevalence of genre fiction on the bestseller lists of the twenty-first century may be considered evidence to the audience's desire for orientation or a reassuring sense of place vis-à-vis the text in an era of globalization.

Nevertheless, the rather salubrious function of genre here described does have its baleful flipside, as Vonnegut had bemoaned. In many ways, this determination of genre is restrictive, shutting off in advance certain avenues of interpretation and rerouting readers onto another, all too familiar path. If it is suggested or agreed upon in advance of reading that a given text is a work of science fiction, say, then it will be read as such, perhaps to the detriment of other possible lines of inquiry. For Vonnegut, it was less a matter of how the work would be interpreted, and more whether it would be interpreted at all; that is, Vonnegut was concerned with whether it would be taken seriously as *meaningful* work. Serious fiction, what we had been accustomed for a century or so to calling "literature," was worth the effort, whereas genre fiction still seemed simple, if not simplistic, entertainments.

However, in recent decades, it has become clear that the distinction between serious writing and genre fiction can be productively blurred, but without losing the sense of seriousness or the generic parameters of the ostensible subgenres. For one thing, a host of very well regarded and even award-winning novels have been written, if not entirely within the mold of genre fiction, then at least with such fiction's generic conventions in mind. Don DeLillo's *White Noise*, like Vonnegut's *Slaughterhouse-Five* before it, partakes of science fiction; Toni Morrison's *Beloved* is a ghost story, as well as a work of real horror, while also being a literary masterpiece; Yann Martel's *Life of Pi* is a fantastic travel narrative; Junot Díaz's *The Brief and Wondrous Life of Oscar Wao* also incorporates fantasy; Haruki Murakami's *1Q84* is pure speculative fiction; Thomas Pynchon's *Inherent Vice* is detective fiction; and McCarthy's *The Road* is a post-apocalyptic dystopia. This list does not even get to well-respected or "serious" writers who have typically embraced certain genres, such as Larry McMurtry and the Western or Hilary Mantel and the historical romance; nor does it consider those, like Margaret Atwood or Ursula Le Guin, who have generally refused to shun the label of genre fiction, openly embracing speculative fiction, utopia, or fantasy in their novels. One might conclude that so-called "literary" fiction is itself an unstable, perhaps undesirable category, and that the blurring of literary and genre fiction over the past century or more decisively calls these categories into question. For all the talk of literary fiction *versus* genre fiction, are they not engaged in the same sorts of projects? As much as it may seem so, maybe not. Even as more and more literary fiction seems to employ generic models or characteristics, there is still a sense of resistance to the categorization.

For example, not long ago Le Guin made waves when she castigated Kazuo Ishiguro for apparently belittling fantasy in a *New York Times* article. Discussing the ways in which his novel *The Buried Giant* employed "surface elements" of fantasy, such as dragons, knights, ogres, and pixies, Ishiguro seemed anxious about how this would be received by his audience. "I don't know what's going to happen [...] Will readers follow me into this? Will they understand what I'm trying to do, or will they be prejudiced against the surface elements? Are they going to say this is fantasy?"[17] Le Guin saw this as a provocation, one with which she took some umbrage. As she stated on her blog entry dated March 2, 2015, "It appears that the author takes the word for an insult. To me that is so insulting, it reflects such thoughtless prejudice, that I had to write this piece in response." Le Guin defends fantasy as "probably the oldest literary device for talking about reality," and notes that the presence or absence of "surface elements" is not what constitutes fantasy. Rather, "Literary fantasy is the result of a vivid, powerful, coherent imagination drawing plausible impossibilities together into a vivid, powerful and coherent story." She concludes that Ishiguro's novel fails, partly because of the author's lack of respect for fantasy itself. As she puts it,

> I respect what I think he was trying to do, but for me it didn't work. It couldn't work. No writer can successfully use the "surface elements" of a literary genre—far less its profound capacities—for a serious purpose, while despising it to the point of fearing identification with it. I found reading the book painful. It was like watching a man falling from a high wire while he shouts to the audience, "Are they going say I'm a tight-rope walker?"[18]

Look out below! In Le Guin's view, Ishiguro's fear that the presence of fantasy would inhibit the reader's enjoyment or appreciation of his serious literary text actually serves to undermine the text's serious literariness. As it happens, the fantastic and the real are more likely to overlap or interact than some are willing to believe.

The Allure of Alterity

There is a delightful scene in Nathaniel Hawthorne's *The House of the Seven Gables* in which Holgrave, a daguerreotypist (amongst other pursuits), reads one of his short stories to Phoebe. The story is filled with fantastic elements, as a mysterious Matthew Maule, who may or may not also be a warlock, casts a spell over young Alice Pyncheon and, unwittingly, causes her death. Meanwhile, Holgrave discovers that by his own storytelling, he has momentarily bewitched Phoebe, who, now enchanted, appears to be totally within his power. For a moment, Hawthorne allows the reader to linger on this narrative precipice, wondering whether Holgrave will somehow reenact his own tale, and "complete his mastery over Phoebe's yet free and virgin spirit."[19]

Whenever I teach this novel, with its themes of wizardry and wild romance, I like to pause at this point, and invite my students to consider the "magic" of storytelling and the implications of this scene. Inevitably, the question arises:

"What's a daguerreotype?"

Admittedly, even in a fictional universe that might contain ghosts, sorcery, and curses from beyond the grave, the outdated technology of the daguerreotype is perhaps the weirdest thing my students encounter in *The House of the Seven Gables*. That the daguerreotype is, within the time of the novel, a cutting-edge technology is stranger still, as my students struggle to picture the historical situations evoked by the novel. The nineteenth-century society in which daguerreotypes are new and perplexing, rather than so thoroughly outdated as to be nearly unknown, is almost as otherworldly as a realm inhabited by dragons and goblins. Oddly enough, then, the introduction to, and exploration of, such worlds is among the most exhilarating delights for the student of literature, and is most likely to create the conditions for the possibility of a life-long love of reading. Fantasy, understood as a genre or as a discursive mode, is no more outlandish that the literary itself, when it comes to twenty-first century readers.

My thinking on this matter emerges from the overlapping territories of my own teaching, often focused on fairly canonical texts in American and European literature, and my amateur's interest in fantasy, including Tolkien, *Game of Thrones*, or Harry Potter, for instance. As noted above, fantasy is a genre that seems to have taken over the publishing industry in recent years. In teaching "classic" or canonical texts, I have found that they provide to student-readers the sort of imaginative pleasures quite similar to that of works of fantasy, and I believe a big part of it is the radical alterity of both "literary" and "fantasy" stories. That is, whether a given work presents a fully formed "Otherworld," such as Dante's Inferno or Tolkien's Middle-earth, or they develop fictions taking place in a recognizable setting (London, for instance, which is a geospace equally "real" in both *Harry Potter and the Order of the Phoenix* and *Our Mutual Friend*), the estrangements of the literary texts are captivating.

Although teachers sometimes try to use texts that more directly jibe with their students' own experiences, that are "relatable" (as people say), or that allow student readers to identify personally with familiar characters, I have found that nearly the opposite strategy may be more effective, particularly if one of the goals is to produce readers who will go on to read further, outside of the course. (As a side note, I have never quite understood this siren-call of the "relatable," which suggests that, like some perverse version of the Lacanian mirror stage, students can only enter into literature's Symbolic Order when they have looked into the mirror and seen, *not* the face of the Other, but the already identified and embraced Same or Self.) Narratives depicting an all-too-familiar world, with easily recognizable characters and experiences, are certainly well liked, especially in the context of a required course, where ease of understanding makes for less anxiety over grades. However, it seems that many students grow weary of such fare, eventually conceding that they "already know" this stuff. *Strange* people, places, and events, by contrast, may be more difficult to get a grip on at first, but this frequently leads to greater interest and enjoyment, as well as to the desire to read or learn more about the subjects involved.

This is not an argument against realism, exactly, but the fantasy-versus-mimesis dichotomy, to cite Kathryn Hume's marvelous study, might offer an instructive example.[20] In a recent controversy over the status of genre fiction in the publishing world—the particular instance, in this case, was the Man Booker Prize and whether its judges were willing to take seriously books written in the fantasy or science-fiction genre—China Miéville suggested that the distinction between realism and fantasy was not really useful or accurate. Miéville suggested another way of thinking about it, distinguishing between fictions of "recognition" and of "estrangement." In response to the question of "what the Booker Prize *really* excludes," Miéville observed that

> the tradition of, if you like, 'mainstream literary fiction' […] has tended strongly to celebrate the former over the latter [i.e., *recognition* over *estrangement*]. There's an obvious relation with realist versus non-realist work (thinking on these lines might help map links between the pulpiest SF and more celebrated Surrealist and avant-garde work), though the distinction maps only imperfectly across the generic divide. All fiction contains elements of both drives (to different degrees, and variably skilfully). That very fact might be one way of getting at the drab disappointment of, on the one hand, the clichés of some fantasy and the twee and clunking allegories of middlebrow 'literary' magic realism (faux estrangement, none-more-mollycoddling recognition), and on the other at those utterly fascinating texts which contain not a single

impossible element, and yet which read as if they were, somehow, fantastic (*Jane Eyre, Moby-Dick*, etc.). Great stuff can doubtless be written from both perspectives.

Miéville concludes by adding that he thinks "there is something more powerful, ambitious, intriguing and radical about the road recently less feted. I'd rather be estranged than recognize."[21]

Miéville's broader category of "fiction of estrangement" usefully brings together so-called genre fiction such as fantasy or science fiction and those more culturally valued productions like romanticism or surrealism, but Miéville do not suggest that realism is to be avoided. For one thing, a great deal of literary realism is remarkably strange, if I can put it that way. Dickens, for example, is usually thought of as a rather realistic writer, but part of his power lies in the way his novels reveals the magical aspects of the real-world, as in the marvelous anecdote of the "MOOR EEFFOC." According to G. K. Chesterton, a young Charles Dickens discovered these magical words by seeing the sign "Coffee Room" from the other side of a glass door. Chesterton concludes that "it is the masterpiece of the good realistic principle—the principle that the most fantastic of all is often the precise fact," and he referred to this as "that elvish kind of realism Dickens adopted everywhere."[22]

However, as my example of Holgrave in *The House of the Seven Gables* demonstrates, one need not even look for the "elvish realism" in many classic texts, since the historical situation itself may appear so strange, particularly to those of us or among our students who have "forgotten how to think historically," as Jameson would have it (i.e., we postmoderns). Part of the immense allure of Tolkienesque fantasy, indubitably, is the quite real, but relatively unrecognizable, medieval world itself. It contains such a radically different social formation, so intriguing to modern readers, that it may as well be otherworldly. I sometimes feel this way about the *Game of Thrones* saga, a television show based on George R. R. Martin's as yet unfinished *Song of Ice and Fire* series of novels, which a colleague of mine charitably referred to as a mix of Tolkien and *Dallas* (the then-risqué, 1980s primetime drama about Texas oil barons); in print and on screen, it definitely "reads" like a soap opera, right down to its seemingly interminable length. Yes, dragons and ice-demons and blood magic appear in Martin's imaginative universe, but one can go hundreds of pages at a time without thinking of them, as we are compelled to focus instead on court intrigue, war strategy, love stories, or the complexly interlacing plotlines. That the plot itself seems loosely modeled on the War of the Roses only underscores the point: the past is itself otherworldly.

In the end, the question is not whether a sober realism or a romantic fantasy offers the best mode in which to engage artistically with the world, but rather how we are to engage at all. Otherworldliness may indeed be the best way of seeing our own world with fresh eyes, and, in an age which seems to have forgotten how to think critically, historically, or speculatively, the sort of conceptual work accomplished by literature is all the more necessary. As the Tolkien scholar and medievalist Tom Shippey notes, an opposition to the strange or unrecognizable often corresponds to the poverty of one's imagination. Speaking of a character in Tolkien's "Smith of Wootton Major," Shippey writes: "He has only a weak [...] notion of fantasy himself, but assumes that this is all there can ever be; and since he is well aware of the feebleness of his own imagination, he assumes all images of the fantastic, of Faerie, must be feeble too."[23] Coming from a very different critical tradition, Jameson has said something similar about our own postmodern condition, in which for many it is easier to envision the end of the world than an end to the present economic system; but, Jameson adds, "perhaps that is due to some weakness in our imaginations."[24]

How does one strengthen the imagination? Another great critic, theorist, and teacher provided the answer: through the study of literature, explained Northrop Frye, in his passionate defense of that field of study, titled *The Educated Imagination*. The individual student needs literature the way that a starving man needs food, writes Frye, for literature will disclose to students a second world largely unknown to them. It is *not* a secondary world in which to escape, but above all the window into a place far more real than the illusory society to which students were previously limited. The strange world discovered by the educated imagination is not illusory. "It is the real world, the real form of human society hidden behind the one we see. It's the world of what humanity has done, and therefore can do, the world revealed to us in the arts and sciences."[25] Readers who explore this world are less likely to find comfort in the ironically false, "real-world" of the crass, familiar, and everyday life. Perhaps, with strengthened imaginations, they will even find ways to change it.

All of this is to say that, in an era in which the literary seems devalued and in which genre-fiction represents the dominant form of literature, the situation may not be so dire. As noted, not long after his famous complaint about being labeled a science fiction writer, Vonnegut achieved his greatest fame and critical acclaim with *Slaughterhouse-Five*, and the epoch in which serious literature blends its themes, techniques, and characteristics with genre fiction has also made for more interesting, innovative novels. If, as Arac suggests, the novel is today a residual cultural form, then the residue is ample, rich, and rewarding. And if the literary moment has passed, the diffusion of literature across various genres and forms may prove momentous after all.

Notes

1. Kurt Vonnegut, Jr. "Science Fiction," *Wampeters, Foma, and Granfalloons* (New York: Delacorte Press, 1974), 1–5.
2. Vonnegut, "Foreword," *Player Piano* (New York: Dial Press, 1980), n.p.
3. Vonnegut, "Science Fiction," 1.
4. See Dinitia Smith, "The Times Plans a Children's Best Seller List," *New York Times*, June 24, 2000: http://www.nytimes.com/2000/06/24/books/the-times-plans-a-children-s-best-seller-list.html.
5. Jonathan Arac, "What Kind of History Does the Theory of the Novel Require?" *NOVEL: A Forum on Fiction* 42.2 (2009), 190–195.
6. See Raymond Williams, *Marxism and Literature* (Oxford: Oxford University Press, 1976), especially 121–127.
7. Arac, *The Emergence of American Literary Narrative, 1820–1860* (Cambridge: Harvard University Press, 2005), 2.
8. Terry Eagleton, *Literary Theory: An Introduction* (Minneapolis: University of Minnesota Press, 1983), 15.
9. Arac, "Literary History in a Global Age," *New Literary History* 39.3 (2008), 757.
10. Franco Moretti, *Atlas of the European Novel, 1800–1900* (London: Verso, 1998), 160.
11. Arac, "What Kind of History," 193.
12. Arac, "Literary History in a Global Age," 757.
13. "Literature" may have more or less expansive meanings depending on institutional context or disciplinary field as well. For instance, in the sciences, "literature review" often refers to a discussion of all the relevant published articles or books on the subject, which of course has nothing to go with questions or literary genres or aesthetics.
14. Anecdotally, I would note that many students—perhaps whole generations of readers—in the United States have begun to use the word *novel* to refer to any book, much to the chagrin of literature professors. I have found this new convention to hold not only for literary texts that are not novels, such as when students refer to Shakespeare's *Hamlet* or T. S. Eliot's *Selected Poems* as a "novel," but also for books completely outside of the literary humanities, as when students refer to their textbook in their Introduction to Psychology course as a "novel." Ironically, the "age of the novel" may thus persist without any need for what had formerly been called novels.
15. Terry Pratchett, "Why Gandalf Never Married," 1985: http://www.ansible.co.uk/misc/tpspeech.html.
16. Fredric Jameson, *The Political Unconscious: Narrative as a Socially Symbolic Act* (Ithaca: Cornell University Press, 1981), 106–107.
17. Quoted in Alexandra Alter, "A New Enchanted Realm," *The New York Times*, February 20, 2015, C19.
18. Ursula K. Le Guin, "95. 'Are they going to say this is fantasy?'" *Ursula K. Le Guin's Blog*, March 5, 2015: http://www.ursulakleguin.com/Blog2015.html.
19. Nathaniel Hawthorne, *The House of the Seven Gables*, ed. Milton R. Stern (New York: Penguin, 1986), 212.
20. See Kathryn Hume, *Fantasy and Mimesis: Responses to Reality in Western Literature* (New York: Methuen, 1984).
21. Quoted in Sarah Crown, "What the Booker Prize Really Excludes," *The Guardian*, October 11, 2011: http://www.theguardian.com/books/booksblog/2011/oct/17/science-fiction-china-mieville.

22 G. K. Chesterton, *Charles Dickens: A Critical Study* (New York: Dodd Mead and Co., 1906), 47–48.
23 Tom Shippey, *J. R. R. Tolkien: Author of a New Century* (Boston: Houghton Mifflin, 2000), 299.
24 Jameson, *The Seeds of Time* (New York: Columbia University Press, 1994), xii.
25 Northrop Frye, *The Educated Imagination* (Bloomington: Indiana University Press, 1964), 152.

Part II

POST-AMERICANIST INTERPOLATIONS

Chapter 6

"BELIEVING IN AMERICA": THE IDEOLOGY OF AMERICAN STUDIES

Leo Marx recounts a story, told to him by the eminent British literary historian Richard Hoggart, of an encounter in the mid-1950s between Hoggart and a young Fulbright scholar who identified himself as a teacher of *American Studies*.

> "And what is *that*?" Hoggart had asked. "An exciting new field of interdisciplinary teaching and research." "What is *new* about that?" "It combines the study of history and literature." "In England we've been doing that for a long time," Hoggart protests. "Yes," said the eager Americanist, "but *we* look at American society as a whole—the entire culture, at *all* levels, high and low." But Hoggart, who was about to publish his groundbreaking study of British working-class culture—*The Uses of Literacy* (1957)—remained unimpressed. After a moment, in a fit of exasperation, his informant blurted out: "But you don't understand, I *believe* in America!"

At this point, Hoggart understood completely just what the young man meant, although he also noted that no British scholar would ever be heard saying, "I believe in Britain!"[1]

The anecdote is representative of the degree to which American Studies, as practiced by Americans in the United States at least,[2] developed out of the political (and personal) convictions of its adherents. Although certain aspects of its work could be tied more directly to this or that program that is explicitly in the service of national and international political aims, such as the CIA's involvement with literary magazines or the operations of *UNESCO*, it is clear that American Studies as a whole was always already ideological. As a disciplinary (or interdisciplinary) field, American Studies functions not only to study America, but to promote it: *it* being the idea of "America" itself, something that was not coextensive with the political or geographic entity known as the United States. Contrary to the many accusations by revisionist critics or even apologias by supposed traditionalists, the early practitioners of American Studies were not blind adherents to a particular government or political policy (far from it!). Rather, they were or became something like disciples of a new religion, one whose system of belief they were in fact helping to create. In studying "America," they could reveal its mysteries and uncover its spiritually uplifting significance like apostles spreading the Gospel, thereby also making the mundane world of U.S. social life better. *Believing* in America appeared to be something of a prerequisite for the study of America.[3]

Establishing a Belief System

The excitement felt by the young Americanist in Marx's anecdote, as well as his chagrin in being forced to recognize that his enthusiasm was so deeply rooted in his personal (rather than merely scholarly) investment in the putative subject, had much to do with the feeling that he was part of something new and grand. As American Studies consolidated its interdisciplinary energies into a field, with its own disciplinary terms and practices, the elements of its belief system became more recognizable. Like a new religion, the fervent ideas and ideals become concretized in formal rites and rituals, such that its novices have a canon to study and its adepts are fluent in the catechism. To *believe* in America, then, would involve the identification of various individual and related beliefs. In particular, certain figures, tropes, and symbols began to become concrete terms in the overall ideology or myth of "America." These include, but are not limited to, the following features: an image of the nation founded as a beacon to humanity, a model for the world; a national community that developed from the space of a pastoral ideal or an encounter with the wilderness that defined the nation; a primordial innocence, by which the American can be distinguished from the world-weary European; a frontier that imbues the American with a sense of destiny, like Manifest Destiny, where a westering movement is ideologically associated with mankind's improvement; and so on. These and various other ideas had been part of the American national ideology for some time, of course, unfolding in various ways through variously told national narratives across the nineteenth century especially, but with the advent of American Studies in the twentieth century, they become almost fixed figures in the belief system.

The crisis in American Studies over the last forty or so years derives, at least in part, from a crisis in belief. The halcyon days of the early practitioners of American Studies gave way to a generation of scholars and critics who wanted to challenge the perceived consensus about what "America" means. The new Americanists could no longer bring themselves to believe in *that* "America."

Although it has been characterized by both proponents and detractors as part of a critical project that undermining the "belief" in America, the bulk of the new Americanist energy in fact went into making the belief system work better. For example, by pointing out the ways that standard Americanist literary studies ignored the contributions of minorities and then by including those figures who had been previously excluded (women, Black Americans, American Indians, and so on), the new Americanists ultimately strengthened the underlying mythology, making it now more believable, and more worthy of one's devotion. Some of the terms would be altered, but the American Way would include more Americans, rightly so. This enhanced inclusiveness filled in crucial gaps of the American national ideal, making "America" something to believe in again.

Others, however, came to believe that the "America" of American Studies was thoroughly corrupt to the core. *Écrasez l'infâme!* These Americanists called for radical revaluation, in which the colonial settlements, the institution of slavery, and the western frontier be understood for the directly imperialist (and immoral) activities that they were. Racism, sexism, and ethnocentrism were thus posited as *inherently* American characteristics, not as unfortunate side-effects of an otherwise laudatory national *ethos* and history. This has given rise to what has been called "Anti-American Studies" by one distraught critic.[4] Here, it seems, the more vitriolic of new Americanists not only denounce the "American Way" as a false idol, they recast it as a demon.

It goes without saying that these are caricatures. But it goes better *with* saying that the practitioners of American Studies have often used caricatures, sometimes even acknowledged as such, to make their points about "America," what it means, and what one should or should not believe. The field of American Studies, as its label indicates, arises out of a profound sense of the national, of the importance of the nation in itself and in the world. Arguably, at least, in our era of globalization, we are now living in something of a postnational era, one in which the very categories of the nation, national identity, and the nation-state are being redefined. As such, the belief system that marks the coherence of an American national narrative inevitably changes. Can one still believe in "America"? If possible, is that even desirable?

"Sancho Panza in a land of Don Quixotes"

Remembering his first encounter with "the ritual of American consensus" in the mid-1960s, the Canadian-born literary critic Sacvan Bercovitch explained that it was, perhaps surprisingly, most clearly audible in protest, where the dissident voices aimed to recall America to its sacred mission. In other words, the protesters who had every reason and motivation to criticize what they saw happening in the United States nevertheless still *believed* in America, and particularly in the American Way or "American dream." As Bercovitch marveled,

> I felt like Sancho Panza in a land of Don Quixotes. It was not just that the dream was a patent fiction. It was that the fiction involved an entire hermeneutic system. Mexico may have meant the land of gold, and Canada might be the Dominion of the North; but America was a venture in exegesis. You were supposed to discover it as a believer unveils scripture. America's meaning was implicit in its destiny, and its destiny was manifest to all who had the grace to discover its meaning. To a Canadian skeptic, a gentile in God's Country, it made for a breathtaking scene: a poly-ethnic, multi-racial, openly materialistic, self-consciously individualistic people knit together in the bonds of myth, voluntarily, with a force of belief unsurpassed by any other modern society.[5]

From this contemporary experience of seeing the overwhelming and unaccountable power of the mythic or ideological "America," even among—or maybe *especially* among—those who had good reason to find fault with it, Bercovitch eventually discovered the long national narrative empowered by what he called "the American Jeremiad," which extended from the earliest days of English colonization of New England in the seventeenth-century to the present.[6]

In the protests of the 1960s that Bercovitch witnessed, we find the overlapping territories of American Studies and the object of study: "America" was something that one *believed in*. Today, because of the interventions of recent revisionist work, it is commonly thought that the main figures in the development of American Studies were cultural conservatives, manufacturing an American ideology that valorized U.S. policies at home and abroad, particularly with respect to the civil rights movement and the Cold War. But as Bercovitch notes, the American dream was perhaps most often used as an ideological tool to criticize those very policies. There was an intense sort of nationalism in the rhetoric of America, but that does not always translate into a whole-hearted acceptance of the means and ends of U.S. power, and both those who claim the mantle of the "patriot" and those who criticize such patriotism have embraced the figure of an "America" in countering what they see as the real world's failures to live up to its ideals. The founders of American Studies were, by and large, motivated by good intentions. As Leo Marx points out, somewhat defensively, almost all of the earlier figures in the field were liberal New Dealers or outright

Leftists.⁷ If the results of their efforts turned out celebrating U.S. capitalism and imperialism, that certainly was not their goal.

What is true is that they believed in America; they were deeply embedded in an American ideology or mythology that they also helped to foster, wittingly or otherwise. Bercovitch points out that many of the early Americanists were hesitant to acknowledge the ideological bases and effects of their work. In some cases, they were reluctant to call this "ideology," which at the time had a negative connotation, being associated with Marxist *Ideologiekritik*, preferring instead to think in terms of *myths* and *symbols*. "Since ideology pretends to truth, the task of analysis is to uncover, rationally, the sinister effects of its fictions," explain Bercovitch explained. "Since myths are fictions, the task is to display, empathetically, their 'deeper truths'—the abiding values embedded in simple plots, the range and richness of formulaic metaphors."⁸

By embracing myth, and thereby failing to place the ideological in the foreground of their work, these old Americanists set themselves up for harsh criticism by the new Americanists who specifically identified the project of American Studies as ideological. Yet Bercovitch believes that these later critics, by focusing almost exclusively on the negative aspects of American ideology, seem unable to see how ideology operates both for ill and for good, as with the discourse on civil rights. "We come to feel, in reading these critics, that the American ideology is a system of ideas in the service of evil rather than (like any ideology) a system of ideas wedded for good and evil to a certain social and cultural order."⁹ Like their predecessors, these revisionist critics seem to *believe* in America nearly as much as Marx's young Americanist of the 1950s, only these critics, especially in the minds of their opponents on the political right, seem to believe that America is a Great Satan. In any case, the quasi-religious aspect of this, including the belief system involved, remains intact.

"America": An Image Repertoire

A brief survey of the evolution of American Studies illustrates the power of the underlying belief in America. Although its disciplinary roots lie in the late nineteenth century, the rise and expansion of American Studies coincided with World War II, and, not insignificantly, the beginning of the Cold War. Prior to the war, American Studies found its voice in a variety of sources, foreign and domestic: V. L. Parrington's immense literary history, Lewis Mumford's criticism, and D. H. Lawrence's magisterial little *Studies in Classic American Literature*, among others, helped to put both U.S. literature and the "national character" it represented on the cultural map.

This culminated, in a sense, in F. O. Matthiessen's field-establishing *American Renaissance*, published in 1941, in which five mid-nineteenth-century figures—Ralph Waldo Emerson, Henry David Thoreau, Nathaniel Hawthorne, Herman Melville, and Walt Whitman—are chosen to embody the artistic achievement and promise of self-consciously American expression. In leaving out such major popular and influential writers as Washington Irving, James Fenimore Cooper, George Bancroft, Fredric Douglass, or Harriet Beecher Stowe, Matthiessen established the aesthetic basis of American literary studies, with its clear preference for irony, ambiguity, and complexity. Of course, the most famous omission, one requiring a specific comment in explanation, was of Edgar Allan Poe. Although the principle reason Poe was left out was strictly historical (i.e., that book focused on works produced between 1850 and 1855, and Poe died in 1849), Matthiessen gives other reasons for excluding him: "Poe was bitterly hostile to democracy," and "his value, even more than Emerson's, is now seen to consist in his influence rather than in the body of his own work"; Poe's "stories, less harrowing upon the nerves as they were, seem relatively factitious when contrasted with the moral depth of Hawthorne and Melville."[10] In other words, Poe is neither American enough nor artist enough to be included, which is itself telling, especially since Matthiessen also confirmed that the principle purpose of art in America was to challenge the regnant orthodoxy. American literature, the literature worth studying at any rate, was in some sense *subversive*, and a generation of critics set out to celebrate this paradox. The greatness of the greatest American literature lies not so much in its celebration of America but in its powerfully *American* critique of the United States.

Although *American Renaissance* is a major landmark, Matthiessen still belongs to the formative period or prehistory of American Studies as an established field. Leo Marx's anecdote above hails from the giddy moment of the field's realization in the 1950s. For better or for worse, American Studies came to maturity during the Cold War. Many of its leading figures were combat veterans, a number of whom might not have attended university at all were it not for the G. I. Bill. The defeat of fascism in Europe and totalitarianism in Japan, combined with Marshall Plan-inspired good feelings about America's positive role in world affairs, undoubtedly emboldened these scholars and critics not only to "believe" in America but to believe, sincerely, that this America was something to be championed. Delving into U.S. history and literature, the newly formed American Studies would identify and create an "America" that could symbolize freedom itself, not only for its own citizens but for the outside world. The mythic America was alluded to in the *ur*-texts of American literature already, from the Puritan sermonizing about the New Jerusalem through the Enlightenment rhetoric of "the Rights of Man" during the Revolutionary period to Lincoln's redefinition of the United States as a nation "dedicated to a proposition, that all men are created equal."[11] The pre-war generation undoubtedly *believed* in America as well, and "America" came to be defined by such figures as Frederick Jackson Turner, Van Wyck Brooks, and Parrington. What changed was the role of that America in a geopolitical configuration markedly altered by the war. The rhetoric of America as leader of the "free world" (indeed, the very idea of a "free world") provides a telling instance of this change. Hence, the emergence of American Studies was timely.

The excitement of the Americanists of this era had much to do with the perceived novelty of the enterprise, evident in the anecdote above. As Hoggart indicated, English literary studies had long been concerned with the historical, and had often focused attention on its culture as a whole. Thus, Hoggart had his reasons to be skeptical that this American Studies was doing anything particularly new, at least with respect to their methods and aims. But, as the historical context reveals, the fact is that American Studies *was* new, or at least its practitioners were somewhat justified in believing it to be. The Americanists were not just studying American civilization; they were *creating* American civilization.[12] Many of the important literary historical and critical works of this period established, or perhaps reinscribed, the fundamental national ideology or mythology upon which American Studies as a field rested. Elizabeth Renker has offered a more positive assessment of these origins, noting that the discipline of American literary studies arose through the inclusion of women, minorities, and the working class, and that the discipline's sense of inferiority within the academy had to do with diverse "teacher and student populations [...] The social functions associated with American literature as a curricular product were thus a foundational part of its identity *as* a product, quite apart from the content of its canon."[13] But then the more representative of "America" American Studies became, arguably, the more it could effectively, if unconsciously, reinforce a kind of nationalist ideological mission, as I discuss below.

In many ways, the American national narrative was being written or rewritten in the 1950s, even if its foundational myths, images, figures, and examples would be revealed to have emerged far earlier. As Donald E. Pease has put it,

> these national narratives constructed imaginary relations to actual sociopolitical conditions to effect imagined communities called national peoples. The image repertoire productive of the U.S. national community can be ascertained through the recitation of its key terms in the national meta-narrative commonly understood to be descriptive of that community.

Those images interconnect an exceptional national subject (American Adam) with a representative national scene (Virgin Land) and an exemplary national motive (errand into the wilderness).[14]

While it is true that these images appear in various guises throughout American history, it is not surprising that they also appear as the titles of three major contributions to American Studies in the 1950s: R. W. B. Lewis's *The American Adam* (1955), Henry Nash Smith's *Virgin Land* (1950), and Perry Miller's *Errand into the Wilderness* (1956).[15] With the image repertoire of American national narrative, the resulting "America" was established and reinforced through the practice of American Studies.

The Great Divide

Then came a period of reevaluation, the "Great Divide," as Marx referred to it, in the "misnamed political upheaval" called the "Sixties," which occurred between 1965 and 1975, occasioned by the crises of the Vietnam War and civil rights movements.[16] The integral, seamless unity of the "America" developed by and through American studies could no longer hold up to scrutiny. The vivid and daily spectacle of the injustices countenanced and, indeed, facilitated by the American Way, whether in Mai Lai or in Selma, Alabama, could not but undermine that mythic American self-image. As a generation of marginalized, disgruntled, or simply disappointed people "discovered" that the American Way was in fact merely a myth, that there was no providential national mission (errand into the wilderness), that America was not a "shining city on the hill" or a "beacon to humanity," that the *idea* of America was in fact disconnected to the reality of the United States—in other words, that they could no longer bring themselves to *believe in America*—this is the point at which American Studies should be fundamentally altered. Or so it would seem.

As Bercovitch makes clear, the power of the American myth is perhaps even more strongly felt by the dissidents within the United States than by the apologists for the status quo. Indeed, one of the cornerstone beliefs in the national narrative was that America is founded on dissent, from the radical Protestant pilgrims through the Revolutionary Founding Fathers, extending onward to the abolitionists and up to the present time, embodied in civil rights leaders, feminists, environmentalists, and so on. The continuing force of *that* "America" can be illustrated by Bercovitch's clear, straightforward contrast between an outsider's and an insider's respective points of view on the undermining of the regnant American mythos. Asking the rhetorical question, "What would happen, in short, if 'America' were severed once and for all from the United States?" Bercovitch answers:

> Nothing much, from an outsider's point of view: only a fresh, non-apocalyptic sense of the exigencies of industrial capitalism; a certain modesty about the claims of nationality; a more mundane distinction between the Old World and the New, as denoting metaphor of geography, rather than the progress of humanity; a more traditional sense of "frontiers," as signifying limits and barriers rather than new territories to conquer; a relativistic assessment of the prospects and constraints of liberal democracy (the benefits of open competition, for example, or the abuses or representative individualism), none of these heaven-ordained either as a sign of national election or as an augury of doom.
>
> But that (to repeat) is an outsider's perspective. Considered from within the culture, the de-mythification of "America" meant everything. It would dissipate the very core of personal and communal identity. It would undo this society's controlling metaphors and narratives, its long-ripened strategies of cohesion, assimilation, and crisis-control. To imagine a liberal United States without "America" was like imagining feudal Europe without the myths of aristocracy and kingship. It seemed a contradiction in terms.[17]

Rather than exploding a myth in favor of a more rational explanation, the crisis of American Studies becomes a crisis of faith. What happens when the Americanist can no longer believe in America?

The first and most visible effect of this crisis is not a turn to atheism but a strengthening of the initial faith. American Studies after the Great Divide may have appeared to turn away from the beliefs of the 1950s' Americanists, but in reality the new American Studies built upon those beliefs. The principal achievement was the recognition of the ways in which the regnant American myth involved the exclusion of various people, notably nonwhite men and all women, American Indians, immigrants and other "foreigners," the working classes, gay men and lesbians. Often, however, the major contribution to American Studies was to write these groups back into the national master narrative. This effort has been largely salutary, and the literature and history of the United States has been made both richer and more accurate by virtue of the more inclusive and complete picture. But the overarching myth of "America" has not thereby changed much. In many instances, the greater inclusiveness has reinforced the myth by emphasizing that idea of America as a nation of nations, containing the entire world, which is one of the central motifs of an American national narrative going back to J. Hector St. John de Crèvecœur's *Letters from an American Farmer* (1782) at least. The greater inclusiveness also underscores another theme of American ideology, that of constant progressive movement, a teleology as ingrained as the Puritan theological beliefs in Divine Providence, assuring Americans that today is better than yesterday and tomorrow looks even brighter, as the promise of the American Way is extended to those previously left out. This further allows practitioners of American Studies to feel that they themselves are part of the progressive movement of American history, for by calling attention to those who had been excluded from the "official" narrative of American history they are in effect helping to extend liberty and freedom to all. Now *that* is an America to believe in!

Others have been less sanguine about the ruling *mythos* of American Studies. Not content to preserve the national narrative, extending it to previously marginalized populations, the so-called New Americanists embrace an avowedly postnational position.[18] The term "New Americanists" was coined, and not as an endorsement, by Frederick Crews in a length review article in the *New York Review of Books* titled "Whose American Renaissance?" in which crews lambasted the recent work of number of critics, including Bercovitch, Pease, Jane Tompkins, Walter Benn Michaels, and Myra Jehlen, for re-introducing ideology and politicizing literary studies.[19] Perversely, perhaps, Pease embraced the term, both for himself and his own work, and as the title of what would be an extraordinarily influential book series published by Duke University Press. In one of its first volumes, in fact, Pease writes a programmatic essay specifically addressing Crews's critique, pointing out what he takes to be misunderstanding and errors, but by and large agreeing with Crews about the aims and methods of the "new" Americanist critics.[20]

By approaching their subject from the vantage of non-national subjects, often through the lens of race, class, and/or gender, these critics have openly denounced the national metanarrative that undergirds the belief system of American Studies. It is not enough to simply include formerly excluded subjects. As Pease argues, the American national narrative developed through and *depended on* the exclusions of subjected peoples ("women, blacks, 'foreigners,' the homeless"). A rewriting of the national narrative with these "national subject peoples" now included, therefore, would not be the same national narrative, no matter how much a liberal imagination might wish it so. As Pease puts it,

> When understood from within the context of the construction of an imagined national community, the negative class, race, and gender categories of these subject peoples were not a historical aberration

but a structural necessity for the construction of a national narrative whose coherence depended upon the internal opposition between Nature's Nation and peoples understood to be constructed of a "different nature."[21]

It is in this sense that Pease uses the term *postnational*: that the national narrative cannot stand once these "subject peoples" have asserted themselves, and above all, asserted their difference from the national symbolic system; this difference cannot be wholly integrated within the national narrative. When these figures "surge up," as "unintegrated externalities, they expose national identity as an artifact rather than a tacit assumption, a purely contingent social construction rather than a meta-social universal."[22]

Pease's use of the term *postnational* is arguably somewhat misleading.[23] In his view, the New Americanists have destabilized the coherent and integrated wholeness of national narrative, exposing it to be an artificial construct, but there is nothing specifically *post*-national about the project, for the sense of America as a distinctively national space and concept remains.[24] As Milette Shamir observes, the "post" in *postnational* is not to be understood as a temporal marker, but rather indicates the New Americanists' antagonistic relationship to national narrative. However, as with the disillusioned or disappointed American Left encountered by Bercovitch in the mid-1960s, the New Americanist project effectively replicated the older one, exhibiting the same features that Bercovitch had identified from the American Jeremiad. As Shamir puts it, the New American Studies "resembled the Jeremiad in its propensity for self-criticism, lament over past moral failings, and, particularly, in its disguised notion of a promised land, a better, more inclusive, more multicultural America in the act of becoming, an act understood to include speech acts of the New Americanists themselves."[25] Far from being postnational, these narratives served to emend and amend the old Americanist national narrative. In other words, by replacing the old national narrative with a new one, the New Americanists similarly create an "America" to believe in.[26]

In his exquisite genealogy of American literature as a field of study, David Shumway has shown that American literature's "most significant achievement was to secure for Americans a belief in their success as a culture. [...] The discipline, in other words, produced a widely accepted representation of American civilization that not only defined its character but 'verified' its existence."[27] As Shumway concludes,

> The effect of the collective work of the discipline of American literature was to celebrate American civilization. Thus American literature was used to reinforce the pervasive political messages of the postwar era that

America had achieved a legitimate global supremacy, threatened only by the potential illegitimate supremacy of communism. America in this view was not merely a civilization, but the savior of civilization itself. The existence of a great and unique tradition of American literature helped Americans believe this vision.[28]

In some respects, then, one could say that "American Studies" is inseparable from the "American Century." The same cultural work that Henry Luce hoped to accomplish in bestowing upon the century that name was being performed in how American literature, history, and culture was studied.

Indeed, the project of the New Americanists has largely served to monumentalize and solidify the field of American literature even more at the time its century was expiring. The insights of their diverse work have reinvigorated the study of American literature, which has had the perverse side-effect of sending more and more students into a nationalistic program of study at the very moment when the nation-state has ceased to be the principal organizing power in the world system. The American Century derived its power from an ideology of American literature and American Studies well prepared to shape the past in the service of the present, but quite unprepared for a future in which America's place was diminished in a postnational (and also post-American) world system. But the articles of faith are no longer valid in a world in which the gods are shown to be false idols. As Shumway has noted, with irony, when "America" became a world power, it "discovered" that it had a unified national literature.[29] After the American Century, can there really be an American literature?

Secular Criticism and U.S. Literature

The *postnational*, if it is to be a useful term in dealing with American Studies, must not replicate the problems of the national. By *postnationality*, I refer specifically to the current condition, in the era of globalization, in which the nation-state is no longer the locus classicus of culture, the economy, or even politics. As Jürgen Habermas has recently written, the "phenomena of the territorial state, the nation, and a popular economy constituted within national borders forms a historical constellation" that globalization has now put into question.[30] Under the auspices of globalization, the national models—including those used for the study of literature and culture—are no longer reliable or even desirable. Hence, the "belief in America" that typified early American Studies and continues to affect new American Studies is not entirely relevant, and may be detrimental, in a postnational world. One cannot effectively approach a postnational study of the literature, history, and culture of the United States with a particular belief in America established at the outset. In other words, one should not *believe in America* as did the young Americanist of Leo Marx's anecdote. But neither should one *believe in America* as have the despondent critics of the Bercovitch's Sixties or the disenchanted New Americanists later, either as a hope deferred and unfulfilled or as an ideological apparatus designed to repress this or that version of the masses. The underlying belief remains the same, and it remains suspect in a postnational era.

Edward W. Said, writing in a different context, urged that criticism be secular. By this he meant that criticism must sever its ancient connections to mysticism and the exegesis of Scripture and recognize its situatedness and affiliations in the world. Throughout this essay I have been suggesting that American Studies, as it was originally constituted as a field and as it continues to be practiced in the United States, has had a quasi-religious aura, such that its leading practitioners have subscribed to and fostered a belief system that is, in effect, an American nationalist ideology. Whether Americanists acknowledge this belief in America, the result has often been the creation, elucidation, and even derogation of an American national narrative. This sacred narrative then elevates and removes from the real world the purported object of study: the histories, literatures, and cultures of the inhabitants of the United States. Said elegantly explains the problems associated with a criticism based on such grand ideas.

> To say of such grand ideas and their discourse that they have something in common with religious discourse is to say that each serves as an agent of closure, shutting off human investigation, criticism, and effort in deference to the authority of the more-than-human, the supernatural, the other-worldly. Like culture, religion therefore furnishes us with systems of authority and with canons of order whose regular effect is either to compel subservience or to gain adherents. This in turn gives rise to organized collective passions whose social and intellectual results are often disastrous. The persistence of these and other religious-cultural artifacts testifies amply to what seem to be necessary features of human life, the need for certainty, group solidarity, and a sense of communal belonging. Sometimes of course these things are beneficial. Still it is also true that what a secular attitude enables—a sense of history and human production, along with a healthy skepticism about various official idols venerated by culture and by system—is diminished, if not eliminated, by appeals to what cannot be thought and explained, except by consensus and appeals to authority.[31]

Said is referring specifically to Orientalist discourse, but his words could easily apply to promoters of an American national narrative. An American Studies that still requires and still fosters a *belief* in America impedes the interdisciplinary study of the history and literature of the United States and the wider world of which it is a part. A more secular approach is needed.

One of the first great works in postnational American Studies actually emerged around the same time that American Studies was forming itself into a cognizable and distinctively nationalist field. Written by a "foreigner," in atrocious conditions that further amplified his foreignness, it is a landmark of the sort of secular and postnationalist work. I am speaking, of course, of C. L. R. James's brilliant study of Herman Melville, published in 1953 and written in Ellis Island while James was awaiting deportation, under suspicion of being a communist at the height of McCarthyism. James's profound, personal commitment to the postnational is evident in his dedication to the book: "For my son, Nob, who will be 21 years old in 1970, by which time I hope he and his generation will have left behind them forever all the problems of nationality."[32] While that dream remains unfulfilled, the James elegantly suggests the hope for an imagined community without borders, a postnational world, and for the sort of cultural criticism best suited to it. A truly postnational American Studies would bring secular, worldly criticism to bear on the still important questions concerning the United States, the role of that place in the wider world, and the relations of the world to it. Practitioners of the reconstituted field may no longer truly *believe* in "America," but the resulting studies would be more credible and worthwhile to its global laity.

Notes

1. Leo Marx, "On Recovering the 'Ur' Theory of American Studies," *American Literary History* 17.1 (Spring 2005), 120.
2. For the purposes of this essay, I limit my discussion to American Studies as practiced in the United States, which may ironically serve as an example of my talking the talk, but failing the walk the walk with respect to my overall critique, which ultimately requires the advocacy of more thoroughly international or transnational approaches. But this particularly "American" feature of a nationally constituted American Studies, the quasi-religious fervor of many practitioners of American Studies in the United States, is itself worthy of further inquiry.
3. In this chapter, the focus is limited to the establishment of American Studies, in particular American literary studies, as a disciplinary field or subfield in the mid-twentieth century, as well as the response of the "new" Americanists in the 1980s and 1990s.
4. See Alan Wolfe, "Anti-American Studies," *The New Republic* (February 10, 2003), 25–32.
5. Sacvan Bercovitch, *The Rites of Assent: Transformations in the Symbolic Construction of America* (London: Routledge, 1993), 29.

6 Indeed, there is no questions that what Bercovitch refers to animates such powerfully effective rhetorical slogans as "Make America Great Again," but it also undoubtedly contributes to the critical energy and educational goals of something like *The 1619 Project* as well.
7 Marx, "On Recovering the 'Ur' Theory of American Studies," 125.
8 Bercovitch, *The Rites of Assent*, 358. For a concise analysis of the "Myth and Symbol" school and the Cold War origins of American Studies, see Janice Radway, "What's in a Name? The Presidential Address to the American Studies Association, 20 November 1998," *American Quarterly* 51.1 (March 1999): 1–32.
9 Bercovitch, *The Rites of Assent*, 359.
10 F. O. Matthiessen, *American Renaissance: Art and Expression in the Age of Emerson and Whitman* (Oxford: Oxford University Press, 1941), xii, note 3. It should be noted, however, that Matthiessen wrote a thorough and largely laudatory entry on "Edgar Allan Poe" for *The Literary History of the United States*, eds. Robert Spiller et al. (New York: Macmillan, 1948), 321–332.
11 On the rise of nineteenth-century American national narrative, and the local, personal, and literary narrative forms that competed with it, see Jonathan Arac, *The Emergence of American Literary Narrative, 1820–1860* (Cambridge: Harvard University Press, 2005).
12 See David R. Shumway, *Creating American Civilization: A Genealogy of American Literature as a Discipline* (Minneapolis: University of Minnesota Press, 1993).
13 Elizabeth Renker, *The Origins of American Literature Studies: An Institutional History* (Cambridge: Cambridge University Press, 2007), 3.
14 Donald E. Pease, "National Identities, Postmodern Artifacts, and Postnational Narratives," in *National Identities and Post-Americanist Narratives*, ed. Donald E. Pease (Durham: Duke University Press, 1994), 3–4.
15 See R. W. B. Lewis, *The American Adam: Innocence, Tragedy, and Tradition in the Nineteenth Century* (Chicago: University of Chicago Press, 1955); Perry Miller, *Errand into the Wilderness* (New York: Harper & Row, 1956); and Henry Nash Smith, *Virgin Land: The American West as Symbol and Myth* (Cambridge: Harvard University Press, 1950).
16 Marx, "On Recovering the 'Ur' Theory of American Studies," 122.
17 Bercovitch, *The Rites of Assent*, 65.
18 I refer primarily to those identified by Donald Pease as New Americanists, especially in his two collections of essays, *Revisionary Interventions into the Americanist Canon* (Durham: Duke University Press, 1994) and *National Identities and Post-Americanist Narratives* (Durham: Duke University Press, 1994). See also John Carlos Rowe, *The New American Studies* (Minneapolis: University of Minnesota Press, 2002).
19 See Frederick Crews, "Whose American Renaissance?," *New York Review of Books* (October 27, 1988), 68–81.
20 See Pease, "The New Americanists: Revisionist Interventions into the Canon," in *Revisionist Interventions into the Americanist Canon*, ed. Donald E. Pease (Durham: Duke University Press, 1994), 1–37.
21 Pease, "National Identities," 4.
22 Ibid., 5.
23 Pease has since revised his use of the term to make it more consistent with the exigencies of globalization and the waning influence of the nation-state form. See his "National Identities."

24 To a certain extent, the prefix indicates postnationality's association with postmodernity. That is, for Pease (following Lyotard), if the postmodern condition entails the dismantling of the master narratives of the Enlightenment (including, presumably, national metanarratives), then the postmodern condition might also occasion a postnational one.
25 Milette Shamir, "Foreigners Within and Innocents Abroad: Discourse of the Self in the Internationalization of American Studies," *Journal of American Studies* 37.3 (December 2003), 380.
26 As suggested above, this is actually a duel belief: a belief that the America invented by old American Studies is ideologically corrupt, a "bad" America, and a belief in the New Americanist vision (or revision), a "good" America that is more multicultural and hence less hegemonic. The dynamics of "believing in America" are not very different as one moves from old to new visions of America.
27 Shumway, *Creating American Civilization*, 7.
28 Ibid., 339.
29 Ibid., 299.
30 Jürgen Habermas, *The Postnational Constellation*, trans. Max Pensky (Cambridge: The MIT Press, 2001), 60.
31 Edward W. Said, *The World, the Text, and the Critic* (New York: Columbia University Press, 1983), 290.
32 C. L. R. James, *Mariners, Renegades, and Castaways: The Story of Herman Melville and the World We Live In* (Hanover: University Press of New England, 2001), 2.

Chapter 7

"SOME MEN RIDE ON SUCH SPACE": CHARLES OLSON'S *CALL ME ISHMAEL*, THE MELVILLE REVIVAL, AND THE AMERICAN BAROQUE

Call Me Ishmael, Charles Olson's 1947 study of Herman Melville and *Moby-Dick*, is an anomalous book. On the one hand, it is a foundational text of Melville Studies, establishing Melville as an American Shakespeare and helping to solidify Melville's elevated position in a canon of American literature.[1] On the other hand, *Call Me Ishmael* also offers a bizarre recasting of Melville's entire *oeuvre*, transforming the image of the nineteenth-century writer at a moment in which early practitioners of American Studies were consolidating a specifically "national imaginary" with respect to literature and history. *Call Me Ishmael* is simultaneously a key document of an emerging American Studies and a proleptic critique of the nationalist project of the disciplinary field. Blurring the lines between literary artist and scholarly critic, Olson sought to rethink Melville's leviathan by reimagining Melville's own imaginative reshaping of the world system in 1851. Olson accomplishes this in part by establishing Melville's literary and historical project as a discrete segment of a grand, 3,000-year exploration of time and space. Olson thereby wrenches the author from the hands of a nascent American Studies, whose practitioners were in this process of enshrining Melville as the central figure in a national program coded as the American Renaissance, and Olson projects a baroque Melville not confined to or emblematic of any nationalist cultural project.

In this chapter, I look at Olson's *Call Me Ishmael* in the context of the Melville Revival and the academic canonization of Melville in the emergent field of American Studies, particularly as associated with an imagined American Renaissance. Olson arguably occupied significant positions in both movements. Through his early interest in Melville, Olson came of age during the Melville Revival of the 1920s and 1930s. He befriended Melville's granddaughters, Eleanor Melville Metcalf and

Frances Osborne, who gave him access to a wealth of material, including Melville's own set of Shakespeare volumes, with which Olson was able to develop so much of his own argument. And, as a student of Perry Miller, among others, in the newly established History of American Civilization program at Harvard University, Olson stood at a ground zero of the new and burgeoning field of American Studies. There Olson worked closely with F. O. Matthiessen, who would effectively christen the new discipline by publishing *American Renaissance* in 1941, and Matthiessen explicitly acknowledged Olson's assistance. Thus, Olson could be viewed as an important figure of both the Revival and the Renaissance, of Melville Studies and American Studies, but in his 1947 study of the great American novel, Olson provided a reading of Melville that effectively frees the author from the ideological uses to which these movements put him. In Olson's reading, Melville is neither a modernist aesthete nor a representative American. Olson imagines a postmodern and postnational *Moby-Dick*, which is at once part of an extensive, global spatiotemporal project that, like baroque art, exceeds the limits of American Studies.

"Beginner—and Interested in Beginnings": An Introduction

Olson's 1947 *Call Me Ishmael* somehow manages to take part in the national project of American Studies and to undermine it at the same time, and this eccentric study of Melville still resonates today, after "the American Century."[2] Following the Melville Revival in the 1920s, which elevated the awareness of Melville's work and canonized *Moby-Dick* in particular as an American masterpiece, a widespread industry of Melville criticism and scholarship emerged. Although the early interventions of Raymond Weaver, Van Wyck Brooks, Carl Van Doren, Lewis Mumford, and others laid a substantial groundwork, one might say that academic criticism on Melville did not really begin in earnest until the publication of F. O. Matthiessen's landmark *American Renaissance* in 1941, which, despite both the author's own intentions and the subtitle's declaration of its purported topic ("Art and Expression in the Age of Emerson and Whitman"), did much to establish Melville as the representative writer of the era and nation. Into this arena comes Olson, with a foot in each camp as it were, as he represented both the lay-scholar or fan of Melville and an academic researcher whose work with Matthiessen and Perry Miller helped to shape the emerging field of American Studies. Olson's boldly revisionary reading of Melville, at a moment in which Melville's legend is only beginning to be composed and disseminated, simultaneously refined and transformed Melville Studies. But, unlike the majority of his contemporaries and those that followed closely in their wake, Olson recognized that Melville was not really the representative of an American Renaissance, but something else: an American Baroque.

After declaring that "SPACE" is the "central fact to man born in America" and spelling it large "because it comes large here,"[3] Olson maintains that Melville "rode" on such space, rather than settling in or fastening himself to it. In Olson's innovative interpretation, Melville's writings are like the baroque paintings and buildings described by the art historian Henri Focillon in *The Life of Forms in Art*, which "tend to invade space in every direction, to perforate it, to become one with all its possibilities."[4] Unlike the renaissance's careful and beautiful ordering of space, the baroque work of art appears as a grotesque, ornate, and above all extravagant production, one that transgresses the limits of the frame and ventures into the space beyond. In reading Melville, Olson grappled with such space as well, and the baroque text seems particularly apt for an age that Olson himself was the first to name "post-modern."[5] In our era of globalization, the suppression of distance made possible by ever more advanced forms of media, communications, and travel technologies has not dulled the acute spatial anxiety sometimes associated with the postmodern condition. Olson, who after all coined the term "post-modern,"[6] is not interested in promoting the American Renaissance celebrated by many of his contemporaries, but rather in what comes after, the messier, more complex, and altogether more interesting condition of what I have called the American Baroque.[7] The baroque Melville made visible in Olson's study becomes an alternative to the national avatar of the American Renaissance, and a proleptic representative of our own, postmodern condition.

With *Call Me Ishmael*, Olson considered how Melville not only responded to the world of 1851, but projected a kind of cosmological vision in which art and experience blended together in a project of mapping a world, as well as exploring other possible worlds. As Olson observes pointedly, Melville was a "Beginner—and interested in beginnings," a thinker who "had a way of reaching back through time until he got history pushed back so far that he turned time into space" (14). This manipulation of time and space is characteristic of Melville's baroque vision. In *Call Me Ishmael*, Olson blurred the lines between artist and critic, and between writer and reader, in order to show how *Moby-Dick* participated in a seemingly national project while transcending, or rather transgressing, its aesthetic and national limits in order to fashion a global narrative, or worldwide representation that, as Melville puts it in *Moby-Dick*, might actually encompass "the whole circle of the sciences, and all the generations of whales, and men, and mastodons, past, present, and to come, with all the revolving panoramas of empire on earth, and throughout the whole universe, not excluding its suburbs."[8] In the process, Olson cartwheels along a tightrope between the nascent but swiftly developing

American Studies and a proleptically postnational or postmodern condition that allows both Melville and Olson to escape the restrictively nationalist literary tradition in formation and to explore alternative trajectories.

In this way, Olson wrests Melville from the hands of an American Studies that would establish him as its spokesman and as the emblematic figure of an American Renaissance, and projects a baroque Melville whose extravagance guides him beyond the circles of this imagined world, into worlds still to be imagined. Participating in the later phase of the Melville Revival, Olson also anticipates the misuses to which Melville's work will be put by the nationalist critics of the Cold War era, and definitively situates Melville in a global and broadly historical project. Rather than arguing for Melville's place in an emerging American literature, Olson regards Melville as the latest incarnation of a primordial, yet historically and geographically embodied, force: the power of "search" itself. That is to say, it is not the quest whose aim is discovery, but rather unmediated and extravagant transgression in its own right. As Olson once put it in an August 20, 1951, letter to Robert Creeley:

>   my assumption is
> any POST-MODERN is born with the ancient confidence
> that, he *does* belong.
>   So, there is nothing to be
> *found*. There is only (as Schoenberg had it, his
> Harmony) search.[9]

"The Melville People are Rare People": From Revival to Renaissance

According to an old joke among American literature scholars, Melville Studies replaced whaling as New England's largest industry.[10] But the ascendency of Melville and his writings to a place of honor in the literary canon, especially among academic critics, was not inevitable. "In 1900," as David R. Shumway has pointed out, "*Moby-Dick* would not have been recognized by many as American literature; those who did recognize it as such would not have accorded it a privileged position."[11] Melville's fame waxed and waned throughout his lifetime, from his early celebrity as "the man who lived among the cannibals," a label he complained bitterly about in a famous letter to Nathaniel Hawthorne,[12] to his relative anonymity and obscurity in later life. Although his 1891 death occasioned a small flurry of interest, the Melville Revival can be said to have begun only with the centennial celebration of Melville's birth in 1919, along with Raymond Weaver's 1921 biography

Herman Melville: Mariner and Mystic,[13] as well as the publication of "Billy Budd" in 1924, which provided the additional boost of a "new" work by a "classic" American writer.[14] The Melville Revival restored, or perhaps for the first time promoted, the writer to a central place in American literary discourse. However, as Shumway's "genealogy of American literature as an academic discipline" makes clear, it is not only the visibility of an author's work or having that author's books back in print that makes one a canonical presence, but also the interplay of various institutional forces which will shape the dissemination and reception of the cultural artifacts.[15] Between the initial Melville Revival of the 1920s and the canonization, or perhaps hypercanonization, of Melville by the 1950s,[16] the energies of the Revival had to translate into a kind of national renaissance. These forces, in no small part, were conveniently set in motion by a monumental scholarly treatise named *American Renaissance*, as well as by others that followed, and these important works helped to establish and were themselves sustained by a new academic discipline, American Studies. Olson, who was only ten years old when Weaver's biography appeared and who was still a graduate student when Matthiessen's field-establishing study went to press, turns out to have been a crucial, albeit mysterious, figure in the process of Melville's canonization and in the advent of American Studies.

In an influential, if provocative, history of the Melville Revival, *Hunting Captain Ahab*, Clare L. Spark notes that the principal actors involved in promoting Melville and his writings had diverse agendas. Many were deliberately reacting to political and cultural debates that bore little direct relation to the work of a mid-nineteenth-century romance writer and poet. Frequently, this cultural work by early practitioners of American Studies involved disputes between various factions of left-wing radicals, populist progressives, and cultural conservatives. As Melville's work became a dominant touchstone for these debates, the character Ahab in particular emerged as a Protean shape-shifter, transmogrifying from the Shakespearean tragic hero to the Byronic romantic one and then into a Hitler- or Stalin-like dictator, all within a few years. Referring to these often conflicting interests, Spark demonstrates that the "Melville Revival, then, is only tangentially about the author of *Moby-Dick*."[17]

Moreover, as William V. Spanos has observed with some irony, the modernist sensibilities of those critics involved in the Melville Revival informed their decisions in canonizing Melville, and *Moby-Dick* in particular.[18] That is, Melville was less valued as a representative author of his own time, than as a proto-modernist whose wealth of allusions, diversity of materials, and complexity of style made his work both more worthy as an aesthetic accomplishment and in greater need of critical treatment.

Where some readers, like Fred Lewis Pattee, would disqualify Melville precisely because his baroque narratives lay outside of the mainstream of American civilization, the "early criers" of Melville, as Olson calls them, embraced Melville in part *because* of his eccentricity with respect to the purported literary or cultural tradition. Paradoxically, then, Melville's centrality to an emerging American literary canon was based on precisely the same criteria that would have previously disqualified him: namely, the extravagance that made Melville and *Moby-Dick* so unrepresentative of the cultural norms of his own time.

For example, Carl Van Doren made a virtue of *Moby-Dick*'s unpopularity, stating that it was "too irregular, too bizarre" for the popular audience, but that its "immense originality" warrants its inclusion among the great romances of world literature.[19] "The Modernist revival," as Spanos puts it, "chose to celebrate precisely that differential speculative extravagance of style, form, and content which, in the eyes of Melville's early critics, interrupted the promise latent in the documentary veracity of his first romances and disqualified him from a place in the emergent American canon."[20] In a ruse of history or dialectical reversal, the biographical critics of the Melville Revival established Melville as a powerful national icon by virtue of his distance from the everyday life of the nation's people. That is, unlike narratives more engaged with matters of national importance—Harriet Beecher Stowe's *Uncle Tom's Cabin*, for instance—*Moby-Dick* did not address such timely controversies directly, but transcended them to establish a kind of individual, mythic, and essentially "American" spirit. "This shift in evaluative emphasis from 'low' to 'high' culture resulted in the apotheosis of *Moby-Dick* not simply as Melville's 'masterpiece' but as an American 'masterpiece'."[21] In sum,

> The Melville revival inaugurated by such biographers and critics as Raymond Weaver, John Freeman, Van Wyck Brooks, and Lewis Mumford was not, in other words, simply a revival of interest in Melville; it was also an ideological victory over the problematic of a previous generation of critics. It went far, if not the whole way (a project fulfilled by the next generation of Americanists), to reverse the judgment of the earlier critics, without, however, disturbing the *logos* informing the earlier representation of American's cultural identity and its canon. These critics of the revival apotheosized *Moby-Dick* as an American masterpiece because it intuited and expressed an essentially *human* "spiritual" Real that, in its integral and universal comprehensiveness, transcended the ideological partiality [...] of American sociopolitical existence.[22]

Of course, the "next generation of Americanists" would include Olson himself. However, given his eccentric reading of *Moby-Dick* and his declaration of a "post-modern" condition, Olson would hardly be representative of the burgeoning field of American Studies as it came into its institutional form in the 1950s and 1960s.

The establishment of Melville's proto-modernist and canonical credentials during the Melville Revival was not uncontested. As Shumway has discussed, the profoundly elitist perspective of a Van Doren was vigorously countered by other critics, including Pattee, who "reflects an older, populist conception of the canon."[23] Pattee took issue with the enshrinement of relatively minor literary figures, writers—like Melville, in fact—who did not register much popular success in their own time and who therefore could not be said to be particularly representative of the American spirit. Indeed, Pattee was repulsed by the critical attention given to such authors and their works at the expense of bestsellers like *Little Women*. "Melville, I prophesy, will wane back to the fifth magnitude to which his own generation adjudged him."[24] Notwithstanding Pattee's unfulfilled prophesy, the initial successes of the Melville Revival in the 1920s and 1930s did not assure Melville's canonicity or lasting influence in American Studies. That would require the academic institutionaliztion of Melville Studies, and Olson himself would function as something of a bridge between the early Melville enthusiasts like Weaver and Van Doren and the more rigorously academic critics like Matthiessen, Henry Nash Smith, Perry Miller, Richard Chase, and others who followed in that line, most of whom may not have been "Melville people."

Olson says that "[t]he Melville people are rare people," curiously and pointedly in "A note of thanks" placed a good third of the way into *Call Me Ishmael*, rather than in a more traditional "Acknowledgements" section, which is where Matthiessen explicitly thanks Olson for his contributions to *American Renaissance*, for instance. As if to highlight this eccentric decision further, Olson's "rare people" sentence continues by noting that "this is the right place to tell," and then Olson's lists the names of those "Melville people" deserving of his gratitude (40). This placement may well be fitting, insofar as it introduces a section of Olson's study devoted most thoroughly to Melville's personally owned, physical books, a section in which Olson analyses some of Melville's handwritten marginal notations and underlinings in these texts. Hence, Olson places his acknowledgments to Melville's family in close proximity, literally, to the argument derived from the fruits of their generosity. However, in addition to thanking Eleanor Melville Metcalf, Henry K. Metcalf, and "another granddaughter, Mrs. Frances Osborne," Olson also thanks Weaver, Henry A. Murray, Jr., and "those early criers of Melville," Van Doren and Brooks (40). That is, Olson's list of "Melville people" includes not only his personal relatives, but biographers, critics, and "early criers," who apparently make up an extended family or perhaps a (not so?) secret society or guild, ideally suited to summoning a spectral presence previously absent. As Spanos and others have observed, the Melville Revival was not simply a rediscovery of an unjustly forgotten writer, but an almost incantatory, mystical, Promethean rebirth-through-resurrection. Although it may at first seem to be a rebirth of one author in particular, the Melville Revival was actually part of a collective project of renascence that heralded and made possible the invention of an "American Renaissance."

Even if he had not written a word on Melville himself, Olson's contribution to this emerging field would have been immense, given the value of his initial research. As Spark points out, "[h]ad he chosen, Olson could have dominated Melville studies, for he had the support of important allies in American letters (besides the devoted friendship of [Melville's granddaughter] Eleanor Metcalf and her family)."[25] By contacting Melville's granddaughters, he was able to gain access to Melville's own library, which in turn allowed him to analyze handwritten marginalia in those volumes that Melville read and reread with such intensity. Such marginal notations became the source of Olson's groundbreaking essay on Melville and Shakespeare, which also forms the central section of *Call Me Ishmael*. Matthiessen himself acknowledged what a tremendous boon to his own scholarship this research had been, and Matthiessen expresses gratitude for "Olson's generosity in letting me make use of what he has tracked down in his investigation of Melville's reading."[26] Nevertheless, Olson's contributions to the academic study of Melville's work and to the processes of consolidating the author's reputation within American literature are perhaps ultimately less interesting than his astonishing, creative interpretations of *Moby-Dick* in *Call Me Ishmael*. This text also envisions a Melville quite different from the canonical figure established in Cold War-era American Studies.

Originally based in part on an M.A. thesis and drafted in connection with his Ph.D. research in Harvard University's History of American Civilization program, a ground zero of the coming disciplinary field of American Studies, *Call Me Ishmael* is a book whose rigorous scholarly research is evident on every page. But it is also a bewilderingly poetic and freewheeling work, juxtaposing Freudian theories (especially drawing from Freud's late, hence then recent,[27] book, *Moses and Monotheism*) with Frederick Jackson Turner's "frontier thesis," mixing mythology with history, and scientific data with pure, fanciful speculation. As James Zeigler has observed, the book was not initially well-received by established authorities of American Studies, though it was reviewed favorably in non-academic journals.[28] The tension between the older, biographical tradition and the new, more aesthetically minded and academic criticism is visible at times in the pages of *Call Me Ishmael*. Coming out of the Melville Revival himself, Olson makes his own entry into the discourse of the American Renaissance, which really took flight, not so much with Matthiessen's 1941 title, which was one crucial launching pad to be sure, as with the academic domestication of Melville by a more formalized American Studies in the 1950s, as represented by those whom Donald E. Pease has referred to as "Cold War critics."[29] This American Studies went on to become a kind of secular (and sometimes, not-so-secular) religion for many practitioners and devotees. But despite its role as a catalyst in sparking further academic study of Melville and what came to be the field of American Studies, Olson's bizarre little book also goes well beyond this modern renaissance, as Olson takes Melville with him on a baroque exploration of postmodern American, or perhaps post-American, space.

"I Take SPACE to be the Central Fact": From Renaissance to Baroque

Olson's notorious beginning to *Call Me Ishmael* announces a matter of "fact," as he calls it, while also establishing a new way of thinking: Using all-capital-letters for the keyword of the entire study, Olson writes: "I take SPACE to be the central fact to man born in America, from Folsom cave to now. I spell it large because it comes large here. Large, and without mercy." As he continues, Olson quickly extends the spatiotemporal scope of his study from the national to the continental and then global: "It is geography at bottom, a hell of wide land from the beginning. [...] Something else than a stretch of earth—seas on both sides, no barriers to contain as restless a thing as Western man was becoming in Columbus' day" (11). After thus establishing the terrain on which his investigation will take place, Olson suggests a fundamental opposition at the heart of the American experience: "Some men ride on such space, others have to fasten themselves like a tent stakes to survive. As I see it, Poe dug in and Melville mounted. They are the alternatives" (12).

Leaving aside for the moment whether the nomadic, peripatetic Edgar Allan Poe really did "dig in" and fasten himself to this space,[30] one might say that the key to Olson's reading of Melville lies in this alternative: Melville did not dig in, but "rode" on such space. For Olson, everything about Melville's literary project involves aspects of "riding" this space. So, for example, "Melville went to space to probe and find man," and "Melville had a way of reaching back through time until he got history pushed back so far he turned time into space" (14). This space-riding, this pushing back of time until it becomes space, is in no way a sense of rebirth. Olson, writing just a few years after *American Renaissance*, already disputes the notion that Melville takes part in such a project of national renaissance. Even Matthiessen was wary of the term, and Harry Levin was apparently responsible for *American Renaissance*'s title; Matthiessen had wanted to call the book *Man in the Open Air*, "after an apt phrase in Whitman," but the publisher desired a title that was more "descriptively categorical."[31] Although Matthiessen conceded that "re-birth" was not really the best term for the literary movement of Melville's day, the word *renaissance* stuck, both in the field of American Studies and in university course catalogues around the country.

Matthiessen was well aware that the word *renaissance* was a loaded term. As Jonathan Arac has pointed out, "[e]ver since the historiographic notion was elaborated by Michelet and Burckhardt—in 1845 and 1860, exactly bracketing Matthiessen's period—'renaissance' has carried with it a glamorous freight of secularism, progress, and preeminent individuality."[32] In other words, the notion of an American renaissance fit neatly into a larger national narrative, one developed during the nineteenth century and extrapolated in the twentieth by practitioners of American Studies.[33] Against his own wishes, Matthiessen's label helped establish a profoundly nationalist enterprise; Matthiessen, who was among other things a Shakespeare scholar, was deeply committed to a comparative or international approach to literary studies. As Arac notes with irony, "Matthiessen's title promoted a euphoria of America that gained power against the grain of his own methodological precepts and critical practice," notes Arac with irony. "American studies has not followed Matthiessen's precept or practice, even while drawing its warrant to exist from him."[34] Applied to the rhetoric of an intensifying cultural nationalism in the nineteenth-century United States, and employed as part of the rhetoric of a post-war and Cold War nationalism in the mid-twentieth century, the term *renaissance*, with its uniformly positive or even celebratory nuances, becomes a vote of approval for a nationalist literary project.

By the mid-twentieth-century, the phrase carried an almost evangelical meaning, as the study of American literature comes to be associated with the proselytizing mission of transmitting American ideals and values to the rest of the world. For example, Leo Marx has recounted the story, as told to him by the British critic Richard Hoggart, of an enthusiastic young scholar in the emerging field of "American Studies" in the 1950s who justified his enthusiasm for the work by blurting out "But you don't understand, I *believe* in America!"[35] The "American Century," as Henry Luce optimistically named it in *Life Magazine* in 1941 (the same year that *American Renaissance* was published), required and received a scholarly field worthy of its ideological mission.[36] The nationalist literary project formed the basis for a well nigh religious "belief in America," for good or for ill, inherent in the discourse of American Studies as the field took shape in the immediate post–World War II years. Such religiously functioning belief-system is still visible in the discourse of new Americanists, even those quite critical of the discipline, in the present era.[37] Notwithstanding the secularism implied by the term, who does not believe in a renaissance? Who opposes renaissance or rebirth? It is almost universally valued.

This is not so with the term *baroque*, which since its original coinage has almost always carried with it a somewhat negative connotation. Originally a jeweler's term referring to "a rough or imperfect pearl" (a lovely epithet, perhaps, for both *Moby-Dick* and Olson's *Call Me Ishmael*), the word *baroque* was applied to the arts at least as early as 1765, and it was not used in a laudatory manner. As René Wellek relates, "[i]n the late eighteenth and early nineteenth centuries the adjective 'baroque' was widely used as an equivalent of 'bizarre,' and the noun 'baroque' became established as a term for 'bad taste' in architecture."[38] By the late nineteenth century, German historiography had consolidated the meaning of the term, bestowing upon it an inherent sense of artistic decadence, specifically with respect to the period during which the unity of Renaissance art and architecture seemed to disintegrate. Heinrich Wölfflin, in his 1888 study *Renaissance and Baroque*, a book which effectively standardized the use of the term, wrote that "[i]t has become customary to use the term *baroque* to describe the style into which the Renaissance resolved itself or, as it is more commonly expressed, into which the Renaissance degenerated."[39] Such usage would be expanded to encompass any period of aesthetic decadence; however, the *baroque* largely remained associated with, and unfavorably contrasted to, the *renaissance*. Whereas the renaissance calls to mind formal ingenuity, rules, models, science and progress, the baroque is defined by excess, extravagance, anarchy, and ridiculousness. "Unlike the Renaissance, the baroque style is not accompanied by theoretical rules: it developed without models."[40] The relative formlessness of baroque productions, or perhaps more so the inscrutability of the baroque forms, underscored the negative impression of the baroque in general. Although the term no longer refers to "bad taste" *per se* by the late nineteenth century, *baroque* still carried an unfavorable connotation, if not denotation. "As an art-historical term *baroque* has lost its suggestion of the ridiculous," writes Wölfflin, "but its general use it still carries a suggestions of repugnance or abnormality."[41]

The re-evaluation of the baroque by such twentieth-century critics as Walter Benjamin was less a change in definition as a change in attitude toward the excesses of the baroque, in which ornateness, complexity, difficulty, or extravagance become terms of approval rather than of opprobrium.[42] This revaluation of baroque excess was also part of the embrace of a modernist aesthetic, which contributed to the revaluation of Melville's own work, and *Moby-Dick* in particular, during the Melville Revival, as I discussed earlier. Ironically, then, the modernist sensibilities of the "early criers" of Melville may have made them more likely to embrace the baroque extravagance of his work.

These characterizations of the baroque could apply to Olson's view of *Moby-Dick*, including the study's eccentric form, which might be said to reflect the novel's own. Just as Van Doren had considered that the novel was "too bizarre" to be popular, a contemporary reviewer of *Moby-Dick* declared that the novel was "distressingly marred by an extravagant treatment of the subject."[43] Not unlike the creators of baroque art and architecture, Melville (and Olson, too) tended to break the rules.

In language well suited to a discussion of Melville's and Olson's projects, the art historian Henri Focillon described the fundamental character of the baroque:

> In the life of forms, the baroque is indeed but a moment, but it is certainly the freest and most emancipated one. Baroque forms have either abandoned or denatured that principle of intimate propriety, as essential aspect of which is a careful respect for the limits of the frame, especially in architecture. They live with passionate intensity a life that is entirely their own; they proliferate like some vegetable monstrosity. They break apart even as they grow; they tend to invade space in every direction, to perforate it, to become one with all its possibilities. This mastery of space is pure delight to them.[44]

The surprisingly flexible contours and shattered frames visible in the form of *Moby-Dick* offer images of the baroque in Melville's text, but the content of the masterpiece also suggests how Melville "rides on" such space.

Melville's delightful "mastery of space," in Olson's view, enables him to form a new conception of the Pacific, the liminal zone in which the wandering Western Civilization has become Eastern once again. In his conclusion to *Call Me Ishmael*, Olson assets that the three great stories of the West are Homer's *Odyssey*, Dante's *Commedia* (in which Odysseus, now consigned to Hell for his sins of deception, including the ruse of the Trojan Horse, recounts his further voyages west of the Pillars of Hercules and south of the equator), and Melville's own *Moby-Dick*, with its "full stop" in the Pacific. (119). Embarking upon an odyssey from the beaches of Troy, venturing through Hell and Heaven, and circumnavigating the globe to find the absolute limits well within one's own sense of space, this vision of ancient, modern, and postmodern literary cartography forms the basis for

Olson's interpretation of both Melville's writings and American civilization in the mid-twentieth century.

Notwithstanding some of the imperial pomp of his language, Olson's Pacific, which he refers to as one of Melville's "inventions" in *Moby-Dick*, is not simply the American imperium extended westward towards Asia. As Zeigler has argued persuasively, Olson "anticipates the Pacific Ocean will become a kind of space of exchange between the U.S. and the nations of Asia until such national designations cease to signify the world's dominant political agencies."[45] Somewhat like C. L. R. James, who in his own magisterial book on Melville expressed his hope that "all the problems of nationality" would evanesce before 1970,[46] Olson's baroque Melville finds in the Pacific a pervasively postnational space. Thus, at the very moment when the Melville Revival gives way to an American Renaissance, which characterized a certain image of Melville and of *Moby-Dick* as paradigmatic representatives of a national literary tradition, Olson strikingly and yet subtly projects an alternative trajectory.

"The Creative Act of Anticipation": From Baroque to the Future

If, as Focillon would have it, baroque forms have no respect for the limits of the frame, then the extravagant work of Melville and of Olson, or of the Olson-Melville complex of *Call Me Ishmael*, is another testament to their baroque sensibilities. Etymologically—surely both Melville and Olson give us license to reflect on the origins of words, as they so often and so enthusiastically do—the word *extravagance* refers to a "wandering out of bounds" or movement across boundaries or limits. Such transgressive movement also characterizes both Melville's art and Olson's vision of Melville's broader project, one that graphs onto an even larger spatiotemporal projection which extends to the limits of the terraqueous globe and for some "3,000 years," according to Olson (117). Melville's originality, and Olson's, derive and expand outward from this overall project, whose genealogy Olson traces back to Homer.

In the closing pages of *Call Me Ishmael*, Olson discovers that Homer, with the figure of Odysseus in particular, had already begun to map the baroque spaces of Melville's world, which is to say, our own. "Homer was an end of the myth world from which the Mediterranean began. But in Ulysses he projected the archetype of the West to follow. It was the creative act of anticipation" (117–118). This anticipation or *prolepsis* registers that foresight and the headlong rush of Melville's own baroque fiction. It is not only that Odysseus started the wandering, which was then taken up by others, eventually leading to a temporal end in some future postmodernity and a spatial end in the paradigmatically alternative zone of the Pacific, although it is that too. But it is also that the projection, beyond the boundaries of time and space and into new spatiotemporal territories, becomes for Olson "the central quality of the men to come: *search*" (118).

Olson finds that there are three great odysseys that have successively established the collective *search* of postmodern man. The first is that of Odysseus, both within the seemingly vast but closed Mediterranean world and outwards, right to the very boundaries and ambiguous spaces of that world, as with Odysseus' visit to the kingdom of the dead to speak with Tiresias, for instance. The second, with a familiar face, is the Ulysses of Dante's *Inferno*, who could not "quench in myself the burning wish to know the world" and who "set out on the deep and open sea,"[47] west past the Pillars of Hercules and into the Atlantic—as Olson reminds us, Plato's philosophical cartography had located Atlantis beyond those pillars—before sailing south past the equator, only to be swallowed up by the sea, much as the Pequod would ages later. This "Atlantic" Odysseus points to the figures of Columbus and the other explorers, eventually leading to Ahab, whose odyssey "lay around the Horn, where West returned to East," and the endless quest for the setting sun's horizon inexorably draws one toward yet another sunrise. For Olson, "Ahab is full stop," the end of a 3,000-year project into the "UNKNOWN which Homer's and Dante's Ulysses opened men's eyes to" (118–119). But, of course, Olson does not really believe this, else he would not have given the final word or image to Proteus, whom Olson casts as the shape-shifting sea god. Flux, change, transgression, movement. Ahab's "full stop" is Heraclitus' river: never the same thing twice.

The originality of all this lies in a poetic resistance enacted in *Call Me Ishmael*. Olson's book resists the ultimate stasis that American Studies and national literature would impose upon the baroque extravagance of *Moby-Dick*, and Olson refuses to read Melville's novel as part of some nationalist mission, as with those interpretations that posit Ishmael as an "American Adam," for example. But *Call Me Ishmael* goes further than merely exceeding the imagined borders of the United States; it enacts the grander, transnational or global projection of the ultimate power—*search* itself—disclosed in Olson's revisionary analysis.

Despite the enthusiastic assertions of many mid-century Melville scholars in praise of the writer's originality, the effect, and sometimes the intended effect, of their interpretations was to fix or freeze Melville's originality into an identifiable "image repertoire" of American national narrative,[48] effectively discovering in *Moby-Dick*'s extravagant novel the all-too-familiar and well-worn pieties of the national culture. That is, *Moby-Dick*'s eccentric and baroque forces are domesticated. For all of the rhetoric of movement in that nationalist literary ideology—such as the restless westering impulse that animates Frederick Jackson Turner's frontier thesis, for instance, but also the earlier national claims for Providential Manifest Destiny or a Puritan Errand into the Wilderness—the discourse and the practice of American Studies really celebrates settlers, not nomads, as the Turner Thesis in the end makes clear. The American national narrative, and the disciplinary field that engenders and supports that narrative, relies on a people's relative immobility, on *not* moving, on sticking to a place and settling in for good. Despite the influence of his professor (and Turner acolyte) Frederick Merk, the Olson of *Call Me Ishmael* knew that "some men ride on such space" and do not simply plant their tent stakes in a suitably stable spot. Moreover, Olson knew that the stability of the place was itself illusory, and that the movement of such nomads as Melville and his "originals" is perpetual motion, radiating throughout space.

In a famous passage from *The Confidence-Man*, which Olson also cites, Melville asserts that there have only existed three truly "original characters" in world literature, and each comes from literary works of the seventeenth century, the historical epoch most directly associated with the baroque. The characters are the errant Don Quixote, gloomy Hamlet, and the fiery Satan of Milton's *Paradise Lost*. The essence of their originality lies, for Melville, in the way each character affects everyone and everything else, projecting a world, a new creation, *genesis*:

> the original character, essentially such, is like a revolving Drummond light, raying away from itself all around it—everything is lit by it, everything starts up to it (mark how it is with Hamlet), so that, in certain minds, there follows upon the adequate conception of such a character, an effect, in its way, akin to that which Genesis attends upon the beginning of things.[49]

This profound originality, or the "creative act of anticipation," thus becomes a world-making, a baroque projection of that "SPACE" on which Melville rides.

Olson also grappled with such space, at a moment of great "moment" in the United States and world history, with developments of the market and the postwar experience creating more complex international relations among workers of the world over an increasingly global space. The baroque power of Olson's Melville seems to me particularly significant in the postnational era of globalization, with its characteristically postmodern time-space compression and spatial anxiety.[50] If *search*, but not discovery, defined the situation of "post-modern" man for Olson, then the oscillatory, shifting constellations of the postmodern condition in the twenty-first century world system call all the more urgently for a baroque art that may exceed the limits of the frame, in order to more effectively attempt to represent the seemingly unrepresentable totality of our present *Lebenswelt*. As with Melville's own project in *Moby-Dick*, the baroque art of the present moment must strive to "manhandle this Leviathan," to be "omnisciently exhaustive," and to pursue its quarry "throughout the whole universe, not excluding its suburbs."[51]

Olson's *Call Me Ishmael* represents an early, rather odd, attempt at bolstering the Melville Revival with a novel interpretation, while also retrieving Melville's baroque masterpiece from the sanctimony and triumphalism of the American Renaissance. In its own post-war and early Cold-War emergence, *Call Me Ishmael* sounded a strange alarum, both celebratory and foreboding, which today hits the ear as starkly melodious music, a fugue that anticipates new refrains. Or, one might say that such baroque excess and eccentricity makes more sense today, with a postnational world system whose formerly reliable coordinates are so frequently called into question by navigators on its shifting, open seas. Olson's baroque Melville in *Call Me Ishmael* thus re-emerges, with even greater urgency than in its own time, as a vital force within a post-American Studies for the twenty-first century.

Notes

1 One might say that the idea of Melville as an "American Shakespeare" was initially suggested by Melville himself, in "Hawthorne and His Mosses," in which he compares "Nathaniel of Salem" to "William of Avon" and asserts that, "if Shakespeare has not been equalled, he is sure to be surpassed, and surpassed by an American born now or yet to be born." See "Hawthorne and His Mosses," in *The Piazza Tales and Other Prose Pieces, 1839–1860*, eds. Harrison Hayford, Alma A. MacDougall, G. Thomas Tanselle et al. (Evanston and Chicago: Northwestern University Press and the Newberry Library, 1987), 245–246. But Olson's study was among the first to recognise and to highlight the connections between Melville's *Moby-Dick* and Shakespeare, which in turn influenced F. O. Matthiessen, who acknowledges Olson's valuable assistance in *American Renaissance*, among many others later.

2 See, e.g., John Carlos Rowe, ed. *Post-Nationalist American Studies* (Berkeley: University of California Press, 2000); Lawrence Buell, "Are We Post-American Studies?" in *Field Work: Sites in Literary and Cultural Studies*, eds. Marjorie B. Garber, Paul B. Franklin, and Rebecca L. Walkowitz (London: Routledge, 1996), 87–93; and Donald E. Pease and Robyn Wiegman, *Futures of American Studies* (Durham: Duke University Press, 2002).

3 Charles Olson, *Call Me Ishmael* (San Francisco: City Lights, 1947), 11; hereinafter cited parenthetically in the text.

4 Henri Focillon, *The Life of Forms of Art*, trans. Charles B. Hogan and George Kugan (New York: Zone Books, 1992), 58.

5 See Charles Olson and Robert Creeley, *The Complete Correspondence: Volume 7*, ed. George F. Butterick (Santa Rosa: Black Sparrow Press, 1987), 75.

6 See Perry Anderson, *The Origins of Postmodernity* (London: Verso, 1998), 7–9.

7 See my *Melville, Mapping and Globalization: Literary Cartography in the American Baroque Writer* (London: Bloomsbury, 2009), especially 1–18.
8 Melville, *Moby-Dick, or, the Whale*, eds. Harrison Hayford, Hershel Parker, and G. Thomas Tanselle (Evanston and Chicago: Northwestern University Press and the Newberry Library, 1988), 456.
9 Quoted in Ralph Maud, *Charles Olson's Reading: A Biography* (Carbondale: Southern Illinois University Press, 1996), 91.
10 See Richard H. Brodhead, "Trying All Things: An Introduction to *Moby-Dick*." *New Essays on* Moby-Dick, or, the Whale, ed. Richard H. Brodhead (Cambridge: Cambridge University Press, 1986), 19.
11 David R. Shumway, *Creating American Civilization: A Genealogy of American Literature as an Academic Discipline* (Minneapolis: University of Minnesota Press, 1994), 1–2.
12 See Melville, *Correspondence*, ed. Lynn Horth (Evanston and Chicago: Northwestern University Press and the Newberry Library, 1993), 193.
13 Raymond Weaver, *Herman Melville: Mariner and Mystic* (New York: George H. Doran, Co., 1921).
14 It is not clear that "classic" is an appropriate term for Melville's (or any American's) writing, but D. H. Lawrence provocatively inserted the word into the title of *Studies in Classic American Literature*, which includes two chapters on Melville, one on *Typee* and *Omoo*, another on *Moby-Dick*. Lawrence's book might thus be considered another early effort at canonizing Melville, although, like Olson, Lawrence takes a rather unconventional approach to his subject. See Lawrence, *Studies in Classic American Literature* (New York: Viking, 1923), especially 131–161.
15 See Shumway, *Creating American Civilization*.
16 On the idea of "hypercanonization," see Jonathan Arac, *Huckleberry Finn as Idol and Target: The Functions of Criticism in Our Time* (Madison: University of Wisconsin Press, 1997), especially 133–153.
17 Clare L. Spark, *Hunting Captain Ahab: Psychological Warfare and the Melville Revival* (Kent: Kent State University Press, 2001), 11.
18 William V. Spanos, *The Errant Art of* Moby-Dick: *The Canon, the Cold War, and the Struggle for American Studies* (Durham: Duke University Press, 1995), 16.
19 Carl Van Doren, *The American Novel* (New York: Macmillan, 1921), 74.
20 Spanos, *The Errant Art of 'Moby-Dick'*, 16.
21 Ibid.
22 Ibid., 16–17.
23 Shumway, *Creating American Civilization*, 188.
24 Fred Lewis Pattee, "Review of *American Literature: An Introduction*, by Carl Van Doren; *American Literature*, by Stanley T. Williams," *American Literature* 5.4 (January 1934), 380.
25 Spark, *Hunting Captain Ahab*, 269.
26 F. O. Matthiessen, *American Renaissance: Art and Expression in the Age of Emerson and Whitman* (Oxford: Oxford University Press, 1941), xviii.
27 The English translation of Freud's *Moses and Monotheism* (1937) was published in 1939.
28 James Zeigler, "Charles Olson's American Studies: *Call Me Ishmael* and the Cold War," *Arizona Quarterly* 63.2 (Summer 2007), 50–51.
29 See, e.g., Donald E. Pease, "*Moby-Dick* and the Cold War," in *The American Renaissance Reconsidered*, eds. Walter Benn Michaels and Donald E. Pease (Baltimore: Johns Hopkins University Press, 1985), 144.

30 See, e.g., my *Poe and the Subversion of American Literature: Satire, Fantasy, Critique* (New York: Bloomsbury, 2014), 27–47.
31 See Matthiessen, vii; see also Harry Levin, *The Power of Blackness: Hawthorne, Poe, Melville* (Athens: Ohio University Press, 1958), vii–viii.
32 Arac, "F.O. Matthiessen: Authorizing the American Renaissance," in *The American Renaissance Reconsidered*, eds. Walter Benn Michaels and Donald E. Pease (Baltimore: Johns Hopkins University Press, 1985), 94.
33 See, e.g., Pease, "National Identities, Postmodern Artefacts, and Postnational Narratives," in *National Identities and Post-Americanist Narratives*, ed. Donald E. Pease. (Durham: Duke University Press, 1994), 3–5.
34 Arac, "F.O. Matthiessen," 95.
35 Leo Marx, "On Recovering the 'Ur' Theory of American Studies," *American Literary History* 17.1 (Spring 2005), 120.
36 Henry R. Luce, "The American Century," *Life Magazine* (17 February 1941), 61–65.
37 See Chapter 6 *infra*.
38 René Wellek, *Concepts in Criticism* (New Haven: Yale University Press, 1963), 116.
39 Heinrich Wölfflin, *Renaissance and Baroque*, trans. Kathrin Simon (Ithaca: Cornell University Press, 1964), 15.
40 Ibid., 23.
41 Ibid.
42 See, e.g., Walter Benjamin, *The Origins of German Tragic Drama*, trans. John Osborne (London: Verso, 1977), 55.
43 See Jay Leyda, *The Melville Log* (New York: Harcourt, 1951), 477.
44 Focillon, *The Life of Forms in Art*, 58.
45 Ziegler, "Charles Olson's American Studies," 70–71.
46 C. L. R. James, *Mariners, Renegades, and Castaways: The Story of Herman Melville and the World We Live In* (Hanover: University Press of New England, 2001), 2.
47 Dante, *Inferno*, trans. Mark Musa (New York: Penguin, 1984), Canto XXVI, lines 97, 100.
48 See Pease, "National Identities," 4.
49 Melville, *The Confidence-Man: His Masquerade*, ed. Stephen Matterson. (New York: Penguin, 1990), 282; see also Olson, *Call Me Ishmael*, 66.
50 See David Harvey, *The Condition of Postmodernity* (Oxford: Blackwell, 1990), 284–306.
51 Melville, *Moby-Dick*, 455–456.

Chapter 8

THE SOUTHERN PHOENIX TRIUMPHANT: THE CONSEQUENCES OF RICHARD WEAVER'S IDEAS

The 1950 U.S. Senate race in North Carolina was fiercely contested, featuring what even then was understood by many to be the opposed ideological trajectories of Southern politics: that of a seemingly progressive, "New South," characterized by its support for modernization, industry, and above all civil rights (or, at least, improvements to a system of racial inequality) on the on hand, and that of a profoundly conservative tradition resistant to such change, particularly with respect to civil rights, on the other. The unelected incumbent, appointed by the governor after the death of Senator J. Melville Broughton a year earlier, Frank Porter Graham was notoriously progressive, the former president of the University of North Carolina and a proponent of desegregation. The challenger was Willis Smith, mentor to later longtime conservative senator Jesse Helms, who was himself an active campaigner for Smith in this race. At the time, this election was viewed as a turning point in North Carolinian, and perhaps even Southern, politics, so starkly was the ideological division drawn. The primary election—this being 1950, the Democratic primary *was*, in effect, the election, since no Republican nominee could possibly offer meaningful competition in November—was remarkably vitriolic, as Smith's supporters played on the fears of bigots at every turn. (For example, one widely disseminated pro-Smith flyer announced "Frank Graham Favors Mingling of the Races.") On May 26, a Graham supporter, the idealistic young major of Fayetteville took to the airwaves to castigate the Smith campaign for its repulsive rhetoric and divisive tactics, inveighing:

> Where the campaign should have been based on principles, they have attempted to assault personalities. Where the people needed light, they have brought a great darkness. Where they should have debated, they have debased. [...] Where reason was needed, they have goaded emotion. Where they should have invoked inspiration, they have whistled for the hounds of hate.

Decades before "dog-whistle politics" become a *de facto* political strategy throughout the South (and elsewhere, of course), J. O. Tally Jr. lamented the motives, and no doubt the effectiveness, of such an approach, which had made this the "most bitter, most unethical in North Carolina's modern history."[1]

That was my grandfather, then an ambitious, 29-year-old lawyer and politician, who must have seen himself as fairly representative of a New South intellectual and statesman. A graduate of Duke University with a law degree from Harvard, Joe Tally had returned from distinguished overseas service in the navy during World War II to teach law at Wake Forest University and then to practice at the family firm before running for office in his hometown. His own career in electoral politics ended with a failed 1952 run for Congress, during which his moderate views on segregation likely amounted to an unpardonable sin for many voters in southeastern North Carolina, and he settled for alternative forms of civic and professional service, such as the Kiwanis Club, of which he later became international president. Others of Tally's political circle had better fortunes with the voters. Terry Sanford, for example, went on to become the governor of North Carolina, then long-time president of Duke University, before returning to politics in 1986, when he was elected the U.S. Senate, becoming perhaps the most liberal of the Southern senators. (Ah, to recall the time when an Al Gore was considered quite conservative!) Tally's ex-wife, my grandmother Lura S. Tally, went on to serve five terms in the N.C. House and six in the Senate from 1973 to 1994, where she represented that liberal wing of the old Democratic Party, promoting legislation especially in support of education, the environment, and the state's Museum of Natural History. However, during the same period, former Smith acolyte Jesse Helms carried that banner into the U.S. Senate in 1973, immediately becoming one of the most conservative members of Congress, hawkish in foreign affairs, parsimonious in his domestic policy, and ever ready to protect the public from "indecency" in his well publicized attacks on the National Endowment for the Arts. Perhaps it is part of the legacy of the 1950 Senate campaign, but North Carolina had always seemed rather bi-polar in its politics, often maintaining a far-right-wing and a relatively liberal contingent in the U.S. Congress. That is, until recently. In the past decade or so, North Carolina, like all of the South and much of the country, has lurched ever rightward in politics and policies. Today, the spirit of the old conservatives of Willis Smith's era reigns triumphant.[2]

The same year that the Smith campaign allegedly "whistled for the hounds of hate" in order to secure an election over a liberal vanguard dead set on undermining traditional Southern values, another native North Carolinian lamented that those espousing belief in such values had been forced out of the South. Speaking of the paradoxical fact that so many Southern Agrarians (including himself) had fled from their ancestral homeland to the urban North, there colonizing institutions like the University of Chicago, Richard M. Weaver proclaimed them "Agrarians in exile," who had been rendered "homeless," for "[t]he South no longer had a place for them, and flight to the North but completed an alienation long in progress." Weaver explained that "the South has not shown much real capacity to fight modernism," and added that "a large part of it is eager to succumb."[3] For Weaver, the great Agrarians of the *I'll Take My Stand* generation had been compelled to retreat in the face of those, like my grandparents, who in their "disloyalty" to "their section" of the United States exhibited "the disintegrative effects of modern liberalism."[4] Contrary to appearances, Weaver found that the Southern values which undergirded his preferred form of cultural and political conservatism were under assault, and perhaps even waning, in the South. The baleful liberalism he saw as all but indomitable in the industrial North and Midwest was, in Weaver's view, ineluctably encroaching on the sacred soil of the former Confederacy.

It is strange to look upon this scene from the vantage of the present. In 2015, with the defeat of Senator Mary Landrieu in Louisiana's December 6, 2014, run-off, there were no longer any Democrats from the Deep South in the U.S. Senate. And, as the 114th Congress convened in 2015, the U.S. House of Representatives contained no white Democrats from the Deep South, this for the first time in American history. Of course, the once "solid South" has been steadily trending ever more toward the Republicans since *Brown vs. Board of Education*, Governor Wallace's "segregation forever" speech, and Richard Nixon's notorious Southern strategy of the late 1960s. Native conservatism, gerrymandering, demographics, racial attitudes, and other factors have come into play, and the shift is therefore not wholly surprising, but the domination of the states of the former Confederacy by the Republican Party represents a sea-change in U.S. electoral politics. Furthermore, the hegemony of a certain Southern-styled conservatism within the Republican Party and, increasingly, within social, political, and cultural conservatism more generally marks a decisive movement away from not only the mid-century liberalism against which many Agrarians like Weaver railed, but also against the worldly neoconservatives like the elder President Bush whose embrace of a "new world order" elicited such fear and loathing from members of his own party in the early 1990s. The dominant strain of twenty-first century political discourse in the United States is thus a variation on a sort of neo-Confederate, anti-modernist theme of the Agrarians,[5] or, rather, of Weaver, perhaps their greatest philosophical champion.

In this essay, I revisit the ideas of this mid-twentieth-century conservative theorist in an attempt to shed light on the origins of this distinctively American brand of conservatism in the twenty-first century. Weaver's agrarian conservatism today seems both quaint or old-fashioned and yet disturbingly timely, as the rhetorical and intellectual force of his ideas seems all-too-real in the present social and political situation in the United States. Weaver's mythic vision of the South, ironically, has come to symbolize the nation as a whole, at least from the perspective of many of the most influential conservative politicians and policy-makers today. As a result of what might be called the *australization* of American politics in recent years—that is, a political worldview increasingly coded according to identifiably "Southern" themes and icons, not to mention the growing influence of Southern and Southwestern politicians at the level of national government—we can see more clearly now the degree to which Weaver's seemingly eccentric, often fantastic views have become not only mainstream, but perhaps even taken for granted, in 2015.[6] The "Southern Phoenix," celebrated by Weaver for its ability to survive its own immolation and re-emerge from the ashes, now appears triumphant to a degree that the original Fugitives and Vanderbilt Agrarians could not have dreamed possible. And, as is so often the case when fantasies come to life, the result may be more frightening than even their worst nightmares forebode.

America's "Southern Question"

Outside of certain tightly circumscribed spaces of formally conservative thought such as that of the Liberty Fund, Richard M. Weaver may no longer be a household name. However, his writings and his legacy have been profoundly influential on conservative thinking, and he has been viewed as a sort of founding father or patron saint of the movement. The Heritage Foundation, for example, adopted the title of his totemic, 1948 critique of modern industrial society, *Ideas Have Consequences*, as its official motto when founded in 1973. A devoted student, literally and metaphorically, of the Southern Agrarians of the *I'll Take My Stand* generation, Weaver embraced a certain "lost cause" view of the old Confederacy that informed his wide-ranging criticism of twentieth-century American and Western civilization. He viewed the antebellum South as the final flourishing of an idealized feudalism, doomed to fail as the forces of industry, science, and technology, together with ideological liberalism, secularism, and "equalitarianism," undermined and ultimately destroyed its foundations. Weaver's critique of modernity, somewhat like J. R. R. Tolkien's more distinctively English and Roman Catholic one, thus took the form of an almost fairy-story approach to history, in which a mythic past functioned as an exemplary model and as a foil to the lurid spectacle of the present cultural configuration, a balefully "modern" society characterized especially by its secularism, its embrace of scientific rationality, and its ineluctable process of industrialization. Weaver's jeremiad is thus both dated, redolent of a certain pervasive interwar and postwar malaise, and enduring, as his rhetoric remains audible in social and political discourse today, particularly in all those election-year panegyrics to a "simpler" America, a paradisiacal place just over the temporal horizon, now most known to us by its mourned absence.

Weaver was born in Asheville, North Carolina, in 1910, but he moved to Lexington, Kentucky, as a small child, where he grew up "in the fine 'bluegrass' country," as Donald Davidson noted,[7] and later received his bachelor's degree from the University of Kentucky. In his autobiographical essay, pointedly titled "Up from Liberalism," Weaver described the faculty there as "mostly earnest souls from the Middle Western universities, and many of them [...] were, with or without knowing it, social democrats."[8] This information is apparently supplied in order to explain Weaver's own brief flirtation with the American Socialist Party upon graduation in 1932. Weaver then enrolled in graduate school at Vanderbilt, birthplace of *I'll Take My Stand* in 1930 and thus ground zero of the literary or cultural movement by then known simply as "the Agrarians." At Vanderbilt, Weaver studied directly under John Crowe Ransom, to whom *The Southern Tradition at Bay* was later dedicated, and he wrote a master's thesis ("The Revolt Against Humanism: A Study of the New Critical Temper"), which criticized the "new" humanism of Irving Babbitt and Paul Elmer More, among others.[9] After receiving his M.A. degree, Weaver briefly taught at Texas A&M, but was repelled by its "rampant philistinism, abetted by technology, large-scale organization, and a complacent acceptance of success as the goal of life."[10] Weaver entered graduate school at Louisiana State University, where his teachers included two other giants of the Agrarian and American literary traditions, Robert Penn Warren and Cleanth Brooks. The latter served as director for Weaver's dissertation, a lengthy investigation and celebration of post–Civil War Southern literature and culture, evocatively (and provocatively) titled "The Confederate South, 1865–1910: A Study in the Survival of a Mind and Culture." This book was released posthumously in 1968 as *The Southern Tradition at Bay: A History of Postbellum Thought*, and it may well be considered Weaver's magnum opus, as I will discuss further below. After receiving his Ph.D., Weaver taught briefly at N.C. State University, before embracing his "exile" at the University of Chicago, where he spent the remainder of his professional life, not counting the summers during which he returned to western North Carolina, apparently to replenish his reserves of authentic agrarian experience and to recapture the "lost capacity for wonder and enchantment."[11] As it happens, Weaver's celebratory vision of the Southern culture is comports all-too-well with that of a fantasy world.

Legend has it that the virulent anti-modernist eschewed such new-fangled technology as the tractor, yet he seemed to have little compunction about enjoying the convenience of the railroad and other amenities made possible by modern industrial societies. "Every spring, as soon as the last term paper was graded, he traveled by train to Weaverville [North Carolina, just north of Asheville], where he spent summers writing essays and books and plowing his patch of land with only the help of a mule-driven harness. Tractors, airplanes, automobiles, radios (and certainly television)—none of these gadgets of modern life were for Richard Weaver," writes Joseph Scotchie, admiringly.[12] Yet Weaver also speaks about drinking coffee with pleasure, knowing full well that Appalachia is not known for its cultivation of this crop. As with so much of the fantastic critique of modernity by reactionaries, there is an unexamined (perhaps even unseen) principle of selection that allows one to choose which parts of the modern world to tacitly accept, and which to ostentatiously jettison.

Ideas and Their Consequences

Weaver's most significant and influential work published during his lifetime is undoubtedly *Ideas Have Consequences*, a title given by his editor at the University of Chicago Press but which Weaver had intended to call *The Fearful Descent*, according to Scotchie.[13] It is actually one of only three books published by Weaver during his own life; the others are *The Ethics of Rhetoric* (1953) and a textbook titled simply *Composition: A Course in Writing and Rhetoric* (1957). Weaver recalled that *Ideas Have Consequences* originated in his own rather despondent musings about the state of Western Civilization in the waning months of World War II, as he experienced "progressive disillusionment" over the way the war had been conducted, and he began to wonder "whether it would not be possible to deduce, from fundamental causes, the fallacies of modern life and thinking that had produced this holocaust and would insure others."[14] Weaver's bold, perhaps bizarre, premise was that the civilizational crisis in the twentieth century could be traced to a much earlier philosophical turning point in the trajectory of Western thought, namely the proto-scientific nominalism of William of Occam. Weaver draws a direct line from Occam's Razor to the most deleterious effects (in his view) of modern empiricism, materialism, and egalitarianism.

For Weaver, humanity took a wrong turn in the fourteenth century when it allegedly embraced Occam's Razor as the guiding principle of all logical inquiry, thus condemning mankind to a sort of secular, narrow, bean-counting approach to both the natural and social worlds. Referring obliquely to Macbeth's encounter with the weird sisters in Shakespeare's tragedy, Weaver asserts that

> Western man made an evil decision, which has become the efficient and final cause of other evil decisions. Have we forgotten our encounter with the witches on the heath? It occurred in the late fourteenth century, and what the witches said to the protagonist of this drama was that man could realize himself more fully if he would only abandon his belief in the existence of transcendentals. The powers of darkness were working subtly, as always, and they couched this proposition in the seemingly innocent form of an attack upon universals. The defeat of logical realism in the great medieval debate was the crucial event in the history of Western culture; from this flowed those acts which issue now in modern decadence.[15]

What follows from this is a lengthy, somewhat disjointed analysis of "the dissolution of the West," which will include not only the critique of philosophical tendencies or declining moral codes, but also attacks on egotism in art, jazz music, and other forms of popular entertainments. It is almost a right-wing version of the near-contemporaneous *Dialectic of Enlightenment*, except that Weaver would not have imagined "Enlightenment" to have suggested anything other than "disaster triumphant" to begin with, and Horkheimer and Adorno was all too wary of the latent and manifest significance of the jargon of authenticity as enunciated by writers like Weaver.[16]

Although *Ideas Have Consequences* is not overtly "Southern" in any way, Weaver's medievalism, which was developed not according to any deeply philological study of premodern texts (à la Tolkien) but rather from his own sense of that late flowering of chivalry in the antebellum South, indicates the degree to which his discussion of the West's decline is actually tied to his view of the lost cause of the Confederacy. The first six chapters of *Ideas Have Consequences* constitute a fairly scattershot series of observations on "the various stages of modern man's descent into chaos," which began with his having yielded to materialism in the fourteenth century, and which in turn paved the way for the "egotism and social anarchy of the present world."[17] The final three chapters, by contrast, are intended as restorative. That is, in them Weaver attempts to delineate the ways that modern man might resist these tendencies, reversing the movement of history, and reaping the rewards of a legacy that would presumably have flourished had only the pre-Occam metaphysical tendency ultimately prevailed. In a 1957 essay in the *National Review*, Weaver claimed that, contrary to the assertions of liberals, the conservatives were not so much in favor of "turning the clocks back" as "setting the clocks right."[18] Not surprisingly, Weaver's three prescriptions in *Ideas Have Consequences* would neatly align with the fantastic, medieval, or feudal system he had imagined as the dominant form of social organization in the antebellum South, although he does not highlight his regional allegiance in this book, a work purportedly devoted to the study of (Western) civilization as a whole.

The first is the principle of private property, which Weaver takes to be "the last metaphysical right" available to modern man. That is, while "the ordinances of religion, the prerogatives of sex and of vocation" were "swept away by materialism" (specifically, the Reformation, changing social values, and so on), "the relationship of a man to his own has until the present largely escaped attack."[19] Weaver calls the right to private property a "metaphysical right" because "it does not depend on social usefulness. […] It is a self-justifying right, which until lately was not called upon to show in the forum how its 'services' warranted its continuance in a state dedicated to collective well-being."[20] Private property, which Weaver likens to "the philosophical concept of substance," is depicted as providing a foundation for the renewed sense of self and being in the world. The second principle is "the power of the word": "After securing a place in the world from which to fight, we should turn our attention to the matter of language."[21] Weaver offers a critique of semantics as itself simply a form of nominalism, while arguing for an education in poetics and rhetoric as necessary to reclaim one's connection to the absolute, while also remaining critical of the abuses of language in modern culture. Finally, Weaver concludes with a chapter on "piety and justice," in which he argues that the piety, "a discipline of the will through respect," makes justice possible by allowing man to transcend egotism with respect to three things: nature, other people, and the past.[22] Fundamentally, for Weaver, this piety issues from a chivalric tradition that he imagines as the only real hope for a reformation of the twentieth-century blasted by war, spiritually desolate, and (he does not shrink from using the term) "evil." What is needed, Weaver concludes in the book's final line, is "a passionate reaction, like that which flowered in the chivalry and spirituality of the Middle Ages."[23]

As it happened, according to Weaver, there was a place in the United States which had previously held, and in 1948 perhaps still maintained, this medieval worldview. Weaver's beloved South, even though it was under siege from without by the forces of modernity and in peril from within by a generation of would-be modernizers, retained the virtues of an evanescing feudal tradition, which might somehow be recovered and brought into the service of civilization itself. Indeed, Weaver's first book-length work, which only appeared in print after his death, was an elaborate examination and strident defense of this chivalric culture that once flourished beneath the Mason and Dixon line. If only its message could be distilled and disseminated, this Southern tradition might redeem the entirety of the West.

The Conservative Critic at Bay

The Southern Tradition at Bay occupies a unique and important place in Weaver's corpus. Based on his doctoral thesis but published five years after his death, the book can be read as being representative of his "early" thinking on the subject and as a sort of *summa* of his entire literary and philosophical program at the same time. Many of the ideas that Weaver here identifies as Southern are clearly connected to those he celebrates in *Ideas Have Consequences*. For example, Weaver's elaboration of the "mind" of the Old South focused on four distinctive but interrelated characteristics: the feudal system, the code of chivalry, the education of the gentleman, and the older religiousness, by which Weaver meant a non-creedal religiosity. Combined, these four factors distinguished the unique culture of the "section," clearly differentiating its heritage from that of other parts of the United States.[24]

Weaver's medievalism, as I mentioned before, is not rooted in the formal study of the history, philology, or philosophy of the European Middle Ages, although he draws upon certain imagery from its time and place. One might argue that Weaver's project is literally quixotic, inasmuch as he figuratively dons the rusty armor of a bygone age to tilt at windmills which he imagines to be giants, but in an effort "in this iron age of ours to revive the age of gold or, as it is generally called, the golden age."[25] Weaver's tone is simultaneously elegiac and recalcitrant, mourning the lost cause or the waning of a glorious past and ardently defending its values in the present, fallen state of the world. Methodologically, Weaver's approach is to gather selectively then-contemporary accounts, including public proclamations and individual diaries—or, often, a combination of the two, in the form of published memoirs—as well as more recent historical studies, then add his own assessments of their currency (i.e., in 1943) as evidence of an enduring, twentieth century "Mind of the South."[26] Weaver somewhat disingenuously cautions that,

> [i]n presenting evidence that this is the traditional mind of the South, I am letting the contemporaries speak. They will seldom offer whole philosophies, and sometimes the trend of thought is clear only in the light of context; yet together they express the mind of a religious agrarian order in struggle against the forces of modernism.[27]

Needless to say, perhaps, but such a collective "mind" is likely not to be discovered if the historian were to cast the nets of his research more widely.[28] By identifying only those "true" Southerners whose opinions can thereafter be identified as authentic, Weaver anticipates all of our current politicians and pundits who seem to be forever deferring to these mythical "real Americans" whose viewpoints are curiously at odds with the actual history of the present.

After laying out the feudal heritage which characterizes the mind and culture of the South in the opening chapter, Weaver by turns examines the antebellum and postbellum defense of the Southern way of life, the perspectives of Confederate soldiers and the reminiscences of others during the Civil War (or "the second American Revolution"), the work of selected Southern fiction writers, and then the reformers or internal critics who, in Weaver's view, effectively managed to take the fight out of the "fighting South."[29]

Weaver concedes by the end that "the Old South may indeed be a hall hung with splendid tapestries in which no one would care to live; but from them we can learn something of how to live."[30] It is a disturbing and prophetic line, suggestive of how much the Southern heritage might be abstracted, idealized, and then transferred to distant places and times. Comparing his own situation to that of a Henry Adams, who, "wearied with the plausibilites of his day, looked for some higher reality in the thirteenth-century synthesis of art and faith," Weaver imagines that the old Confederacy, with its feudal hierarchies and chivalric cultural values, may yet become a model for the social formations to come. Calling the Old South "the last non-materialist civilization in the Western world," Weaver concludes:

> It is this refuge of sentiments and values, of spiritual congeniality, of belief in the word, of reverence for symbolism, whose existence haunts the nation. It is damned for its virtues and praised for its faults, and there are those who wish its annihilation. But most revealing of all is the fear that it gestates the revolutionary impulse of our future.[31]

Behind this elevated rhetoric lies the hoary old dream, indistinct threat, and rebel yell: the South will rise again!

The title of *The Southern Tradition at Bay* is provocatively descriptive. Since its purview is the period of American history between 1865 and 1910, following the crushing defeat of the former Confederacy and the disastrous period of Reconstruction—not to mention advances in science, the rise of a more industrial mode of production, and the emergence of modernism in the arts and culture—the study's elaboration of a cognizable "Southern Tradition" rooted in unreconstructed agrarianism and adherence to the ideals of the old

Confederacy is intended to establish it as a preferred counter-tradition to that of the victorious North and to the *united* States in general. Moreover, the phrase "at bay" is suggestive not of defeat or conquest, but of temporary inconvenience; it refers especially to being momentarily held up, kept at a distance, but by no means out of the game. Such an accomplished rhetor as Weaver would no doubt be aware that the phrase derives from the French *abayer*, "to bark," and that it probably referred to dogs that were prevented from approaching further to attack and that were thus relegated to merely barking at their prey. (The image of a group of Southerners barking at an uncomprehending North may be all too appropriate when revisiting *I'll Take My Stand*, come to think of it.) In other words, *The Southern Tradition at Bay*'s title nicely encapsulates two powerful aspects of its argument: that the Southern Tradition exists, present tense, long after its *ancien régime* was disrupted by war and by modernization; and that it was not ever defeated, much less destroyed, but merely kept in abeyance from the then dominant, though less creditable national culture. Weaver's vision of the South does not imagine a residual or emergent social formation, to mention Raymond Williams's well-known formulation,[32] but rather another dominant, yet somehow suppressed or isolated, form which remained in constant tension with the only apparently victorious North. Weaver's mood is sometimes melancholy, befitting his sense of the "lost cause," but his conviction that the South ought to rise again, whether he believed it was practically feasible or not, is clear throughout.

Thus, the idea of a distinctively Southern tradition being temporarily held "at bay" suits Weaver's argument well. However, this was not the original title of the study. When he presented it as his doctoral dissertation at Louisiana State University, where his thesis advisor was Cleanth Brooks,[33] Weaver gave it a much more provocative and politically charged title: "The Confederate South, 1865–1910: A Study in the Survival of a Mind and Culture." The difference is not particularly subtle. Here it is asserted that the "Confederate South," not just a tradition, itself exists outside of the more limited lifespan of the C.S.A., and that *its* mind and culture—not merely those of a South, a recognizable section of the United States, but those of the Confederacy—survived the aftermath of the Civil War, a conflict which Weaver dutifully names the "second American Revolution."[34]

Weaver submitted the manuscript to the University of North Carolina Press in 1943, but it was summarily rejected. I have found no evidence one way or another, but I like to think that the publishing arm of the university presided over by Frank Porter Graham declined to publish the execrable apologia of the Confederacy's "survival," with its idyllic portrait of human bondage and of racial bigotry, on not only academic but also political grounds. The story is probably less interesting than that, for although the book makes a passionate case for a certain worldview, the dissertation's extremely selective portrayal of the postbellum culture of the southern parts of the United States almost certainly rendered its conclusions dubious from the perspective of academic historians and philosophers. Most likely, Weaver's omissions, as well as his renunciation of any sense of objectivity or nonpartisanship, led to the study's remaining unpublished during his lifetime. In any case, its eventual publication in 1968, a transformative moment in U.S. politics and society, makes for a rather intriguing, if unhappy, coincidence. The "Southern strategy," conceived by Harry Dent and launched by the Nixon campaign that very year, had in *The Southern Tradition at Bay* its historico-philosophical touchstone.

"The Alien Race"

It is all too noteworthy that the "mind and culture" that Weaver identifies as surviving in the aftermath of the Civil War is, at once, generalized so as to extend to the entirety of the American South and limited to a fairly tiny slice of that section's actual population. Weaver makes no bones about the fact the he wanted to consider only the elite members of that society as representative of this tradition. Asserting that "it is a demonstrable fact that the group in power speaks for the country," Weaver unapologetically writes that, "[i]n assaying the Southern tradition, therefore, I have taken the spirit which dominated," thus ignoring Southern abolition societies, for example.[35] He also ignores the majority of the people. In order to make his case, Weaver pays little attention to white people who are not aristocratic lords of their own fiefdoms or soldiers who fought in the Civil War, which is to say, Weaver largely overlooks the poor multitudes who vastly outnumbered the wealthy planters, military leaders, and governors. Also, though not unexpectedly, the Black population, a not inconsiderable percentage of the populace in these states, is treated far worse, in this account; Black Southerners are not ignored, but rather are called out for special treatment in assessing their significant role in making possible this culture and its tradition.[36]

Indeed, Weaver refers to Black people in the South as "the alien race," as if he cannot understand that persons of African descent are no more or less alien to the lands of the Americas than are those of European descent. "Alien" cannot here mean "foreign," since Weaver highlights the Southerner's kinship to the Europeans, whether genealogically or with respect to social values. Weaver almost blames the Black servants for being "inferior," the mere fact of which itself could lead to abuse and therefore can reflect badly on the moral constitution of the white superiors. For example, after praising the idyllic state of paternalism in which "[t]he master expected of his servants loyalty; the servants of the master interest and protection," and going so far as to note that even at present, "so many years after emancipation," the Southern plantation owner will routinely "defray the medical expenses of his Negroes" and "get them out of jail when they have been committed for minor offenses," Weaver concedes that

> [t]his is the spirit of feudalism in its optative aspect; some abuses were inevitable, and in the South lordship over an alien and primitive race had less favorable effects upon the character of the slaveowners. It made them arrogant and impatient, and it filled them with boundless self-assurance. Even the children, noting the deference paid to their elders by the servants, began at an early age to take on airs of command. [...] These traits [i.e., irritability, impatience, vengefulness], which were almost invariably noted by Northerners and by visiting Englishmen, gave Southerners a reputation away from home which they thought baseless and inspired by malice.[37]

Weaver never doubts whether the feudalistic and benign paternalism of the plantation owner, prior to or after emancipation, to "*his* Negroes" would have appeared quite so optative in its aspect to the servants themselves. Informed readers, regardless of their own political views, cannot help but question this formulation.

In Weaver's view, all servants—almost exclusively understood to be members of an "alien race" as well as being a subaltern class—on a Southern plantation are either happy and loyal or hopelessly deluded. During the Civil War, for example, "the alien race, which numbered about four millions in the South, kept its accustomed place, excepting those who through contact with the Federal armies were won away from adherence to 'massa' and 'ol' mistis'."[38] This appears in a section called "The Negroes in Transition," within a long chapter titled "Diaries and Reminiscences of the Second American Revolution," and Weaver's unmistakable conclusion is that the Black population of the South was almost entirely better off under the system of slavery. Indeed, from his blinkered perspective, the African Americans under consideration would be better off as slaves precisely because they are more naturally suited to that condition. This position constitutes not only an *apologia* for human bondage but also a casual acceptance of the most foul racial bigotry. Weaver cannot seem to imagine a reasonable reader who would question white supremacy, the inherent racial superiority of white people that he and the authorities he approvingly cites take to be a matter of fact. "The Northern conception that the Negro was merely a sunburned white man, 'whose only crime was the color of his skin,' found no converts at all among the people who had lived and worked with him."[39] Weaver thus intimates that those who believed otherwise were merely ignorant of simple facts familiar to any and all with the least bit of experiential knowledge. Similarly, when Weaver writes that "[m]ore than one writer took the view that it was impossible for the two races to dwell together unless the blacks remained in a condition approximating slavery," he offers not a word to gainsay the view, and he tacitly endorses it throughout the book.[40]

Weaver's somewhat disingenuous assertion that he is "letting the contemporaries speak" for themselves is hardly an excuse for this profoundly racist account. Even if he relied only on direct quotations, which he certainly does not, Weaver had already conceded that he was rather selective in how he would approach his project. Needless to say, perhaps, but "The Negroes in Transition" section makes no reference whatsoever to any Black authorities; in fact, Weaver here seems to rely entirely on the remembrances of Southern belles, as the footnotes in this section refer exclusively to autobiographies or memoirs written by white women, including one titled *A Belle of the Fifties*.[41] (The suggestion that free Blacks represented a threat to white women is not so subtly hinted at in these pages.) Weaver quotes liberally from the women's writings, but he frequently editorializes and supplements their mostly first-person perceptions with an almost scientific assessment, expounding on the laws governing society and nature.[42] For example, having just mentioned both slavery and race, and therefore leaving no doubt in the mind of the readers as to the racial criteria by which a social hierarchy of the type he is endorsing would be established, Weaver asserts: "Out of the natural reverence for intellect and virtue there arises an impulse to segregation, which broadly results in coarser natures, that is, those of duller mental and moral sensibility, being lodged at the bottom and those of more refined at the top."[43] Indeed, Weaver goes so far as to credit the endemic racism of the Southerner with a kind of moral superiority over those who lack this good sense. He argues that, in the Southerner's "endeavor to grade men by their moral and intellectual worth," his defense of slavery and racial hierarchy "indicates an ethical awareness" missing from many Northerners' perspectives.[44]

That politics in the United States has, since 1968, become increasingly characterized by racial division is both controversial and indubitable. The "post-racial" America presided over by Barack Obama has witnessed some of the most acrimonious, racially-inflected public discourse and debate in years. Yet open appeals to racial justice or to discriminatory practices are still considered *gauche* by many liberals, even as "mainstream" conservatism has become more and more transparent with respect to its support of white supremacy. As I mentioned at the beginning of this essay, a form of "dog-whistle politics" has infiltrated nearly all political rhetoric in recent decades. Perhaps the most infamous example of this "dog-whistle" political strategy can be found in Lee Atwater's remarkably candid revelation in a 1981 interview. The former Strom Thurmond acolyte, who served in the Reagan White House, then as George H. W. Bush's presidential campaign manager in 1988, and who later became chairman of the Republican National Committee, Atwater is acknowledged as one of the most astute political strategists of his generation. In speaking (anonymously, at the time) of the Reagan campaign's far more elegant and effective version of the Southern strategy, Atwater explained:

> You start out in 1954 by saying, "Nigger, nigger, nigger." By 1968, you can't say "nigger"—that hurts you. Backfires. So you say stuff like forced busing, states' rights and all that stuff. You're getting so abstract now [that] you're talking about cutting taxes, and all these things you're talking about are totally economic things and a byproduct of them is [that] blacks get hurt worse than whites. And subconsciously maybe that is part of it. I'm not saying that. But I'm saying that if it is getting that abstract, and that coded, that we are doing away with the racial problem one way or the other. You follow me—because obviously sitting around saying, "We want to cut this," is much more abstract than even the busing thing *and* a hell of a lot more abstract than "Nigger, nigger."[45]

The fact that abstract economic issues, which presumably would affect both whites and Blacks in the relatively poor Southern states in more-or-less equal measure, are so effective as code words for traditional, race-baiting tactics of a previous generation—the era of Willis Smith, in fact—demonstrates the degree to which Weaver's feudal hierarchies maintain themselves, now in an utterly fantastic way as a vague threat, well into the late-twentieth century or early twenty-first.

As Atwater suggested, many voters—not just those in the South, of course—are willing to endorse policies that actually harm them or their own interests, so long as a byproduct of those policies is that "blacks get hurt worse than whites." This too, it seems, has much to do with the survival of a mind and culture in the aftermath of slavery and war, and so it is not altogether surprising that Weaver's examination of the Southern tradition "at bay" focuses so intently on demonstrating why the Black population of the South ought to remain subjugated to the white population as the era of civil rights, desegregation, and modernization dawns on the region.[46]

The Australization of U.S. Politics

In his appreciative remembrance of *I'll Take My Stand*, written on the occasion of the thirtieth anniversary of its publication, Weaver invoked the image of the "Southern Phoenix," a mythic reference to a creature that had regenerated itself from the ashes following its own fiery destruction. Weaver uses this figure not so much to recall how the Agrarians whose work constituted that epochal text had themselves gone on to greatness, even if the volume had been ridiculed and dismissed by many Northern (among other) critics in the 1930s. Weaver is also thinking of the tenets and values of the Old South, those that the Vanderbilt Fugitives and Agrarians embraced and promoted, which must have seemed retrograde, even malignant to so many in 1930, but which had reemerged and flourished amid an ascendant conservatism just beginning to take shape nationally in 1960. Yet, for all its usefulness as a metaphor, the phoenix is probably also an apt figure for Weaver's own conservative vision, since—like an imaginary creature taken from the provinces of mythology—Weaver's image of the Southern tradition, whether at bay or on the offensive, is profoundly fantastic. This imaginary tradition is rooted in a world that certainly never existed, not on a wide scale at any rate, and the polemical forces of Weaver's argument are directed at a foe that has been conceived as an immense Leviathan, but which we today know to have been largely chimerical.

At times, this argument becomes almost comical. In explaining the importance of "the last metaphysical right," private property, for example, Weaver cites the example of Henry David Thoreau,[47] although the latter's notorious experiment in living deliberately required him to purchase no private property (as was his "metaphysical right," I suppose), but to live rent free on property owned by another (Ralph Waldo Emerson, in fact). Far from demonstrating the self-sufficiency and resolve of the individual, Thoreau's experiment might be taken as exemplary of a kind of localized welfare system; one need not punch the clock at the local factory if one lives off the generosity and largess of family and friends. However, as we have seen increasingly in the United States in recent years, the receipt of corporate and other forms of welfare in no way prevents the recipients from bashing the government for offering support to others. The Republican Party's adoption of the "We Built It" slogan in 2012 offers a tellingly Thoreauvian fantasy, one where it is possible to accept the public's funding, make use of all those affordances granted by the taxpayers, and profit mightily from these and other windfalls made possible by the social and governmental organizations of which one is a part, all the while insisting upon one's absolute independence from the commonweal.

Given the importance of a sense of place and of community to Weaver's fantastic vision of a medieval heritage, such rampant individualism—an ideology subtending the basic neoliberal projection of free markets and autonomous economic actors—seems quite foreign. Indeed, it is odd to talk about Weaver as a forebear to contemporary conservatism. Certainly, the economic neoliberalism which celebrates unfettered free markets and the geopolitical neoconservatism which glories in globalization and preemptive military engagements are a far cry from Weaver's fanciful nostalgia for an idealistic feudalism founded upon rigid social hierarchies, chivalric codes of ethics, and a powerful, culture-shaping religion or religiosity.[48] In his own writings, we can see Weaver's strong aversion to the emergent globalization and even nationalization, which he views as corrupting the properly regionalist values he favored. Weaver's worldview would not have allowed him to embrace the preemptive war strategies championed by Dick Cheney, Donald Rumsfeld, and Paul Wolfowitz during the various military conflicts of the past forty years. Moreover, Weaver's ardent defense of the humanities— recall his loathing for the educational and cultural aura of Texas A&M, now home to the George [H. W.] Bush Presidential Library—is entirely at odds with the views on higher education, the arts, philosophy, and "high" culture held by the most prominent and visible members of the G.O.P. today. Yet, the sectarianism of Weaver's view paved the way for contemporary neoconservative politics and policies. Weaver's well-nigh Schmittian, Us-versus-Them antagonism, requires us to envision not merely a Western civilization opposed to its non-western rivals but a truer, more valuable "Southern" civilization against the putatively uncivilized rest of the United States. The loathsome, omnipresent discourse about "real" Americans and what constitutes them is a legacy of the Southern Agrarian traditions apotheosized by Weaver's philosophy.

Indeed, the particular labels (e.g., conservative, neoconservative, neoliberal, and so forth) are not necessarily helpful in understanding the dominant political and cultural discourses in the United States in the twenty-first century. As Paul A. Bové has observed, "[m]any critics of the Far Right movement conservatism mischaracterize it. It is not an epiphenomenon of neoliberalism. In fact, the popular elements of this movement, of its electoral coalition, resent the economic and cultural consequences of neoliberalism and globalization in politics and culture."[49] To many of the policies and even most of the ideas of the neoconservatives like Wolfowitz, Cheney, and both Presidents Bush, Weaver and his beloved Agrarians would almost certainly object. However, the cultural and intellectual foundations of the neoconservatives' positions, not to mention the fact of their being elected or appointed to offices of great power In the first place, owes much to an ideological transformation of U.S. intellectual culture whose *fons et origo* may be found in the fantastic vision of a distinctively Southern variant of American exceptionalism.

One might well think of this as the *australization* of American politics, for the purportedly unique culture of the Southern states has tended, since the 1960s, to be more and more representative of a national conservative movement. This movement, which has become perhaps the most influential force within the Republican Party at a moment when the conservative politics has itself become more prominent in the United States, thus tends to be the dominant force in national, and increasingly international, politics as well. It should not be forgotten that the rightward shift even in the Democratic Party can itself be linked to this increasingly australized politics on a national level, as both Georgia's Jimmy Carter and Arkansas's Bill Clinton emerged as the preferable, because more conservative, presidential candidates who would stand up to the old-fashioned liberals in their own party (symbolized by figures like Ted Kennedy, Mario Cuomo, or Jesse Jackson).[50] In their commitment to economic growth, particularly that made possible by increasingly corporate or industrial development, these conservative Southern Democrats would have earned the agrarian-minded Weaver's contempt, but their rhetorical and ideological commitments align far better with the agrarian discourse than did the expansive liberalism of the New Deal or the Great Society. Weaver would undoubtedly decry the rapid growth of the South's population in recent decades, since that growth has been generated in large part by ever more industrial or urban development, but he would probably delight in seeing the rusting of the Rust Belt as unionization, heavy industry, and traditional urbanism has declined in the North and Northeast. The shifting numbers of electoral votes in favor of Southern states is also a real consideration for any political or cultural program interested in preserving or expanding Southern "values" in the United States. The fall of the hated North, in this view, is almost as sweet as the South's rising again.

The costs of this apparent australization of American politics are incalculable, as may be inferred from the increasingly vicious public discourse with respect to all manner of things, including welfare and taxation, education, science, the environment, individual rights, foreign adventures, war, domestic surveillance (a form of paternalism), and so forth. As far back as 1941, W. J. Cash had concluded his study of *The Mind of the South* by noting the "characteristic vices" of that culture:

> Violence, intolerance, aversion and suspicion toward new ideas, an incapacity for analysis, an inclination to act from feeling rather than from thought, an exaggerated individualism and too narrow concept of

social responsibility, attachment to fictions and false values, above all too great attachment to racial values and a tendency to justify cruelty and injustice in the name of those values, sentimentality and a lack of realism—these have been its characteristic vices in the past. And, despite changes for the better, they remain its characteristic vices today.[51]

Taken out of their original context, these words seem all too timely in the twenty-first century. In Cash's final lines, he abjured any temptation to play the role of prophet, declaring that it would be "a brave man" who would venture definite prophecies, and it would be "a madman who would venture them in the face of the forces sweeping over the world in 1940."[52] Bravery or madness notwithstanding, Cash likely could not have imagined the degree to which the characteristic vices of the South in his time could become so widespread to have become the characteristics of a national American "mind" *tout court* in the next century.

Moreover, as should be obvious, the australization of American politics is not simply a matter of political leaders or voters residing in the southern parts of the United States. The pervasiveness of certain identifiably Southern cultural signifiers within mainstream political discourse, particularly in the more conservative members of the Republican Party but also throughout the public policy and electioneering rhetoric of both major parties, signals a victory for that fantastic or idealistic "mind and culture" so celebrated by Weaver and his Agrarian forebears. It is a terrifying prospect for many, but the vision of the intransigent Southern traditionalist now operating from a position of broad-based cultural and political power on a national, indeed an international, stage might be the apotheosis of Weaver's grand historical investigation into the region's purportedly distinctive past. As Weaver put it in a 1957 essay,

> [i]t may be that after a long period of trouble and hardship, brought on in my opinion by being more sinned against than sinning, this unyielding Southerner will emerge as a providential instrument for saving this nation. [...] If that time should come, the nation as a whole would understand the spirit that marched with Lee and Jackson and charged with Pickett.[53]

For most people residing in the United States, including many of us in the South (like me, some of whose ancestors likely did march with or in support of some of these men in the early 1860s), the prospect of a neo-Confederate savior of the nation or world is horrifying, like a mythological monster assuming worldly power. Sifting through the ashes of the triumphant Southern Phoenix, we are likely to find much of value has been destroyed.

Notes

1 Quoted in Julian M. Pleasants and Augustus M. Burns III, *Frank Porter Graham and the 1950 Senate Race in North Carolina* (Chapel Hill: University of North Carolina Press), 183, ellipses in original. On the term "dog-whistle politics," see Ian Haney López, *Dog Whistle Politics: How Coded Racial Appeals Have Reinvented Racism and Wrecked the Middle Class* (Oxford: Oxford University Press, 2014).
2 The rise of Donald Trump in 2016 would seem anomalous, particularly as he is (and "brands" himself as) a New Yorker, but there is no question that Trump's political success derives in part from his embrace of what had been coded as "Southern" values, right down to his support for flying the Stars-and-Bars (i.e., what is better known as "the Confederate Flag").
3 Richard M. Weaver, "Agrarianism in Exile," in *The Southern Essays of Richard M. Weaver*, ed. George M. Curtis III and James J. Thompson Jr. (Indianapolis: Liberty Press, 1987), 40, 44.
4 Weaver, "The Southern Phoenix," in *The Southern Essays of Richard M. Weaver*, 17.
5 See Paul A. Bové, "Agriculture and Academe: America's Southern Question," in *Mastering Discourse: The Politics of Intellectual Culture* (Durham: Duke University Press, 1991), 113–142.
6 Recent events concerning the removal of the "Confederate Flag," the notorious symbol of racism wielded by the KKK and others, from state capitols and other official sites in the South appears to be a surprising turn of events, although cynics could argue that, in turning attention away for gun violence and particularly violence against black citizens and other minorities, the flag issue has provided a convenient cover, allowing the media to ignore more urgent social problems in the wake of the Charleston massacre. Still, symbols are powerful, and the removal of this symbol is itself a hopeful sign as even conservative politicians and pundit have realized, all too late, what the embrace of the lost Confederacy has cost them on a moral level. See, e.g., Russ Douthat, "For the South, Against the Confederacy," *New York Times* blog, June 24, 2015: http://douthat.blogs.nytimes.com/2015/06/24/for-the-south-against-the-confederacy/?_r=0.
7 Donald Davidson, "The Vision of Richard Weaver: A Foreword," in Richard M. Weaver, *The Southern Tradition at Bay: A History of Postbellum Thought*, eds. George Core and M. E. Bradford (New Rochelle: Arlington House, 1968), 17.
8 Weaver, "Up from Liberalism" [1958–59], in *The Vision of Richard Weaver*, ed. Joseph Scotchie (New Brunswick: Transaction Publishers, 1995), 20.
9 See Fred Douglas Young, *Richard M. Weaver, 1910–1963: A Life of the Mind* (Columbia: University of Missouri Press, 1995), 56–58.
10 Weaver, "Up from Liberalism," 23.
11 Ibid., 28.
12 Joseph Scotchie, "Introduction: From Weaverville to Posterity," in *The Vision of Richard Weaver*, 9–10.
13 Ibid., 9.
14 Weaver, "Up from Liberalism," 31. Notwithstanding the use of the word "holocaust," Weaver makes no mention of the Nazis or the concentration camps in this essay; rather, his example is "the abandonment of Finland by Britain and the United States" (31).
15 Weaver, *Ideas Have Consequences* (Chicago: University of Chicago Press, 1948), 2–3.

16 See Max Horkheimer and Theodor W. Adorno, *Dialectic of Enlightenment*, trans. John Cumming (New York: Continuum, 1987), 3. See also Adorno, *The Jargon of Authenticity*, trans. Knut Tarnowski and Frederic Will (Evanston: Northwestern University Press, 1973).
17 Weaver, *Ideas Have Consequences*, 129.
18 Weaver, "On Setting the Clock Right," *In Defense of Tradition: Collected Shorter Writings of Richard M. Weaver*, ed. Ted J. Smith III (Indianapolis: Liberty Fund, 2000), 559–566.
19 Weaver, *Ideas Have Consequences*, 131.
20 Ibid., 132.
21 Ibid., 148.
22 Ibid., 172.
23 Ibid., 187.
24 In a later essay, Weaver compares the difference between the American North and the South to that between the United States and England, France, or China. In the same essay, Weaver adds that "The South [...] still looks among a man's credentials for where he's from, and not all places, even in the South, are equal. Before a Virginian, a North Carolinian is supposed to stand cap in hand. And faced with the hauteur of an old family from Charleston, South Carolina, even a Virginian may shuffle his feet and look uneasy." See "The Southern Tradition," in *The Southern Essays of Richard M. Weaver*, 210, 225.
25 Cervantes, *Don Quixote*, trans. J. M. Cohen (New York: Penguin, 1950), 149. Apparently, many conservatives would not object to such a comparison. For example, in his history on the right-wing Intercollegiate Studies Institute, Lee Edwards approvingly begins by saying of its founder, "Frank Chodorov had been tilting against windmills all his life." See Edwards, *Educating for Liberty: The First Half-Century of the Intercollegiate Studies Institute* (Washington, DC: Regnery Publishing, 2003), 1.
26 At no point does Weaver cite Cash's *The Mind of the South* (originally published in 1941), which in this context must be seen as a sort of "absent presence" for Weaver and others who carried the torch for the Agrarians in the 1940s and beyond. *The Mind of the South* appeared while Weaver was working on his dissertation, and Weaver's own study might even be seen as a tactical critique of, or at least alterative to, Cash's celebrated work. See W. J. Cash, *The Mind of the South* (New York: Vintage, 1991). Although these two native North Carolinian authors identify some of the same characteristics and even arrive at similar conclusions about the "mind of the South," they also maintain rather different social and political positions. For one thing, Cash does not see a feudal or aristocratic Southern character as praiseworthy, whereas Weaver's entire defense of the Southern tradition rests on his admiration for and allegiance toward the aristocratic virtues of the archetypal Southerner.
27 Weaver, *The Southern Tradition at Bay*, 44.
28 One legitimate critique of Cash's *The Mind of the South* was that it focused primarily on the attitudes and customary habits associated with Cash's own Piedmont region of North Carolina (which happens to be my native region as well), thus underestimating the divergences to be found in the Tidewater zones to the east or the "Deep South" below and to the west. Weaver's *Southern Tradition at Bay* does not limit its approach by regions, giving more or less equal space to views from all parts of the South, but it does severely restrict itself to materials best suited to make its argument with respect to a feudal system. Hence, Weaver tends to ignore the experiences of

those who did not live on large estates or plantations, which is to say, Weaver omits the experiences of the *vast* majority of Southerners. If Cash's study could be faulted for its Mencken-esque journalistic techniques—Cash's original article, "The Mind of the South," did appear in H. L. Mencken's *American Mercury*, after all—and for its lack of intellectual rigor, Weaver's more academic study (it was a Ph.D. dissertation, of course), in its questionable method and especially in its selectivity, also raises doubts about the "mind" it purports to lay bare.

29 Weaver, *The Southern Tradition at Bay*, 387.
30 Ibid., 396.
31 Ibid., 391.
32 See Raymond Williams, *Marxism and Literature* (Oxford: Oxford University Press, 1977), 121–127.
33 Weaver's advisor had been the cultural historian, literary critic, and biographer Arlin Turner; Brooks stepped in only near the end to serve as the head of Weaver's thesis committee. In his biography, Young reports that "Weaver was in the final stages of writing his dissertation when Turner left LSU to take a position at Duke University; Cleanth Brooks became his advisor at that point and oversaw the work to its conclusion" (78). However, as far as I can tell, Turner did not arrive at Duke until 1953, ten years after Weaver received his Ph.D. degree. The more likely reason for the change in advisor, as Fred Douglas Young writes, was that Turner was "called up for service in the U.S. Navy," which is why Weaver asked Brooks to serve as dissertation director at the last minute (see Young, *Richard M. Weaver*, 67). I am not prepared to speculate on the relationship between teacher and student, but I might note that Turner, a native Texan who wrote a well-regarded biography of Nathaniel Hawthorne and later became the editor of the distinguished academic journal *American Literature*, likely did not share his former student's strictly sectarian views with respect to the opposed and irreconcilable cultures of the North and the South.
34 See Weaver, *The Southern Tradition at Bay*, 41, 231–275.
35 Ibid., 30.
36 Although it lies well outside the scope of the present essay, it would be interesting to consider the other side of Weaver's celebratory medievalism by looking at Eugene D. Genovese's *Roll Jordan, Roll: The World the Slaves Made* (New York: Random House, 1974). Genovese also identifies a patriarchal, paternalistic society in which religion or religiosity played a crucial role, but he focuses attention on the essential contributions of the slaves in forming this distinctively Southern culture. Genovese, then a Marxist historian influenced by Antonio Gramsci, among others, later became a notoriously conservative thinker in his own right, a shift that coincided—perhaps not coincidentally?—with his growing interest in the Agrarians of the *I'll Take My Stand* era, which culminated in a book whose title could have come directly from Weaver's own pen: see Genovese, *The Southern Tradition: The Achievement and Limitations of an American Conservatism* (Cambridge: Harvard University Press, 1994).
37 Weaver, *The Southern Tradition at Bay*, 55–57.
38 Ibid., 259. Being "won away" is, for Weaver, a sign of the servant's delusion. Indeed, this line follows directly from a section which concluded that "the blacks suffered as much maltreatment as the whites, the [Union] soldiery being as ready to snatch the silver watch of the slave as the gold one of his master" (258).
39 Ibid., 261.

40 Ibid., 173. Weaver lists a number of postbellum incidents, including "disturbing reports of Negro voodooism," as evidence that Black people in the South, now lacking the beneficial effects of a civilizing servitude, would "soon relapse into savagery" (261–262).
41 Incidentally, Weaver's overall assessment of women's rights is not much more salutary than his position on civil rights for persons of color, at least with respect to the decline of the West. In *Ideas Have Consequences*, Weaver laments that, although "[w]omen would seem to be the natural ally in any campaign to reverse" the anti-chivalric modern trends that have rendered Western civilization so spiritually vacant, in fact, they have not. "After the gentlemen went, the lady had to go too. No longer protected, the woman now has her career, in which she makes a drab pilgrimage from two-room apartment to job to divorce court" (180). Without chivalry, Weaver concludes, there can be no ladies.
42 See *The Southern Tradition at Bay*, 268.
43 Ibid., 36–37.
44 Ibid., 35.
45 Quoted in Alexander P. Lamis, "The Two-Party South: From the 1960s to the 1990s," in *Southern Politics in the 1990s*, ed. Alexander P. Lamis (Baton Rouge: Louisiana State University Press, 1999), 8.
46 Contrast this view with the lament by which Albert D. Kirwan chooses to conclude his near-contemporaneous, 1951 study of postbellum Mississippi politics: "As for the Negro, whose presence in such large numbers in Mississippi has given such a distinctive influence to its politics, his lot did not change throughout this period. No one thought of him save to hold him down. No one sought to improve him. [...] He was and is the neglected man in Mississippi, though not the forgotten man." See Kirwan, *The Revolt of the Rednecks: Mississippi Politics, 1875–1925* (Gloucester: Peter Smith, 1964), 314.
47 Weaver, *Ideas Have Consequences*, 132. Thoreau seems to be the one Yankee whom Weaver is willing to consider a non-barbarian. See also *The Southern Tradition at Bay*, 41: "Southerners apply the term 'Yankee' as the Greeks did 'barbarian.' The kinship of ideas cannot be overlooked."
48 Space does not permit a full consideration of the matter, but Weaver's embrace of a certain Southern "non-creedal religiosity" would not necessarily seem to fit easily with the rise of the religious right in the 1980s and beyond, particularly when considering the prominence of certain denominations and organization, like the Southern Baptist Convention, in political and cultural debates of recent decades. However, one might also recognize the apparently Southern accent with which must of the new political religiosity has been voiced on a national level, which suggests another aspect of the australization of American politics.
49 Paul A. Bové, *A More Conservative Place: Intellectual Culture in the Bush Era* (Hanover: Dartmouth College Press, 2013), 10.
50 Bill Clinton, then Governor of Arkansas, made his name nationally as the Chairman of the Democratic Leadership Council, an organization founded in the aftermath of the 1984 Reagan re-election landslide. The D.L.C. was established the express aim of promoting more conservative policies within the Party and nationally, and its leadership largely consisted of politicians from Southern states, not coincidentally.
51 Cash, *The Mind of the South*, 428–429.
52 Ibid., 429.
53 Weaver, "The South and the American Union," in *The Southern Essays of Richard M. Weaver*, 256.

Chapter 9

BLEEPING MARK TWAIN?: CENSORSHIP, *HUCKLEBERRY FINN*, AND THE FUNCTIONS OF LITERATURE

Adventures of Huckleberry Finn is perhaps the most famous, most beloved, and most controversial novel featuring a prominent Black character and written by a white author. Extremely popular in its own day and in the decades that followed, Mark Twain's novel became one of the most holy of the canonical texts of American literature once mid-twentieth-century critics discovered in it the key to the American experience and an uplifting illustration of the American spirit. When the influential critic Lionel Trilling, in *The Liberal Imagination*, asserted that Huck Finn and Jim formed a "community of saints," he effectively established the novel as national monument.[1] However, the eupeptic effect of *Adventures of Huckleberry Finn* on the body politic is not as indisputable as many of its apologists would have it, and during the last forty years controversies have arisen over use of the novel in the classroom, particularly given the frequent appearance in the book of a well-known, and offensive, racial epithet. The story is presented as a meandering and quixotic tale of a poor, white boy and his boon companion, a runaway slave, as they make their way down river, deeper and deeper into the slave-holding South, until they reach a problematic but seemingly happy ending, in which the adventures come to an abrupt end with Tom Sawyer and Huck Finn playing a dangerous game with Jim. It is then discovered that, unbeknownst to both Huck and his companion, Jim had already been set free, and so he was not a runaway slave after all, at which point Jim almost disappears from the text entirely. Twain's Mississippi River odyssey, with its local color and vaudeville-styled humor, is narrated by Huck himself, who manages to refer to Jim and to all African Americans by one of the most offensive terms in the modern English language, and he does so over two hundred times in a relatively short book. For many readers, particularly in a classroom setting, the *Adventures of Huckleberry Finn* is therefore a work that causes embarrassment, pain, and resentment. As a hypercanonized text, one that has been frequently included as required reading not only in college courses, but also in high school and even earlier, Twain's 1884–85 novel continues to be a crucial site for discussions of race in the United States today.

The controversy over a modified, some would say Bowdlerized, expurgated, or even censored, edition of *Adventures of Huckleberry Finn* raises once more the question of censorship and of the functions of literature, more generally.[2] Edited by Alan Gribben, an established Mark Twain scholar who teaches at Auburn University at Montgomery, in Alabama, the NewSouth Edition notoriously substitutes what Gribben considers to be less offensive "synonyms" for Twain's original racial epithets, of which the *N-word* is both the most pervasively used term in the novel and the least acceptable in civil discourse today. (A caveat to the reader: I will use the offensive word in the body of the text below, but only in direct quotations, some of which come from books routinely given to schoolchildren as required reading.) Predictably, following the publication of the NewSouth Edition in 2011, a public outcry arose against it. Mark Twain's would-be defenders lashed out against the "censorship," as they rushed to the apparent rescue of a literary masterpiece which was thought to be imperiled by yet another "politically correct" assault. Ironically, Gribben's own justification of the project of this NewSouth Edition is, in part, that it might help to *save* the great American novel by making it more suitable for classroom use in high schools or colleges. Gribben feared that, without a less offensive alternative, the near-omnipresence of such an inflammatory and controversial word might otherwise keep *Huckleberry Finn* off the syllabus. In the cases of both Gribben's expurgations and the defense of Twain's original language, an implicit question is, what is the function of a work of literature, both in the classroom and in the world beyond.

Before examining the controversy over the NewSouth Edition of *Huckleberry Finn* further, I would like to begin with a brief autobiographical anecdote, and I promise to keep it well under 500,000 words (i.e., the length of Twain's own recently published, unabridged autobiography). It occurs to me that I did not read the *Adventures of Huckleberry Finn* in high school; or, rather, I read it on my own during those years, but it was never an assigned text. I entered ninth grade in 1982, the same year that John Wallace, an African American teacher at the Mark Twain Intermediate School in Fairfax, Virginia, famously (or infamously) condemned *Huckleberry Finn* as "racist trash."[3] I do not know if my high school or its teachers made any deliberate decision to avoid *Huckleberry Finn*, but I can imagine that the controversial repetition of the *N-word* might have made both teachers and students uncomfortable. This would have been in what was then thought of as a fairly progressive region of the "New South" (yes!), North Carolina, and more particularly a somewhat urban, industrial, or technological locale, in the Piedmont region of that state, and Winston-Salem specifically. Although the area was, and remains, quite conservative politically, most of its citizens regardless of ethnicity would most likely pride themselves on their enlightened attitudes toward race and race relations, and no one at my high school would have embraced the rhetoric of racial bigotry openly. Thus, I can imagine that it is at least possible that the presence of the *N-word* might have discouraged use of Twain's novel in the classroom.

One book that was in the ninth-grade classroom, both for me and for nearly everyone I know, was William Golding's haunting little novel from 1954, *The Lord of the Flies*. In the unforgettable, climactic moment of that book, the young heroes Piggy and Ralph approach the camp of the "wild boys," and Piggy, entreating them to embrace the mores of civilized society once more, makes this heartfelt plea: "Which is better—to be a pack of painted Indians like you are, or to be sensible like Ralph is?"[4] At least, that is how the line reads in the copy we were given. In the terrific 1963 film adaptation, Piggy's line is slightly different: "Which is better—to be a pack of painted savages like you are, or to be sensible like Ralph is?" However, in the 1954 original, the same line reads as follows: "Which is better—to be a pack of painted niggers like you are, or to be sensible like Ralph is?" Somehow, my edition was expurgated, with the term "Indian" replacing the incendiary *N-word*. In other words, someone had Bowdlerized this passage, substituting "Indians" for a more offensive term, but one which was also apparently intended to refer to a similar though distinct sort of "savage." (Let us leave aside for the moment the proposition that the phrase "painted Indians" might be offensive as well.) One other note about my *Lord of the Flies* experience in high school: nowhere in my volume does it say that anything in the novel has been altered. The copyright date is still listed as 1954, and there is no evidence that the author himself, an editor, or the publisher might have emended any part of the text. I am not sure just who, but *someone* had protected me and my fellow (American) pupils from an offensive word, without comment and apparently without any controversy at all.[5]

Admittedly, one single use of the *N-word* is easier to replace, to "bleep" out or to alter, hundreds of uses, and a logic of comparative "savagery" or of comparative terminological offensiveness would not really rescue *Huckleberry Finn* from the discomfort of schoolchildren, their teachers, or parents. The NewSouth Edition edited by Gribben substitutes the word "slave" for the nearly ubiquitous *N-word*. (It also substitutes "Indian" for the more offensive *Injun* and "half-blood" for *half-breed*, an odd choice, but Gribben credits J. K. Rowling's *Harry Potter and the Half-Blood Prince* for giving that term "a degree of panache" [14].) This editorial decision is obviously fraught with other problems, as I will discuss in a moment, but the intent behind the choice is clearly to make the novel more amenable to schoolteachers and more likely to be read by schoolchildren, both in middle schools and in high schools, and perhaps also at the collegiate level. To put it another way, Gribben's aim is to make a text with "adult" language available to minors who would not, and perhaps should not, be exposed to that sort of diction at that particular time in their lives.

Leslie Fiedler famously suggested that the classics of American literature had come to be seen as children's literature, more particularly "boys' books."[6] Fiedler was thinking of the intrigue and warfare of James Fenimore Cooper's *The Last of the Mohicans*, the sea voyages of Richard Henry Dana's *Two Years Before the Mast* and Herman Melville's *Moby-Dick*, and above all Twain's *Adventures of Huckleberry Finn*, in which the youthful hero narrates his odyssey through a lawless wilderness. Of course, few or none of these writers intended that their audience be limited to, or even include, children, and Fiedler acknowledges this irony when he writes that modern American life seems typified by "its implacable nostalgia for the infantile, at once wrong-headed and somehow admirable."[7] Just as so many Americans long to be youthful, in looks or energy-levels or some perceived innocence, perhaps we want to turn our mature literature back into child's play. But, as we sometimes rediscover on closer inspection, not everything in our library is suitable for all audiences.

The NewSouth edition controversy over the use of *that word* in the *Adventures of Huckleberry Finn* highlights the interactions among writing, editing, teaching, and reading, and this serves as a point of entry into a discussion of the function of literature itself. What is literature? How ought it be used? For many, works like *Huckleberry Finn* are themselves primary and fundamental texts for both enjoying and studying literature, inasmuch as the delights as well as the lessons of the novel spark an interest in further reading. Since its publication in 2011, Gribben's NewSouth Edition has been roundly criticized by scholars and laypersons alike, primarily because of its substitution of the word *slave* for the almost ubiquitous *N-word*. And the word-substitutions do seem like a misguided attempt to clean up Huck's, and Twain's, language. However, as Gribben explains, the intent of this "censorship," as it is most often called, is to expand the readership and extend the influence of the novel. In fact, far from being an "attack" on an American classic, this edition is intended to save *Huckleberry Finn* from the oblivion to which it is destined, as more and more teachers refuse to include the novel on their reading lists. In his introduction, Gribben emphatically endorses the use of other, non-expurgated versions, and he specifically urges scholars to use other editions, but he insists that this NewSouth Edition is intended to bring new and younger readers to Twain's masterpiece. Most scholars and teachers of American literature would consider this a worthy goal. The question, then, is whether this form of "censorship" is an appropriate way to achieve such a goal.

Gribben's introduction straightforwardly explains the alterations in the text, as well as the rationale behind them, and Gribben explicitly directs "academic" readers to the "magisterial edition" produced by "the Mark Twain Project at Berkeley" (16). This honest acknowledgment and helpful guidance for more mature readers is welcome, I should think. This strikes me as far, far less of a sin against literature than the Orwellian erasure of history that occurs when Piggy warns against behaving like "painted Indians" in *The Lord of the Flies*, with no footnote or explanation concerning what had been altered.

Hence, the intent behind the NewSouth Edition, if not the execution, is mostly commendable. Despite the understandable outcry of voices condemning NewSouth's and Gribben's literary crimes against Mark Twain, we all know that it is not uncommon to "bleep" parts of even great works of art when the audience includes minors. For example, if *The Godfather*—to name what is often viewed as one of the greatest films in the history of American cinema—can have its dialogue altered and its brief nudity excised in order to make it suitable for television, then there is no inherent reason why *Huckleberry Finn* could not have its PG-rated version available in grade school, so long as the original can still be enjoyed elsewhere. Surely the "classic" works of American filmmaking deserve their own respect, and the films ought to have aesthetic integrity preserved, yet most of us will understand that certain words and images may be deemed unsuitable for this or that audience, and we can make allowances accordingly. This brouhaha over the expurgated version of *Huckleberry Finn* again raises the question of how appropriate certain "classic" works of American literature may be for teenaged students. The publisher's rationale, in part, is that this edition will be more suitable for high school and college students embarrassed (or worse) by the repeated use of the offensive term. This is why Lorrie Moore, who is no fan of the NewSouth Edition, wants *Huckleberry Finn* to go to, and remain in, college.[8]

In this as in other controversies over the novel, some of Twain's would-be defenders have rolled out the old arguments about the sanctity of literature, the "realistic" language of the time, and the book's generally salutary depiction of a poor white boy and an African American man as bosom companions. In this effort, they sometimes overlook the textual and historical evidence that makes these positions much more problematic than they appear. Further, as Jonathan Arac pointed out in his *Huckleberry Finn as Idol and Target*,[9] such arguments frequently pit (largely white) persons of ostensible goodwill against (largely Black) students, teachers, and parents, who are told that they are ignorant or that they are plain wrong for not whole-heartedly endorsing the required reading of the book—a book, I might note, which could not possibly be read aloud, word-for-word, on primetime network television.

Defending Twain's use of the *N-word*, rather ironically, has sometimes meant forcing it upon the very people most hurt by its use.

Anyone who teaches early American literature regularly encounters the *N-word* in print. In the main, however, students reading these texts are seldom encouraged to sympathize or to identify with the utterer of the word, as they are likely to be when Huck uses it. The *N-word* appears a few times in *The Adventures of Tom Sawyer*, but that book is narrated by an omniscient and sometimes ironic third-person narrator, not by the actual hero of the story. A handful of Edgar Allan Poe's narrators use the term—surprisingly few, in fact—but readers never confuse any Poe narrator with a representative figure of a distinctively American national culture. In Frederick Douglass, it appears as a dirty word, used only by those whom the intended reader is invited to revile. Quite unlike many other such characters, Huck, while narrating his own story and using this word on nearly every page, is rarely seen as an odd-ball rube who doesn't know any better, which, after all, may have been closer to Twain's original intent, but as the heroic and iconic American whom all students should applaud. Not only is Huck not "wrong," but he is celebrated for being "right," a person to admire and even emulate. This can cause discomfort for many students, African American or not, who are suddenly told that the offensive term is not only acceptable in this context, but implicitly authorized by their teacher, by their school, and by the institution of American literature itself.

As James S. Leonard and Thomas Asa Tenney note in *Satire or Evasion?: Black Perspectives on 'Huckleberry Finn'*,

> it goes without saying that the word was at the time of Twain's writing, and remains today, a slap in the face for black Americans. It is inevitable that black children in a classroom with whites should feel uncomfortable with a word and a book in which it appears so often, and that black parents should wish to protect their children from what the word represents.[10]

And, as Arac notes with some dismay, the institution of American literary criticism, particularly in its public face in newspapers and magazines, is at least as much to blame as the original text. Reviews appearing in such mainstream organs as the *New York Times* and the *Washington Post* have perpetuated a false impression of both the novel and the *N-word*, often to the detriment of concerned teachers, students, and parents, "who find themselves pained, offended, or frightened by the permission *Huckleberry Finn* gives to the circulation of an abusive term in the classroom and schoolyard."[11] Arac is referring in part to the long-standing critical usage of the name

"Nigger Jim" to refer to the principal African American character in the novel. Astonishingly, given their apparently anti-racist positions and generally liberal political leanings, critics and writers such as Lionel Trilling, Leslie Fieldler, C. Vann Woodward, Perry Miller, Harold Beaver, and Norman Mailer (among scores of others), have had no compunction about employing this moniker *even though* the phrase never appears in the *Adventures of Huckleberry Finn* at all. Let me repeat that: the phrase "Nigger Jim," used by critics and scholars and writers for over 70 years and presumably on the putative authority of Mark Twain himself, *never* appears in the novel. Not once.

The NewSouth Edition's attempt to ameliorate such problems in the text of *Huckleberry Finn*, while not wholly laudable, is therefore at least understandable and reasonable. Furthermore, it is certainly not the first attempt. The publishing house of Harper & Brothers released a 1931 edition, according to Robert B. Brown, "specially prepared to let 'Huck [...] step down from his place on the library shelf and enter the classroom.'"[12] And ironically, the central complaint in a 1957 controversy in New York was that an edition of *Huckleberry Finn* did not capitalize the word "Negro," a word that does not actually appear in Twain's original text.[13] Apparently, as with my own experience with *The Lord of the Flies* in the 1980s, the New York students were already getting an expurgated version, unbeknownst to them.

Still, although I think that its goals are praiseworthy in the main, I cannot endorse the NewSouth Edition, since its means for achieving these aims are ham-fisted and sometimes outright stupid. Gribben has chosen to replace the *N-word* with the word "slave," which (astoundingly!) he claims is a "synonym," as if he cannot imagine an African American person living in the antebellum era could be a free man or woman, a surmise rather obviously overturned by the merest glance at the historical record. Indeed, Gribben seems to have temporarily forgotten that the most prominent African American character in *Huckleberry Finn* is *himself* a free man! Hence, we must grit out teeth through the nonsense of this famous (now-revised) line from the novel's denouement: "so, sure enough, Tom Sawyer had gone and took all that trouble and bother to set a free slave free!" (517). Slavery and racism in the United States are related, but quite distinct, matters, and the *N-word* certainly did not go away after abolition, as Gribben knows all too well. The offensive epithet was applied to Jim in the book regardless of his status with respect to ownership. While Twain notoriously cautioned the illustrator of *Huckleberry Finn*, E. W. Kimble, not to make Huck look "too Irishy," for instance, Jim's looks had nothing whatsoever to do with his bondage or his freedom, and neither did the word with which his friend Huck constantly refers to him.

In fact, one could argue that Gribben's decision to conflate the historical condition of antebellum slavery with the seemingly perpetual problem of racism does *more* damage than the original, bigoted language of the novel was doing. Gribben cites a well-known moment in the text where Huck, disguised as Tom, lies to Sally Phelps, telling her that the steamboat "blowed out a cylinder-head," which leads to the following exchange:

"Good gracious! anybody hurt?"
"No'm. Killed a slave."
"Well, it's lucky; because sometimes people do get hurt." (453)[14]

Referring to this scene, Gribben explains that "the synonym 'slave' expresses the cultural racism that Twain sought to convey" (13). However, common sense alone suggests that Gribben is incorrect here. Were a "slave" to have been killed, then someone's valuable property would have been lost, and the tragedy of the accident, at least in the mind of Sally Phelps, presumably would be enhanced. By switching the terms, Gribben has lessened the power of any potential critique of racism that Twain (dubiously, in my view) may have had in mind. For example, Sacvan Bercovitch, pointing to the exact same spot in *Huckleberry Finn*, notes that Huck's use of the *N-word* is "profoundly racist" here. Observing the "full-stop" between Huck's "No'm" and "Killed a ...", Bercovitch writes: "We can't argue (as too many critics have) that it's just slang—a poor, ignorant boy's way of saying African American. What Huck *means* is far worse than what a bigot means by 'wop' or 'wasp.' Huck is saying that a 'nigger' is a *no one*, a nonhuman." Huck's use of the term here is also entirely gratuitous; "Huck could have just as well stopped at 'No'm.'" The term was a "vicious slur," in the 1880s as today—for Huck, for Twain, for contemporary readers, and for other readers up to the Civil Rights movement.[15] No, the word "slave" is not, *in any way*, a synonym for the far more offensive and still incendiary word uttered throughout in Twain's novel.

As is well known even among high school students, by the 1880s the question of abolition in the United States was settled, and chattel slavery no longer had serious proponents or apologists in the mainstream social and political spheres. Thus, Huck Finn's "decision" to "go to Hell" by electing not to return Jim to bondage was unlikely to be considered a controversial or even difficult choice by the contemporary reader. (This, despite how much some critics have wished to turn that scene into a moment of great racial and moral triumph, while conveniently forgetting an earlier scene in which Huck expressed his preference for Hell over Heaven, given what he was taught about each place.) However, the bigoted perspective that sees a person who is referred to by the *N-word* as inferior to whites or even as not-wholly-human *has* persisted long after abolition, and this is the world in which the *Adventures of Huckleberry Finn* circulates. Owing to the NewSouth Edition's flat-out foolishness in confusing race and slavery, I would not use this edition in a college-level class, and I would advise against its use in grade schools as well. But, in sum, it is not the NewSouth Edition's so-called "censorship" that makes the project objectionable, but the specific means chosen.

Twain's heirs in comedic and incisive satire have found ways to use the mechanisms of censorship to their advantage. I think that television satires, for instance, *The Daily Show* or *The Colbert Report*, are very much in the tradition of modern American humor that Twain helped to establish, and these shows routinely use those seven words that George Carlin taught us cannot be uttered on television.[16] They "get away with it," as we know, by "bleeping" the words. The use of the bleep does not really erase the word entirely—that is, we all know what word is being bleeped—but the offensiveness is somehow mitigated. It would become very frustrating to have to hear that bleeping sound over two hundred times over the course of *Huckleberry Finn*, I readily concede, but it might still be preferable to the hundreds of instances of a word that even the fiercest defenders of the novel would hesitate to use in polite company, if at all.

The very existence of the silly term I have been using, the *N-word*, demonstrates the degree to which this is true. As Arac points out, the term *N-word* gained popular currency during the O. J. Simpson trial, when Deputy District Attorney Christopher Darden argued that admitting into evidence Detective Mark Fuhrman's use of "the filthiest, dirtiest, nastiest word in the English language" would "blind the jury."[17] As Arac observes, "many broadcast media bleeped out Fuhrman's use of the term, and *USA Today* would not print the term even in their front-page story revealing the contents of the Fuhrman tapes." Arac then asks pointedly, "should people of goodwill unhesitatingly maintain that a word banned from CNN and *USA Today* must be required in the eighth-grade schoolroom?"[18]

Of course, I'm not really suggesting that a textual equivalent of the "bleep" should be inserted in place of the *N-word* in the *Adventures of Huckleberry Finn*, only that the sort of "censorship" we see in the NewSouth Edition is actually done all the time, with no real damage done to the original, to the reader, or to the institution of literature itself. Undoubtedly many young readers can profitably read the unexpurgated *Huckleberry Finn*, as well as *Moby-Dick*, *The Scarlet Letter*, and other great and complex books, just as they could watch great films like *Chinatown* or *Raging Bull*, but whether they should do so might be another question, and whether all schoolchildren should be required to do so is a different matter entirely. Perhaps *Huckleberry Finn* does belong in college, as Lorrie Moore suggests, but if a PG or PG-13 version can be used in the high schools, so much the better.[19]

This is less a question of censorship than a question of how we wish for literature to function in culture and society more broadly. Are these texts to be worshipped as idols, which *Huckleberry Finn* has most certainly become for some, or can they become active participants in a vibrant, changing social milieu? My own terminology and phrasing give me away, of course, as I find the value of Twain's novel to lie not in our scrupulous attention to a boy's repetition of a naughty word but in the narrative's ability to help us imagine new and more interesting ways of seeing ourselves (white, Black, and other) and the world we live in. Just because Huck himself wished to avoid being "sivilized" doesn't mean we or our students need to do so.

Notes

1 Lionel Trilling, *The Liberal Imagination: Essays on Literature and Society* (New York: Doubleday, 1950), 104, 106.
2 See Alan Gribben, ed. *Mark Twain's Adventures of Tom Sawyer and Huckleberry Finn* (Montgomery: NewSouth Books, 2011). Unless otherwise noted, all references to *Huckleberry Finn* and to Gribben's "Editor's Introduction" cited parenthetically in the text will be to this edition.
3 See Molly Moore, "Behind the Attack on 'Huck Finn': One Angry Educator," *Washington Post*, Metro Section (April 21, 1982): 1. Wallace went on to publish his own edition of the novel, which removed all instances of both the *N-word* and, for reasons presumably unrelated to racism, the word "Hell."
4 William Golding, *The Lord of the Flies* [1954] (New York: Perigree, 1959), 180.
5 I believe that only the American editions were changed in this manner. As far as I can tell, in the United Kingdom and in Commonwealth nations, the phrase "painted niggers" remained. For example, in the *Encyclopedia of Censorship*, Jonathan Green notes that, according to the Canadian Library Association, in 1988 "parents and members of the black community objected to a reference to 'niggers' and said it denigrates blacks"; see Green, *Encyclopedia of Censorship*, Nicholas J. Karolides, rev. ed. (New York: Facts-on-File, Inc., 2005), 331.
6 Leslie Fiedler, "Come Back to the Raft Ag'in, Huck Honey!" in Steven G. Kellman and Irving Malin, eds., *Leslie Fielder and American Culture* (Cranbury, NJ: Associated University Presses, 1999), 28. Fieldler's "Come Back to the Raft Ag'in, Huck Honey!" was originally published in the *Partisan Review* in 1948. It may be worth noting that the phrase used as the title appears nowhere in *Huckleberry Finn* itself.
7 Fiedler, "Come Back to the Raft Ag'in," 27.
8 See Lorrie Moore, "Send Huck to College," *New York Times* (January 16, 2011): WK12.
9 See Jonathan Arac, *Huckleberry Finn as Idol and Target: The Functions of Criticism in Our Time* (Madison: University of Wisconsin Press, 1997).
10 James S. Leonard, Thomas A. Tenney, and Thadious M. Davis, eds., *Satire or Evasion?: Black Perspectives on 'Huckleberry Finn'* (Durham: Duke University Press, 1992), 5.
11 Arac, *Huckleberry Finn as Idol and Target*, 30.
12 Robert B. Brown, "One Hundred Years of Huck Finn," *American Heritage* (June–July 1985), 84.
13 See Arac, *Huckleberry Finn as Idol and Target*, 63–66.
14 Needless to say, in Twain's original, Huck says "No'm. Killed a nigger."

15 See Sacvan Bercovitch, "Deadpan Huck, or, What's Funny about Interpretation," *The Kenyon Review*, New Series, Vol. 24, No. 3/4 (Summer–Autumn 2002): 106–108.
16 See, e.g., my "I am the Mainstream Media (and So Can You!)" in Amarnath Amarasingam, ed., *The Stewart/Colbert Effect: Essays on the Real Impact of Fake News* (Jefferson: McFarland, 2011), 149–63. Also, since 1998, the John F. Kennedy Center for the Performing Arts has awarded the Mark Twain Prize for American Humor, whose recipients have now included George Carlin and Jon Stewart, the longtime host of *The Daily Show*.
17 See David Margolick, "Simpson Judge Delays Trial Opening and Will Allow Questioning of Detective on Bias," *New York Times*, January 24, 1995: A16.
18 Arac, *Huckleberry Finn as Idol and Target*, 24.
19 Needless to say, perhaps, but it has often been done, and in many cases without "censorship" charges being leveled at the author or publisher. For example, I first read Agatha Christie's bestselling novel *And Then There Were None* (1939) in high school, only to learn that it had also been called *Ten Little Indians*, and even that was an accommodation intended for the U.S. marketplace, for elsewhere it had appeared under its original title *Ten Little Niggers*, under which title it continued to appear in the U.K. until 1985.

Chapter 10

I AM THE MAINSTREAM MEDIA (AND SO CAN YOU!): THE HYPERREALITY OF "FAKE NEWS"

On its February 10, 2010 broadcast, *The Daily Show with Jon Stewart*[1] opened with a satirical monologue in which Stewart explored the possible slogans that a "fake news" program on the Comedy Central television network might use in covering the day's leading story, a massive snowstorm blanketing the eastern seaboard of the United States. Employing what should be recognized as nonsense words appropriate to such a venue (and, by contrast, words that should be entirely inappropriate for "real news" programs), Stewart begins to introduce the terms *Snowmageddon, Snowpocalypse,* and eventually *Snowtorious B.I.G.*,[2] only to be cut off each time by clips of other mainstream network news shows—on CNN, NBC, and MSNBC—using those very words. A mock-chagrined Stewart bemoans the fact that mainstream news channels (the "big boys"), with their greater financial and meteorological resources, have usurped what should have been the birthright of comedy writers on *The Daily Show.*

The humor in this bit, as with similar segments on almost every other episode of the program, derives from the powerful critique of the mainstream media: What is funny about the piece is not so much *The Daily Show*'s own writing or comedian Jon Stewart's performance (although these certainly enhance the experience), but rather that the so-called "real news" programs are so ridiculous. To use phrases like *Snowmageddon* or *Snowpocalypse* in a serious news broadcast, with real news to cover, should be viewed as unprofessional, if not shameful. But, far from it, such silliness had by now the actual stuff of mainstream television news. Stewart's fake news is funny *because* of its trenchant exposure of just how silly real news actually is. As Jeffrey P. Jones has put it, "As a parody of television news shows, it skewers the absurdity and contradictions that pass for 'news'."[3] The key point is not that satirical, fake news is taken as seriously as real news (although hard evidence, as well as hue and cry, suggest it is),[4] but that all "news" has become transformed into entertainment-television that no longer bears much, if any, relation to the "real." The social significance of fake news programs like *The Daily Show* and *The Colbert Report* is disclosed in their assiduous critique, not of the news itself—that is, the underlying reality or story (e.g., in the example above, the February snowstorm)—but of the purported agents of journalistic information-dissemination: the news programs themselves. From the fake news' critique of the real news, one recognizes the hyperreality of the news more generally.

Welcome to the Plenum of the Fake

One can see this clearly in the very form of both Comedy Central programs, *The Daily Show* and its spin-off *The Colbert Report*,[5] produced in mockery of real news shows, yet they are almost entirely faithful replicas of the sort of fare to be found on CNN and Fox News. The satirical simulacrum is nevertheless absolutely authentic, as it happens. In his *Travels in Hyperreality*, Umberto Eco writes that America is "a country obsessed with realism, where, if a reconstruction is to be credible, it must be absolutely iconic, a perfect likeness, a 'real' copy of the reality being represented."[6] This ostensible realism functions equally well for satirical or for more reverent simulations, illustrating Eco's (and Jean Baudrillard's) celebrated notion of *hyperreality*, in which the simulacrum supplants the real by acquiring a kind of experiential authenticity or, perhaps, by showing that there's no such thing. In the hyperreal, the "authentic fake" takes on a reality far more salient than the reality itself, all the more so for being fake. In a ruse of history, perhaps, the idea that fake news, *by being fake*, is actually more real than real news—at least, as it appears on television, an already vexed medium-that-is-also an industry, as Sidney Lumet's then timely but increasingly haunting 1976 film *Network* demonstrates all too vividly—is not only possible, but now seems likely.

The Daily Show and *The Colbert Report* seem humorously apt examples of the hyperreality of fake news, but part of their aptness lies in the effectiveness of their critical agenda. Satire in the form of news is not new, but Comedy Central's duo has become a much more socially significant force, not just poking fun at figures *in* the news, but launching a full-scale attack on the media and the messages simultaneously.[7] Earlier examples of "fake news" include Monty Python's frequent use of the format, along with *Saturday Night Live*'s "Weekend Update," and Canada's *This Hour Has 22 Minutes*, just to name a few. However, in most cases, these programs have presented themselves in the formal raiment of a news show in order to engage in topical humor about items or figures *in* the news (e.g., politicians, celebrities, or events). But this critique of the newsmakers did not usually include a critique of the news-reporters, except perhaps by implication or in cases of comedic impersonation of particular individuals (Gilda Radner spoofing Barbara Walters ["Baba Wawa"], for example). *The Daily Show* and *The Colbert Report*, by contrast, explicitly make the critique of the mainstream media their principal aim; in Colbert's case, this satire of the mainstream media reaches its apotheosis.

A good demonstration of the difference between satire using the fake news format and the more thoroughgoing social critique of the media in these two fake news programs might be seen in the remarkable transformation of *The Daily Show* after its change of hosts. Whereas Craig Kilborn's *Daily Show* was a lighthearted spoof, mainly of local television news shows, which added political humor and sidebar "on location" reports of various characters and oddities, Jon Stewart's was a national and international force, shaping the debates while participating in and poking fun at them, and above all displaying a critical disdain for the very "real" television journalists covering the stories for the cable and broadcast news networks. With Stewart, *The Daily Show* has become a better comedy by also becoming a more *real* fake news show, especially in the sense that it has significant effects on the so-called "real world."[8] *The Colbert Report* goes even further, as it allows Stephen Colbert to adopt the persona of a right-wing pundit, thereby dropping any pretense to objective television journalism, which in turn makes possible an even more savage critique of politics and the media. In Colbert's monologues, even the spoken critique carries with it a further critique: a metacritique or hypercritique, whose on-screen spirit is made manifest in the marginal gloss accompanying Colbert's "The Word" segment. The nonsense of Colbert's book-title, *I Am America (and So Can You!)* embodies the greater sense of immanent social critique, precisely because Colbert can attack the very thing he purports to be, which is a hyperreal personage: the fake newsman who is more real than the supposedly mainstream journalists.

The hyperreality of these fake news programs is not based on the much vaunted or much maligned, and largely dubious, proposition that some people "get their news" from Stewart or Colbert. Rather, what is hyperreal about the shows is that they dramatically enact the underlying critique of the media by showing that the mainstream news is itself altogether artificial, constructed according to formulae and processes easily decoded by comedy writers and attentive viewers. *The Daily Show* and *The Colbert Report* thus shape the social field even as they lampoon it. Above all, these programs impress upon the viewers the profound sense that the mainstream media's real news is not much more real than its satirical or parodic copies. Hence, the distinction between the real and the fake begins to recede, and the television-information nexus reveals itself to be little more than a critical apprehension of various sorts of simulations, some in the form of breathless coverage of a "balloon boy hoax" on CNN, others in the form of mock-breathless accounts of "the threat of global darkening" on *The Daily Show*. This is not so much *the desert of the real*, in Baudrillard's infamous phrase, (1994, 1), as *the plenum of the fake*.[9]

In suggesting that television news, whether understood as fake or real, is actually hyperreal, I do not really mean to say that it comports directly with the semiological meaning of the term. However, I do think that certain aspects of the notion of hyperreality are revealing in the context of the social significance of fake news. In his notorious essay, "The Precession of Simulacra," Baudrillard delineates the process by which the representation of reality withers away in what Guy Debord had notoriously called the "society of the spectacle."[10] Baudrillard's examination of the *image* (that is, the purported representation of reality) offers a view of the image produced by and in the news as well. Baudrillard lists and interprets "the successive phases of the image" as follows:

> it is the reflection of a profound reality;
> it masks and denatures a profound reality;
> it masks the absence of a profound reality;
> it has no relation to any reality whatsoever: it is its own pure simulacrum.
> In the first case, the image is a *good* appearance—representation is of a sacramental order. In the second, it is an evil appearance—it is of the order of maleficence. In the third, it plays at being an appearance—it is of the order of sorcery. In the fourth, it is no longer of the order of appearances, but of simulation.[11]

In the context of fake news and the social significance thereof, one could add that one of the key things that *The Daily Show with Jon Stewart* and *The Colbert Report* do, on an almost nightly basis, is guide their viewers through just this process, substituting the mainstream media's news imagery for Baudrillard's image.

Examples are simply too numerous to go into, but one can easily see the ways that both shows contrast, say, Fox News' or CNN's presentation of an event with the "reality" of what happened. At this first level, the joke reveals just how incompetent the mainstream news is, as it frequently seems to "get the story wrong," or, in Baudrillard's terms, it does a poor job of "reflecting" the underlying reality. At the next level, the fake news shows may look into the active masking or concealing of reality by purportedly objective news organization, thus allowing fake news to serve the traditional function of ideology-critique, revealing the truth underneath the deliberate or negligent falsehoods of the mainstream media. (For example, in a 2010 episode of *The Daily Show*, Stewart exposed Fox News' use of footage from an entirely different event to make it seem as though more people attended a certain rally in Washington.) In the third case, the fake news shows may reveal that the mainstream media's coverage is of something nonexistent entirely, or perhaps it is coverage of a news item of such little consequence that any coverage is a clear misuse of resources, as with the many "threats" with no substantial menace behind them or the non-news that is celebrity gossip and the like. Finally, there is the inevitable notion of news as a self-perpetuating image-generation machine, in which the very news to be reported is only that of other news reports. This becomes the most vicious of vicious cycles, where the news reports only that others are reporting upon it, back and forth, signifiers without signified, signs without referents.[12] In the end, and this is the most devastating critique leveled by the fake news of *The Daily Show* and *The Colbert Report*, all news is disclosed to be a hyperreality of its own, largely if not completely cut off from any actual and meaningful reality "out there."

Obviously, this is not to say that there is no real news to cover, or that no one actually does any real journalism. The demystifying operations of fake news, *contra* a more properly Baudrillardian analysis, require that there be something real to hold up in opposition to the CNNs, Foxes, MSNBCs and so forth. Stewart and Colbert must bear in mind some real world, if only a proxy for reality, that the mainstream media is somehow misrepresenting, whether through incompetence, lack or conflict of interest, corruption, or what have you. Hence, the phenomenon may not be entirely *hyperreal* in the more technical sense in which the term used by Baudrillard or Eco, but the notion that fake news may serve the journalistic profession more faithfully (and therefore be more "real") than real news leads one to rethink the terms a bit. In Baudrillard's metaphor, drawn from Jorge Luis Borges's famous imperial cartographers whose map was coextensive with the territory it purported to represent, the "territory" of the real news is subsumed by the "map" of its Stewart and Colbert spoofs. Of course, in the society of the spectacle, juiced up even more by the accelerated spectacles available through cable television and the internet, the *real* events that the *real* news program is supposedly covering may be further lost to us the viewers, as we find ourselves deeper and deeper in Plato's cave.

Indeed, the fakery of fake news makes it all the more interesting in its hyperreality. As Eco has pointed out, "Disneyland is more hyper realistic than the wax museum, precisely because the latter still tries to make us believe that what we are seeing reproduces reality absolutely, whereas Disneyland makes it clear that within its magic enclosure it is fantasy that is absolutely reproduced."[13] In this formulation, real news programs present false representations but insist on their representative accuracy, and the fake news of *The Daily Show* and *The Colbert Report* that provides the authentic fakery of the hyperreal.

Yet I also want to suggest that in their hyperrealism, *The Daily Show* and *The Colbert Report* perform that critical function that most real news cannot, or at least is less likely to be able to do than in an earlier epoch. Many apologists for the mainstream news organizations like to imagine that journalists serve a watchdog function, using their investigative powers to uncover wrongdoing and using their information-dissemination media to broadcast the results. In this, as one jeremiad after another has noted in recent years, the decline of the press is directly linked to a decline in democracy, as the sacred role of the Fourth Estate is to maintain vigilance over those in power and to speak to and for those outside of it.[14] This is indeed part of the thrust of Jon Stewart's own notorious appearance on *Crossfire* in October 2004, when he accused the show—and, by implication, all others like it—of ignoring real problems while they instead generated much heat and little light in meaningless partisan squabbling. The comedians' fake news pokes through the pretense of journalistic solemnity, and calls attention to the seemingly hypocritical or self-serving activities of the mainstream media. In a sense, the fake news is able to perform more critical social critique than investigative journalism could in an era of 24-hour news cycles and constant commercial interruption. Perhaps the kitschy, parodic play of the signifiers can (and in this case does) serve as viable social critique; indeed, it can do so better than merely oppositional forms of the actual mainstream media precisely *because* it operates in the form of satirical fake news.[15]

Comedy is no laughing matter, as they say. Although *The Daily Show* and *The Colbert Report* are first and foremost television shows, with audiences to entertain and sponsors to satisfy, they have also exerted no small influence on the political discourse in the United States and abroad. Of course, the same could be said for those other television news programs, which also have audiences to entertain and sponsors to satisfy, and whose ratings tend to far exceed those of comedy shows.[16] What sets the two Comedy Central shows apart, both from other news programs and from other comedy programs, is their profoundly critical spirit. As both Jon Stewart and Stephen Colbert have proved, in many cases this form of critical satire does not necessarily allow itself to be funny, and certainly does not try to appeal to the broadest audiences, as would most shows designed for mere entertainment. The movement from political satire, as ancient as comedy itself, to this immanent critique of the mainstream media itself, has real-world effects. The social significance of these two fake news programs can be illustrated by looking at how *The Daily Show* transformed itself from mere comedy to biting social critique, and at how the persona of Stephen Colbert has disrupted the sign-system of political and media discourse.

From Topical Humor to Fake News: On the Structural Transformation of *The Daily Show*

Using a fake news format to lampoon public figures or to entertain is nothing new. Satire, especially political satire, is well suited to the format of fake news, since the underlying substance of the jokes (i.e., politics, politicians, political issues) are known to the audience largely through the medium of news programming. *Saturday Night Live*'s "Weekend Update," as much a staple of the long-running comedy sketch show as the opening monologue or the musical guest, has had great success in re-presenting the week's key news stories with humorous effects or as set-ups to jokes. To a certain extent, the very form of "Weekend Update" also allows it to poke fun at the television news broadcasts. Sometimes this is explicit, as in Jane Curtin's and Dan Aykroyd's now legendary "Point/Counterpoint" (itself the name of an actual segment of CBS's *60 Minutes* at the time) sketches, and at others it may be implied, as with the deliberately crafted "inane banter" between co-anchors Amy Poehler and Seth Meyers in their era. Yet, in the main, the objects of the show's derision were the people *in* the news, not those broadcasting the news.

A telling example of the formal and substantive difference can be gleaned from the remarkable transformation of *The Daily Show* from its inception in 1996, with Craig Kilborn as its host, to what it then become in the Jon Stewart era (and subsequently). Formally, at least, *The Daily Show* with Craig Kilborn was above all a spoof of *local* news, and its forays into national and international affairs were presented in such a way as to highlight the glib superficiality of a smarmy local-news anchor, rather than with the *gravitas* (a word journalists so love) of a national news anchorman, of a Walter Cronkite, Dan Rather, Tom Brokaw, and others of their ilk. The original *Daily Show* program underscored its resemblance to local news shows by introducing, along with its anchorman, its use of a news van and of such technology as the "TDS 5000 color copier" in parody of local news programs' hype over "eye in the sky" helicopters, Doppler radar, and other technological marvels. Although many of Kilborn's jokes dealt with national news stories—this was the era of the Monica Lewinsky, after all—the overall feel of the show was less *newsy*, and the television-news format was really just a framing device for the joke-telling. The field reports filed by such intrepid journalists as Stephen Colbert himself certainly had little or nothing to do with the "news" presented by Kilborn.[17] *The Daily Show* was actually developed to replace the more topical, and more intelligent, program *Politically Incorrect*, which used a talk show (rather than news) format as the platform for its political satire. In the beginning, *The Daily Show* was set up to allow a bit of topical, political humor on what was manifestly a comedy, not news, program.

The very look of the anchor tells part of the story. Craig Kilborn, a former college basketball player, embodies a stereotype of the tall, blond, handsome all-American boy from the heartland (Minnesota, in fact). He had previously worked as an ESPN *SportsCenter* anchor, and maintained the on-screen persona of an athletic, mischievous frat-boy, a character-type he easily reprised in the film *Old School* (2003). Kilborn's look accentuates the jokes, as the clean-cut, fresh-faced smart-aleck smirks at the news of the day. At about 5'7", with dark hair, projecting himself as a self-conscious (one might even say, self-promotional) Jewish nebbish from New Jersey, Jon Stewart cuts the figure of an anti-Kilborn, the corporeal embodiment of a franchise's "change-of-direction." Although he is also handsome and clean-cut, Stewart's humor frequently comes from the disjunction between the clever but impotent little guy and the larger powers that be (a franchise that Woody Allen has made his stock and trade). Kilborn's boyish Goliath breezily strode alongside and among the powerful, genially giving them "what-for" without concern for the consequences, whereas Stewart's on-screen persona vacillates between cowed underling and outraged outsider, a mouse that might sometimes roar.

More noteworthy in the transformation of *The Daily Show* were the changes to the guest list after Stewart seized the reins, although one might note a bit of a chicken-and-egg conundrum in this, since it is obvious that the increased newsiness of *The Daily Show with Jon Stewart* is both the cause and the result of the greater participation by politicians and others working more directly in the political arena. Nevertheless, during the two years of Craig Kilborn's term as anchorman, not a single politician, government official, or even politically oriented writer or journalist appeared as a guest on the show. Kilborn's guests included actors (Jason Priestly), comedians (Janeane Garofalo), and musicians (Travis Tritt); only one journalist appeared as a guest, Deborah Norville, and Norville's own "news" show (*Inside Edition*), which also focused primarily on the entertainment industry, was not much more newsy than *The Daily Show* itself. In 1999, the year Jon Stewart took over, the guest list remained limited to entertainers, with the possible exception of former Senator Bob Dole, who was thoroughly entertaining during his two-part interview on December 7–8, 1999. By the next year, however, *The Daily Show* devoted an entire episode to a New Hampshire primary (featuring Senator Dole), as well as two full weeks to the Republican and Democratic Party conventions respectively. The show hosted such politically oriented guests as Bob Dole (again), journalists Wolf Blitzer, Sam Donaldson, Peter Jennings, David Frost, and Greta Van Susteren, Senator Arlen Specter, the vice-presidential nominee Joe Lieberman, and consumer advocate and presidential candidate Ralph Nader. Considering Comedy Central's commercial reluctance to allow political positions to be aired for fear of alienating viewers, this was already a leap forward into a much more "real-news-like" fake news show. Of course, space would not permit the listing of "real news" guests on *The Daily Show* in recent years; suffice it to say that in 2009, such guests actually outnumbered those in the strictly-speaking "entertainment industry." (This very fact should offer occasion to question that distinction further, and the result of that questioning might not reveal anything particularly salutary about the contemporary practices of politics or of entertainment.)

The look of the anchor and the type of guests were not the only changes. Much of the substance of the writing changed as well. Referring to his own time as a *Daily Show* correspondent in the Kilborn era, Stephen Colbert noted: "Those were more character-driven pieces. First of all, there were no desk pieces. Correspondents didn't do stuff like editorializing at the desk. The field pieces we did were character-driven pieces—like, you know, guys who believe in Bigfoot. Whereas now [2003], everything is issue- and news-driven pieces, and a lot of editorializing at the desk. And a lot of use of the green screen to put us in false locations."[18] Asked whether the change was a budgetary decision, Colbert emphasized: "No, no, no. It's editorial tone that Jon has changed. We're more of a news show—we were more of a magazine show then."

Colbert also pointed out that Kilborn was not involved with field reports at all; Kilborn did the studio bits, and correspondents like Colbert would film the field reports, almost as if they were two separate shows. As Colbert put it, referring to the transition from the Kilborn to the Stewart eras:

> it really wasn't night-and-day, because you had the same writers, the same executive producer [...] You had the same correspondents—at first. And so, it was a gradual evolution. Jon didn't come in and say, "It's closing time, folks." He came in and said, "And let's see if we can't push this in this direction. Let's see if we can't maybe make the field pieces reflect something that's happening in the headlines of the day, so there's more of a natural transition, the show doesn't change tonally, completely." Which it would often do, from headlines into field pieces. It would be, like, something fairly clever about the Clinton administration—and then straight into a guy who was a Bigfoot hunter. It was quite jarring. That was the first thing I noticed, was that our field pieces were coming out of the news, and not in sort of opposition to them.[19]

With the integration of the anchorman's (or comedian's) in-studio commentary and the field reports, *The Daily Show* became more like the real news, and much more capable of performing the social-critical function of fake news.

Stewart's renovation and transformation of *The Daily Show* reveal the extent to which television needed, and audiences craved, what I have been calling (somewhat tongue-in-cheekily) "immanent critique," the satirical critique *of* the media *by* the media, here in the form of fake news. Stewart was less interested in jokes about Bill Clinton *per se*, and more interested in the ways that Clinton-jokes were dominating mainstream media while other crucial social issues were being overlooked. As Jeffrey P. Jones notes in his book *Entertaining Politics*, Stewart expresses "dismay over the artifice of public life—whether it is news reporting, political rhetoric, or entertainment talk" and "ridicules politicians and journalists for being fakes."[20] *The Daily Show with Jon Stewart*, a fake news show, was almost perfectly suited to expose the fakery of real news in its time.

Authentic Fakery: Stephen Colbert and *The Colbert Report*

The Colbert Report began as a spinoff of *The Daily Show*, with Stephen Colbert adopting a full-time persona of a conservative commentator along the lines of Rush Limbaugh, Sean Hannity, or especially Bill O'Reilly. Colbert had occasionally used this persona earlier on *The Daily Show* as a foil to liberal commentators or to Stewart himself; in their back-to-back time slots, with Stewart normally introducing *The Colbert Report* at the end of his show, the two were able to reprise their rivalry to humorous effect. That he chooses to give his persona the name "Stephen Colbert" only adds to the glorious ambiguities of fake and real news, and Colbert frequently supplements his own real biographical details (like being a Roman Catholic from Charleston, South Carolina) with fake ones (like being a local anchor in the 1980s for a small-town, North Carolina TV station). Colbert's show permits him to present the worldview of a character whose politics are both conservative and risible, thus allowing his show to be more overtly political than *The Daily Show*, since *The Colbert Report* is not so much fake news as reversed punditry.

Perhaps the *coup de grace* of Stephen Colbert's career up to that point was his triumphant and controversial appearance at the White House Correspondents Association dinner on April 29, 2006, later reprinted as the appendix to *I Am America (and So Can You!)*. An immediate YouTube sensation that originally aired on C-SPAN, Colbert's speech satirically assailed President Bush and his administration, as expected, but it also reserved much of its biting and ironic criticism for those very members of the mainstream media who cover the White House. In Colbert's view—a view not at all dissimilar to Jon Stewart's deliberately less funny, but still trenchant critique of the media in his infamous *Crossfire* appearance in 2004—the mainstream media had not only failed in its duty as a public watchdog, allowing the government to get away with policies that ought to have outraged many news readers or viewers, but it had actively facilitated these outrages, going along with if not promoting an anti-democratic agenda, and allowing itself to become a mere megaphone for the powers that be. The mainstream Washington-based journalists, who so like to think of themselves as essential checks on political power, were not watchdogs, but lapdogs, in Colbert's scathing yet hilarious critique.

Under the circumstances, it is perhaps unsurprising that the vociferous, negative reaction to Colbert humorous speech emerged at such a loud volume and over such a widespread area in the so-called "mainstream media." For all of the claims that Colbert's piece was a "lame," "insulting," or that "He was a bully,"[21] the rush to defend President Bush's honor by some in the affronted media seems more a form of wounded self-defense. After all, there was nothing surprising or unseemly about Colbert's political remarks in and of themselves: Colbert, Stewart, *Saturday Night Live*, Jay Leno, and hundreds of comedians had been delivering similar critiques of the administration on a nightly basis, and non-comedians elsewhere had not reserved their venom either. Nor were his remarks inappropriate in their setting, contrary to the misleading spin of some critics outraged by Colbert. For example, despite the claim that the White House Correspondents Association dinner was supposed to be a staid, respectful affair, it had frequently if not always been an occasion to "roast" the President, and Colbert's very presence there—that is to say, a *comedian* (not a statesman) was the invited speaker—shows just how much satire was *meant to be* guiding tone of the event. The speaker for the 2010 dinner was Jay Leno, and headliners in the 2000s have included Wanda Sykes, Craig Ferguson, Cedric the Entertainer, and Drew Carey, all comedians; indeed, Bob Hope headlined the first ever such occasion in 1944, and most recently (in 2022) *The Daily Show*'s own Trevor Noah was the host. In fact, Colbert's supposedly inappropriate remarks were *exactly* the type of discourse one would expect to hear at this event, but for the fact that he attacked the members of the media, rather than chiding the political figures alone.

The most damning critique of Colbert's speech was directed at the White House correspondents and by extension the mainstream media journalism. Mock-praising reporters for underplaying if not actually turning a blind eye to such stories as the effects of irresponsible tax cuts, faulty intelligence over apparently nonexistent weapons of mass destruction in Iraq, and the potentially devastating effects of global warming, Colbert reminded the press of its place in the nation:

> We Americans didn't want to know, and you had the courtesy not to try to find out. Those were good times, as far as we knew.
>
> But listen, let's review the rules. Here's how it works: the President makes decisions. He's the Decider. The press secretary announces those decision, and you people of the press type those decisions down. Make, announce, type. Just put 'em through a spellcheck and go home. Get to know your family again. Make love to your wife. Write that novel you got kicking around in your head. You know—the one about the intrepid Washington reporter with the courage to stand up to the administration. You know—fiction!

"Or Fantasy," adds the marginal gloss, à la *The Colbert Report*'s "The Word" segment.[22] And this is Colbert's point. During the Bush Administration, much of the mainstream media operated as the administration's stenographers, allowing dubious if not downright misleading information to circulate as real news. That such a critique is delivered by a leading member of the "fake news" establishment adds to its satirical power, to be sure, but it also suggests that the underlying reality being satirized is all the more dismal.

The real outrage came not from Colbert's venue, his bad taste, or even his actual comments; rather, the nerve touched by Colbert was so acutely felt because his speech, delivered in his persona as a media-pundit (and not as a comedian), revealed to many in the mainstream media exactly what they had become: simulacra of simulacra. Far from the real journalists they took such pride in being—let us not forget that the WHCA is a rather elite organization among mainstream journalists—they were at best hyperreal, becoming almost indistinguishable from the fake journalists in the world of satire, and less capable than they of recognizing their own fakery.

The media critics Jonathan Gray, Jeffrey P. Jones, and Ethan Thompson have nicely summed up the effects of the Colbert event, naming five particular aspects of media culture in the twenty-first century that this event disclosed:

> First, it speaks of the immense popularity of satire TV: being funny and smart sells and has proven a powerful draw for audiences' attention. Second, the rapid spread of the clip highlights satire's viral quality and cult appeal, along with the technological apparatus that now allows such satire to travel far beyond the television set almost instantaneously. Consigned to basic or pay cable channels (as it often is in the United States),

satire has nevertheless frequently commanded public attention and conversation more convincingly than shows with ten times the broadcast audience. Third, since multiple commentators criticized the speech for not being funny, the speech illustrates how the presence of "humor" in political humor can rely quite heavily on one's political worldview. It demonstrates that some satire may not even intend to be funny in a belly laugh kind of way. Fourth, Colbert's boldness as a comedian in a room full of politicians and journalists crystallized the sad irony that contemporary satire TV often says what the press is too timid to say, proving itself a more critical interrogator of politicians at times and a more effective mouthpiece of the people's displeasure with those in power, including the press itself. Good satire such as Colbert's has a remarkable power to encapsulate public sentiment. Finally, then, the incident tells us of how satire can energize civic culture, engaging citizen-audiences (as few of Colbert's press corps audience can), inspiring public political discussion, and drawing citizens enthusiastically into the realm of the political with deft and dazzling ease.[23]

Colbert's speech ushered in a new phase of political satire in the context of fake news, establishing a different relationship to the media and its audience than political satire and humor had previously.

Colbert's persona, drawn largely as a caricature of various right-wing pundits (e.g., Fox News' Bill O'Reilly), makes him an even more effective fake-newsman and social critic than Jon Stewart in a way. In *The Daily Show*, Stewart's persona is that of the relatively objective journalist, and he has proven himself to be a fiercely sardonic critic of Democrats Bill Clinton and Joe Biden as well as Republicans George W. Bush and Sarah Palin. As Stewart himself has put it, "The point of view of the show is we're passionately opposed to bullshit. Is that liberal or conservative?"[24] But Colbert, by posing as a right-wing conservative blowhard, need not oppose bullshit; he can *promote* bullshit, make sure everyone *knows* that it is bullshit, and even *insist* that such bullshit is in fact core principle at the very foundation of conservative political philosophy. Indeed, by portraying the very thing he is parodying, Colbert can more actively undermine the authority of his targets. This was partly what was on display in the WHCA dinner, even though many of those correspondents in the audience likely imagine themselves to be politically liberal.

The upshot of this fake news is that the already blurred lines between fake and real become even less distinguishable. Take, for example, this bit of trivia: Colbert's book *I am America (and So Can You!)* reached No. 1 on the *New York Times* nonfiction best-seller list on October 28, 2007 and stayed there until

December 2, 2007. The title that preceded it was Clarence Thomas's "real" autobiographical memoir, *My Grandfather's Son*, and the one that succeeded Colbert's was right-wing pundit Glenn Beck's satirical *An Inconvenient Book*. As the risk of making a churlish point, I would say that this particular chain of book-publishing events in the autumn of 2007 parallels the sort of social and cultural transformations that have made fake news so significant. However one views his political or judicial views, Thomas is an important, "newsworthy" figure, an associate justice of the United States Supreme Court, only the second person of color to occupy such a position, and someone whose life story—particularly in its compelling narrative of a black child rising from the segregated South to one of the highest positions of power in the country— is inherently worthy of the attention of socially aware readers. Colbert's "fake" autobiography, offering parodic faux-politics and self-aggrandizing cultural commentary, makes no actual claim to cultural relevance, aside from the comedian's desire to poke fun at the current state of affairs. Its presence on the bestseller list does not diminish the importance of Thomas's memoir, but it does offer another kind of discourse entirely. But Beck pushed this process even further. Like Colbert's book, his was fundamentally a work of satire; the title itself is a playful jab at former Senator and Vice President Al Gore's book and film, *An Inconvenient Truth*. Yet Beck's adoring fans apparently did not view his political opinions, even when presented in a clearly satirical manner, to be fake in any way. That is, Beck has taken a form of "fake news" to an extremity whereby it collapses back upon itself in the form of "real" news commentary. The absolute evacuation of *gravitas* has therefore led to the weightlessness of the media in general, and the gravitational pull of "fakery" becomes the only ground upon which the news-media can rest at all.

Here again we see the hyperreality of fake news, where *The Colbert Report* actually becomes far more grounded in reality than many television news programs can be. By staking out a position, Colbert actually maintains a position—the opposite of that held by his fictional persona—something the news cannot allow itself to do in good conscience, whatever the far right or far left believes about media bias. (The exception is when partisan shamelessness and outright mendacity take over the networks or their programs, at which point there can no longer be such a thing as journalistic "good conscience.") In establishing itself only as the transparent eye of a society of the spectacle, the news dissipates its own reality in favor of a hyperreal or nonreal that becomes indistinguishable from it. Of all news on television, fake or real, Colbert's then stands as the most real.

Again, this is not to say that the fake news replaces real news, or to repeat the nonsense about how Jon Stewart and Stephen Colbert should be viewed as real journalists. When asked about whether audiences "get their news" from *The Daily Show*, Colbert expressed doubt, then explained: "I wish people would watch the real news before they watch our show, because we have two games. Our game is we make fun of the newsmakers, but we also make fun of the news style. They're missing half our joke if they don't keep up with the day-to-day changes of mass media news."[25] Yet, so effective has been the fake news of Stewart and Colbert that some have asserted that they are actually *real* journalists after all. For example, in an article on Stewart's controversial *Crossfire* appearance (tellingly titled "If You Interview Kissinger, Are You Still a Comedian?"), Dan Kennedy is quoted as saying that, "by offering serious media criticism," Stewart must assume the responsibilities of a journalist; "you can't interview Bill Clinton [and others] and still say you're a comedian."[26] In other words, whether they like it or not, the fake news comedians Stewart and Colbert are now real news journalists and commentators. This astonishing claim may indicate the most hyperreal, or perhaps surreal, aspect of the blurring of the lines between journalism and entertainment, implicitly revealing the social significance of these fake news shows: Fake news is more real than real news precisely because it discloses just how fake the real news can be.

Here it is, your moment of Zen.

And that's the word.

Coda (October 2022)

The term "fake news" as used in this chapter refers to a particular form of satire, mostly that employed in comedic television shows (two in particular, of course), although such print or online comedic forms as *The Onion*, along with similar sorts of radio programs or works in other media would also count. In this chapter I do not address the burgeoning and now pervasive use of "sponsored content" in news media, which quite literally dissolves the line between journalism and advertising, not to mention conflicts of interest among those supposedly presenting "objective" reports and corporations that have paid for those reports to happen (as with scandals affecting *The New England Journal of Medicine*, for example) or even more egregious examples of flat-out lying. Such breaches of journalistic ethics undermine the authority of the news media far worse than television satire ever could. The undermining of journalistic authority in all media has set the stage for even worse abuses of the idea of "fake news" in recent years.

This essay was originally written in 2010, and although I have made some updates and revisions to this chapter as it appears here, I could not begin to address the way that the term "fake news" has come to be used by many in the United States since 2016; such a study is beyond my capabilities and, in any case, would likely require a depressingly extensive book project or projects to do it justice. In recent years, many people—including the president of the United States from 2017 to 2021—have insisted on labeling as "fake news" virtually any news story with which they personally disagree, even in cases where the "news" in question is little more than a statement of what used to be understood as incontrovertible facts. In some cases, the "mainstream media" itself has been derided as producers and purveyors of fake news, regardless of the specificities of a given story being reported on. In the United States at least, "fake news" is increasingly invoked to dismiss all news that does not fit neatly within one's beliefs not only about *what happened*, but about *what must have happened* or even *what ought to have happened*, regardless of evidence one way or another. Moreover, it is clear that some are deliberately obfuscating or dissimulating in their use of what is now an epithet intended to dissuade others from approaching even the outskirts of the truth—even Stephen Colbert's vaunted "truthiness" is far too close to the core reality for some—such that anything at all deemed objectionable from the speaker's point of view is derided as "fake."

My discussion of the effects of *The Daily Show* and *The Colbert Report* on U.S. political culture in the early part of this century does not support this negligent or intentional attack on journalism *tout court*. Nevertheless, I think it is clear that this perversion (literally) of the satirical form and its intent represents a dialectical reversal or ruse of history that, in retrospect, is not as surprising as it would seem. The blurring of the lines between serious journalism, editorial commentary, and comedic satire at the turn of the twenty-first century undoubtedly encouraged further blurring and blending. Alas, the sarcasm at the heart of effective humor can itself undermine productive political discourse, and I am less assured today that satire can influence change for the better, particularly when its most ardent supporters seem willing to trade any real-world policies or programs that they were supposed to have supported for a cherished sense of moral superiority, while those who feel they are not in on the joke (or worse, that they are the butt of the joke) are understandably irritated by the whole business. As satirical fake news and "real" journalism overlap, such feelings of superiority and resentment can only become more intense. "Politics" as presented in news media in the U.S. is a form of entertainment, not unlike sports-fandom, which only exacerbates these problems, as no expertly delivered and devastatingly funny sermon by a John Oliver, Samantha Bee, or Trevor Noah will ever convince right-wing voters to change their minds (or vice-versa, if such a thing is imaginable), but it will perhaps make partisans more resolved in their opposition to the enemy who seems intent on denigrating their views, particularly if doing so for laughs.

I suppose it should come as no surprise that the hyperreality of fake news should reflect the hyperreality more generally. The already vexed sphere of politics had plenty of hyperreality to begin with, but it seems evident that whatever contribution culture workers—journalists, comedians, and others—can make in effecting social or political reforms will necessarily have to confront this postmodern discursive network in which the meaning of terms like *real* and *fake* are not going to be widely agreed upon, and in which satire cannot save us.

Notes

1 *The Daily Show*, as it was originally called, first aired on the U.S. cable television network Comedy Central on July 22, 1996, and was developed by comedians Lizz Winstead and Madeleine Smithberg. As noted *infra*, the show was hosted by Craig Kilborn until his last episode on December 17, 1998. When Jon Stewart took over as host on January 11, 1999, the show was renamed *The Daily Show with Jon Stewart*. Following his retirement and replacement by Trevor Noah in 2015, it became *The Daily Show with Trevor Noah*, which it remains as of this writing (October 2022), but Noah has announced his impending departure after this year, so the next host's identity or the show's future more generally is uncertain at present.

2 Undoubtedly, a meant-to-be-lighthearted reference to the hip hop star Notorious B.I.G. (a.k.a. Biggie Smalls), Christopher Wallace, who was killed in a "drive-by shooting" in 1997; as such, in addition to its arguably being unprofessional by journalistic standards, the joke is in rather bad taste.

3 Jeffrey P. Jones, *Entertaining Politics: The New Political Television and Civic Culture* (Lanham, MD: Rowman & Littlefield, 2005), 54.

4 See Julia R. Fox, Glory Koloen, and Volkan Sahin, "No Joke: A Comparison of Substance in *The Daily Show with Jon Stewart* and Broadcast Network Television Coverage of the 2004 Presidential Election Campaign," *Journal of Broadcasting & Electronic Media* 51.2 (July 2007): 213–227; see also Damien Cave, "If You Interview Kissinger, Are You Still a Comedian?" *New York Times*, October 24, 2004: https://www.nytimes.com/2004/10/24/weekinreview/if-you-interview-kissinger-are-you-still-a-comedian.html.

5 *The Colbert Report*, a news-talk show loosely modeled on the sort of Fox News bloviating, editorializing political program like *The O'Reilly Factor* (starring conservative pundit Bill O'Reilly), first aired on October 17, 2005. Stephen Colbert had appeared, sometimes in his persona as a conservative-leaning reporter, on *The Daily Show* even before Jon Stewart's arrive, but had taken on an increasingly important role, even serving as guest host, in those intervening years. *The Colbert Report* ended in December 2014, when Colbert moved to CBS to take over hosting *The Late Show* following the retirement of David Letterman.

6 Umberto Eco, *Travels in Hyperreality*, trans. William Weaver (New York: Harcourt Brace, 1986), 4.

7 One indication of Stewart and Colbert's outsized influence on political culture beyond the entertainment industry may be found in their jointly organized "Rally to Restore Sanity" on October 30, 2010, which drew hundreds of thousands of people to Washington, DC—thus approximating a real political event on the order of major

protests and rallies in the past century—but ostensibly intended to militate in favor of nothing more than decorum or good manners among partisans. Would-be protesters carried signs reading "Things are pretty OK" and "What do we want? Moderation! When do we want it? In a reasonable time frame." Needless to say, the past decade has not proved to be a time of bipartisan rapport or politesse, and one might argue that this sort of satire is not only ineffective politically, but counterproductive and ultimately lending unintended support to more extremist positions. See Ben Burgis, *Canceling Comedians While the World Burns: A Critique of the Contemporary Left* (Winchester: Zer0 Books, 2021), 15–16.

8 With Trevor Noah as host, *The Daily Show* has more-or-less continued to follow to formal aspects of the Jon Stewart-led version, while maintaining its social satire of the news media and, in particular, the political coverage by that media. Noah has brought his own comedic presence to bear on the substance, but the basic structure of the show and the targets of its humor are largely the same.

9 See Jean Baudrillard, Jean. "The Precession of Simulacra." *Simulacra and Simulation*, trans. Sheila Faria Glaser (Ann Arbor: University of Michigan Press, 1994), 4. The "desert of the real" reference has achieved greater fame thanks to its use in the Wachowskis' science fiction film *The Matrix* (1999), which in turn was taken up by Slavoj Žižek in *Welcome to the Desert of the Real: Five Essays on September 11 and Related Dates* (London: Verso, 2002).

10 See Guy Debord, *The Society of the Spectacle*, trans. Donald Nicholson-Smith (New York: Zone Books, 1994).

11 Baudrillard, "The Precession of Simulacra," 6.

12 The internet and especially social media has only enlarged and accelerated this phenomenon, such that a news "personality" can post a controversial comment on Twitter, say, which is then the subject of radio and television news and fodder for the talk shows on those media, all while continuing to generate "viral" interest online. As such, the news media quite literally creates its own news, virtually *ex nihilo*, which means that there is an infinite supply of "content" to feed the perpetual motion machine that is the 24-hour and global news media. (Never mind that in so doing, much of what might also be considered by some to be newsworthy is completely ignored if not actively suppressed in favor of this urgently pressing, parthenogenetic "news" to be reported and commented upon.)

13 Eco, *Travels in Hyperreality*, 43.

14 See, e.g., Alex S. Jones, *Losing the News: The Future of the News that Feeds Democracy* (Oxford: Oxford University Press, 2009).

15 See Sophia A. McClennen, *Colbert's America: Satire and Democracy* (New York: Palgrave Macmillan, 2011); see also her forthcoming *Trump Was a Joke: How Satire Made Sense of a President Who Didn't* (London: Routledge, 2023).

16 As of this writing, in 2002, Fox News has nine of the top ten highest rated news programs—i.e., most total viewers—in the United States, including all of the top eight. *The Daily Show* current averages less than a tenth of Fox News' most popular program, *Tucker Carlson Tonight*, but even at its ratings height during the Stewart era, *The Daily Show* never had ratings close to those of many "real news" programs.

17 See Ken Plume, "An Interview with Stephen Colbert," *IGN*, August 11, 2003, http://movies.ign.com/articles/433/433111p6.html.

18 Quoted in Plume, "An Interview with Stephen Colbert."

19 Ibid.

20 Jones, *Entertaining Politics*, 54.
21 Richard Cohen, "So Not Funny." *Washington Post*, May 6, 2006: http://www.washingtonpost.com/wp-dyn/content/article/2006/05/03/AR2006050302202.html.
22 Stephen Colbert et al., *I am America (and So Can You!)* (New York: Grand Central, 2007), 224.
23 Jonathan Gray, Jeffrey P. Jones, and Ethan Thompson, eds., *Satire TV: Politics and Comedy in the Post-Network Era* (New York: New York University Press, 2009), 4.
24 Quoted in Jones, *Entertaining Politics*, 55.
25 Quoted in Plume, "An Interview."
26 Damien Cave, "If You Interview Kissinger, Are You Still a Comedian?" *New York Times*, October 24, 2004: https://www.nytimes.com/2004/10/24/weekinreview/if-you-interview-kissinger-are-you-still-a-comedian.html.

Part III

ERRANT TRAJECTORIES IN POSTMODERN CRITICAL PRACTICE

Chapter 11

NOMADOGRAPHY: GILLES DELEUZE AND THE HISTORY OF PHILOSOPHY

In his *Introduction to the Lectures on the History of Philosophy*, Hegel says that "what the history of philosophy displays to us is a series of noble spirits, the gallery of the heroes of *reason*'s thinking," but that the history of philosophy would have little value if thought of as a mere collection of opinions, in themselves arbitrary: "philosophy contains no opinions; there are no philosophical opinions."[1] Hence, Hegel says, those who wish to understand the history of philosophy by studying the individual philosophers it comprises, rather than achieving a more universal idea of the totality of its thought, will be missing the forest for the trees. "Anyone who starts by examining the trees, and sticks simply to them, does not survey the whole wood and gets lost and bewildered in it."[2] For Hegel, the history of philosophy is the overarching concept, and the evolutionary realization, of philosophy itself.

Gilles Deleuze, it might be said, built a career in philosophy in which he attempted to subvert this view, and he was particularly critical of "the history of philosophy" as an enterprise. In a well-known letter, Deleuze wrote, "I belong to a generation, one of the last generations, that was more or less bludgeoned to death with the history of philosophy," adding that

> Many members of my generation never broke free of this; others did, by inventing their own particular methods and new rules, a new approach. I myself "did" history of philosophy for a long time, read books on this or that author. But I compensated in various ways: by concentrating, in the first place, on authors who challenged the rationalist tradition in this history (and I see a secret link between Lucretius, Hume, Spinoza, and Nietzsche, constituted by their critique of negativity, their cultivation of joy, the denunciation of power [...] and so on).[3]

In the same letter, Deleuze says, "What I most detested was Hegelianism and dialectics,"[4] so perhaps it is not surprising that he would approach the history of philosophy rather differently. However, Deleuze does not abandon or reject the history of philosophy. Rather, he transforms the project into something else, a "nomadography," which projects an alternative history of philosophy that not only allows Deleuze to "get out" of that institution, but allows us to re-imagine it in productive new ways. Deleuze's distaste for the history of philosophy, the quasi-Hegelian institution presented to him and his contemporaries in school and which formed a basic requirement of the profession of philosophy in France, is overcome by his peculiar approach to the history of philosophy, an approach that redeems philosophy as it transfigures it.

Typically, any discussion of Deleuze's career draws a line between his "early" work, those monographs produced between 1953 and 1968 dealing with individual figures from the history of Western philosophy, and Deleuze's later work "written in his own voice," starting with *Difference and Repetition* and *The Logic of Sense*,[5] followed by his 1970s-era collaborations with Félix Guattari, and finally with his diverse post-*Capitalism and Schizophrenia* writings, culminating perhaps in *What Is Philosophy?* (also co-authored with Guattari). Although Deleuze himself has remarked that his early works were devoted to the history of philosophy, readers of his entire oeuvre will notice that the concerns animating those early studies are still engaged in his later work. Moreover, one could say that Deleuze *never* really stopped "doing" the history of philosophy, albeit in his own rather eccentric way. In addition to those early monographs on Hume,[6] Nietzsche,[7] Kant,[8] Bergson,[9] and Spinoza,[10] Deleuze wrote studies devoted to the philosophers Leibniz, Foucault, and his old friend François Châtelet,[11] as well as maintaining an ongoing conversations with his nomad thinkers and other figures from the history of philosophy in the collaborations with Guattari,[12] in his dealings with literature (including a book on Proust and a lengthy essay on Sacher-Masoch,[13] in addition to the Kafka study), and in his books on cinema and on Francis Bacon,[14] to name just the book-length studies; his essays and other shorter works frequently address the history of philosophy, as did his lectures throughout his teaching career. Yet it is in his earlier works that Deleuze most carefully identifies that nomadic line of flight within the Western philosophical tradition, the counter-history of philosophy or nomadography that typifies Deleuze's radically creative engagement with philosophy.

Deleuze's distinction between State philosophy and nomad thought is perhaps best known through his essay on Nietzsche titled "Nomad Thought" and in his more elaborate discussion of "Nomadology" in *A Thousand Plateaus*.[15] However, Deleuze had already made the distinction as early as 1968, in *Difference and Repetition*, in which he identifies a "nomadic distribution" of the various components of Being in Spinoza, opposing it to the Cartesian theory of substances that, like the agricultural or statist model, distributes elements of Being by dividing them into fixed categories, demarcating territories and fencing them off from one another. Deleuze notes that the statist or Cartesian distribution of Being is rooted to the agricultural need to set proprietary boundaries and fix stable domains. Alternatively, there is "a completely other distribution, which must be called nomadic, a nomad *nomos*, without property, enclosure or measure," that does not involve "a division of that which is distributed but rather a division among those who distribute themselves in an open space—a space which is unlimited, or at least without precise limits."[16]

Deleuze's nomad thinkers, like (and, of course, including) Spinoza, would partake in such an ontological and ethical philosophy, in one way or another, which in part constitutes the "secret link" Deleuze refers to in his letter to Michel Cressole. These nomads are themselves distributed throughout the history of philosophy while also standing somewhat outside of it. "I liked writers who seemed to be part of the history of philosophy, but who escaped from it in one respect, or altogether: Lucretius, Spinoza, Hume, Nietzsche, Bergson."[17] For Deleuze, these thinkers stand apart from, or even athwart, a philosophical tradition which has ever associated itself with the State. "For thought borrows its properly philosophical image from the state as beautiful, substantial or subjective interiority. [...] Philosophy is shot through with the project of becoming the official language of a Pure State."[18] Although Descartes and Hegel would seem to be State philosophers *par excellence*, the nomad-versus-State distinction finds an unexpected precursor in Immanuel Kant, an "enemy" to which Deleuze devoted a study.[19]

In the 1781 preface to the first edition of *The Critique of Pure Reason*, Kant names metaphysics "the Queen of all the sciences," emphatically identifying philosophy with the State. Kant writes that the chief threat to this Queen's beneficent government lay in the forces of the skeptics, "a species of nomads, despising all modes of settled life, [who] broke up from time to time all civil society. Happily, they were few in number, and were unable to prevent its being established ever anew."[20] Of course, Kant was also wary of the dogmatists, under whose administration the Queen's government was "despotic," which led in part to the "complete anarchy" that allowed those nomads to breach the walls of the kingdom. Kant's metaphor establishes the conflicting philosophical traditions explicitly as statist on the one hand and nomadic on the other. From this somewhat playful usage, we can see already in Kant the Deleuze's distinction between State philosophy and nomad thought, although, of course, Deleuze view the nomads as a positive force, in more ways than one. Moreover, Kant makes this distinction specifically in the context of the history of philosophy, and one may approach that history as a battle between the contesting forces of State philosophy and nomad thought. Deleuze's interventions into the history of philosophy, then, may be seen as a nomadography, an alternative path through Hegel's dense forest, yielding unexpected discoveries and innovative concepts.

This terrain is the playground and the laboratory of the "early" Deleuze. In fact, even at his "earliest," Deleuze was already known for his transformative analyses of the history of philosophy. In his 1977 autobiography, *The Wind Spirit*, Michel Tournier describes his first encounter with the young philosopher-in-formation when they were still teenagers, but already Tournier marveled at Deleuze's "intellectual rigor and speculative reach": "The arguments my friends and I tossed back and forth among ourselves were like balls of cotton or rubber compared with the iron and steel cannonballs that he hurled at us."[21] Deleuze was "the soul" of the young group, and "philosophy was to be our calling," which meant that they would be steeped in the history of philosophy. As Tournier recalls,

> Most of us would become guardians of those twelve citadels of granite named for their 'placental' progenitors: Plato, Aristotle, Saint Thomas, Descartes, Malebranche, Spinoza, Leibniz, Berkeley, Kant, Fichte, Schelling, and Hegel. As professors of philosophy we would be responsible for initiating young people into the study of these historical monuments, grander and more majestic than anything else mankind has yet to offer."[22]

The unlikely dream would be to *become* a "placental" progenitor, to give birth to a new philosophical system oneself. And, to the extent that Deleuzian thought may be thought of as a system, it is clear that his philosophy were developed and refined throughout his early interactions with those figures in the history of philosophy with which he so frequently grapples.

The Deleuze whom Tournier remembers is certainly "early," but even here Deleuze's prodigious intellect is discernible, especially with respect to his ability to transform traditional ideas into bold new concepts. As Tournier put it, Deleuze "possessed extraordinary powers of translation and rearrangement: all the tired philosophy of the curriculum passed through him and emerged unrecognizable but rejuvenated, with a fresh, undigested, bitter taste of newness that we weaker, lazier minds found disconcerting and repulsive."[23] Deleuze later proved just how rejuvenated the tired old philosophy of certain citadels in the history of philosophy could really be. Deleuze returns again and again to older, perhaps canonical figures in the history of Western philosophy, producing what might have seemed to be fairly straightforward studies by the standards of the profession. Of course, in retrospect, we know that Deleuze's seemingly conservative interventions were actually moments in the development of a radically new philosophy. In these returns to some of the great figures of Western philosophy, Deleuze revives matters fundamental to, say, seventeenth- or eighteenth-century thought, and, at the same time, Deleuze demonstrates the contemporaneity of such philosophical problems in our time.

Some may find it ironic, perhaps, that while Deleuze has paid so much attention to the history of philosophy, he has also been an ardent critic, even adversary, of this institution. In *Dialogues*, for example, Deleuze says that

> [t]he history of philosophy has always been the great agent of power in the philosophy, and even in thought. It is played to repressor's role: how can you think without having read Plato, Descartes, Kant and Heidegger, and so-and-so's book about them? A formidable school of intimidation which manufactures specialists in thought—but which also makes those who stay outside conform all the more to this specialism which they despise. An image of thought called philosophy has been formed historically and it effectively stops people from thinking.[24]

Or, in Nietzschean terms, the history of philosophy is both a product and a producer of a priestly class who would guard over the sacred texts, regulating not only what can, and must, be read, but also how this canon will be read. Deleuze is aware of the institutional power of the history of philosophy, of its relations to State philosophy, and yet he does not avoid it, but rather faces it head-on, enlisting the aid of those nomad thinkers who are both part of the history of philosophy and yet outside of it as well. In Deleuze's early writings, we see this battle unfold.

By now, a number of scholars and critics have examined Deleuze's early writings, and his career is understood as involving what might be considered lifelong projects, even if he clearly also developed difference concepts with different emphases at various times along the way. For a while, Deleuze's "early" work was largely ignored, and in contrast to the work of such contemporaries as Michel Foucault or Jacques Derrida, many of his pre-1968 writing did not appear in English translation until the late 1980s or beyond. Deleuze was best known for *Anti-Oedipus* and then *A Thousand Plateaus*, which are still remarkable books, but the sense was that his prior work was merely preliminary to the important contributions to come.

Michael Hardt's *Gilles Deleuze: An Apprenticeship in Philosophy*, one of the first studies devoted to Deleuze's early writings, offered a nice reading of Deleuze's studies of Bergson, Nietzsche, and Spinoza (Hardt does not really look at Deleuze's book on Hume).[25] Notwithstanding the implication of the subtitle, Hardt's fundamental argument is that Deleuze's political and philosophical thought is constructed through his early interaction with these authors. That is, these works are not merely occasions for Deleuze to practice becoming a philosopher, but important Deleuzian philosophical texts in themselves. Hardt identifies a progressive, evolutionary project in which Deleuze's own thought develops through Bergson's ontology, Nietzsche's ethics, and Spinoza's practice, culminating in a full-blown philosophy already visible prior to Deleuze's works written "in his own voice."

This last phrase is unfortunate and a bit misleading, but it has been the standard view of Deleuze's career. As Brian Massumi had put it, in introducing *A Thousand Plateaus* and again in his *A User's Guide to Capitalism and Schizophrenia*, Deleuze's early work is limited to traditional (and repressive) history of philosophy. "Gilles Deleuze was schooled in that philosophy. The titles of his earliest books read like a who's who of philosophical giants." Massumi includes a backhandedly compliment that is paradoxically inclusive of the early monographs ("Yet much of value came of Deleuze's flirtation with the greats"), before dismissing these works entirely by averring that *Difference and Repetition* and *The Logic of Sense* were "Deleuze's first major statements written in his own voice."[26] The inappropriateness of the phrase, "written in his own voice," is apparent by simply reading Deleuze's early books, which are not simple primers or commentaries on other thinkers. That is, Deleuze is not merely restating or summarizing Hume's theory of human nature, Bergson's ideas of time and being, Nietzsche's transvaluation of values, or Spinoza's philosophy of expression. Rather, as Tournier suggested, Deleuze transformed these philosophies and restated them in such a way that they become new, fresh, and also strange.

Indeed, Deleuze may be at his *most* original when returning to these figures from the history of philosophy—a *return with difference*, one might say—and developing his new monsters from the encounter. In a well-known, mischievous metaphor, Deleuze has described his approach as a form of sexual activity in which he impregnates the philosopher in question who then gives birth to monstrous offspring. Deleuze says that he viewed

> the history of philosophy as a sort of buggery [*enculage*] or (it comes to the same thing) immaculate conception. I saw myself as taking an author from behind and giving him a child that would be his own offspring, yet monstrous. It was really important for it to be his own child, because the author had to actually say all I had him saying. But the child was bound to be monstrous too, because it resulted from all the shifting, slipping, dislocations, and hidden emissions that I really enjoyed.[27]

Hence, even where Deleuze had endeavored to present the philosopher's own thoughts, he undoubtedly, and perhaps inevitably, intended to present his own as well.

Massumi and others may be forgiven for viewing the work of the "early Deleuze" as wholly separate or in another voice from the work of the middle or later Deleuze, since Deleuze himself has invited the comparison by referring to his having "paid off my debts" and writing "yet more books on my own account."[28] But Deleuze had also suggested that the way in which his own philosophy came into being was by a process of philosophical buggery similar to that described above. "It was Nietzsche, who I read only later, who extricated me from all this. Because you just can't deal with him in the same sort of way. He gets up to all sorts of things behind *your* back."[29] Delighting in the mildly scandalous wordplay that allows "doing things behind one's back" (i.e., furtively or covertly) to also suggest sexual acts, Deleuze proposes that his *own* thought is itself the monstrous offspring of his encounter with Nietzsche.

The *enculage* that typifies Deleuze's approach to the history of philosophy thus becomes a two-way exchange, a reversible relation of power—like erotic love, Michel Foucault would say[30]—in which the history of philosophy, the "nomadography" formed by Deleuze's encounters with his nomad thinkers, also creates Deleuzian thought. Hence, the first rule in dealing with Deleuze's early interventions into the history of philosophy is to recognize that we are indeed reading *Deleuze*, and not merely reading any old commentary on Hume, Nietzsche, Bergson, or Spinoza. But the Deleuze we read, whether in the early works or elsewhere, is himself a multiplicity that includes these other thinkers: "Individuals find a real name for themselves, rather, only through the harshest exercise in depersonalization, by opening themselves up to the multiplicities everywhere within them, to the intensities running through them."[31]

Similarly, for all of his trenchant critique of philosophy and the history of philosophy, Deleuze is also committed to philosophy, perhaps more than any of those poststructuralists with whom he is sometimes grouped. Deleuze is frequently seen as a thoroughgoing iconoclast, as someone who desires a radical break from traditional ways of thinking, so much so that many readers fail to perceive just how grounded in philosophy and tied to the principles of properly philosophical thought Deleuze really is. This is true of Deleuze's approach to the history of philosophy as well. Although Deleuze certainly recognizes the damage at the institution of the history of philosophy has done to thinking, he does not advocate ignoring that history, ignoring the institution, or getting rid of such practices entirely. Hence, Deleuzian thought is not a rejection or flight from Western philosophy; it is intensely philosophical, immersed in the very tradition with which it grapples. Even when Deleuze ventures into other disciplinary arenas—for example, art history, mathematics, literature, psychoanalysis, and so on—his articulation of the problems and his painstaking critiques are profoundly philosophical.[32] Indeed, after his panegyric to the discipline in *What Is Philosophy?*, one can hardly doubt that Deleuze—early, middle, and late—is actively *doing* philosophy in his work.

Notwithstanding their sometimes broad titles (e.g., *Nietzsche and Philosophy* or *Bergsonism*), Deleuze's early books selectively engage with the thought of the philosopher in question, addressing concepts that relate to Deleuze's own project. Deleuze's early works are "punctual interventions" into the history of Western philosophy.[33] In describing the "secret" connections between his nomad thinkers, Deleuze offers another meaningful analogy. They are linked in a way similar to the relationships among stars in a constellation, each independent of the others yet also constellated in such a way as to give new meaning to each and to the ensemble or assemblage.

> One might say that something happens between them [i.e., these nomad thinkers], at different speeds and with different intensities, which is not in one or other, but truly in an ideal space, which is no longer part of history, still less a dialogue among the dead, but an interstellar conversation, between very irregular stars, whose different becomings form a mobile bloc which it would be a case of capturing, an inter-flight, light-years.[34]

Deleuze's nomadography charts these interstellar conversations and casts the history of philosophy in a new light.

Examples of Deleuze's fascinating reconstellation of the history of philosophy are abundant, but I would like to look briefly at his first book, *Empiricism and Subjectivity*. Hume's continuing influence on Deleuze is apparent in his later work, and it is hardly accidental that, in 1986, Deleuze chose to begin his "Preface to the English Language Edition" of *Dialogues* with the words: "I have always felt that I am an empiricist."[35] Deleuze's early work on empiricism not only delineates the fundamentals of Hume's philosophy, but also suggests ways in which Deleuze's later work will develop.[36]

For Deleuze, the empiricism that so often appears as a chapter in the history of philosophy is actually a positive force in thinking today. Hume has traditionally been cast in a transitional role, linking Locke or Berkeley to Kant, who would then manage to correct the excesses of Hume and synthesize the abstract strains of rationalism and empiricism. In Deleuze's nomadography, by contrast, Hume bursts from the narrative of philosophical continuity, resisting facile definitions, and escaping the categorizations imposed by the history of ideas. In a 1989 preface to the English edition of *Empiricism and Subjectivity*, Deleuze lists three important concepts that Hume introduced into Western philosophy, and Deleuze's characterization shows just how much he respects the field even as he wishes, with Hume's help, to transform it into something completely different. As Deleuze sees it, Hume "established the concept of *belief* and put it in the place of knowledge. [...] He gave the *association* of ideas its real meaning, making it a practice of cultural and *conventional* formations (conventional instead of contractual), rather than a theory of human mind"; and "He created the first great logic of *relations*, showing in it that all relations (not only 'matters of fact' but also relations among ideas) are external to their terms."[37] These three concepts not only establish the terrain on which his theory of empirical subjectivity will emerge, but also allow us to imagine a history of philosophy that escapes the Hegelian forest-and-trees imagery altogether.

Deleuze insists that empiricism not be confused with a theory of knowledge. Historians of philosophy tend to identify empiricism as the philosophical mode by which knowledge in the form of ideas is obtained through sensuous experience. But Deleuze argues that this epistemological view misses the point. Empiricism is, above all, a practical philosophy, in which questions of knowledge and truth are always ancillary to and activated by material concerns. Belief, which exerts its power in our lives whether we have true knowledge or not, thus becomes more significant. Through belief, the subject comes to constitute itself within the mind. Deleuze affirms, with Hume, that the mind is not all the same as the subject. The mind is a collection of sense impressions, a "given" without order, "a flux of perceptions" which must be organized in order for the subject to develop. *Association* allows the mind becomes systematized under the influence of its principles, such as contiguity, causality, and resemblance. For example, "the principle of resemblance designates certain ideas that are similar, and makes it possible to group them together under the same name." The mind is thus affected by the principles, which give it a tendency or habit. As Deleuze puts it, "the mind is not a subject; it is subjected."[38]

Once the mind becomes a system and the given has been organized, it is possible for subject to constitute itself as that which transcends the given. Deleuze explains that "I affirm more than I know; my judgment goes beyond the idea. In other words, *I am a subject.*" Through *belief*, we are able to transcend the given ("I believe in what I have never seen nor touched"), and this establishes a *relation* (which is not given) among ideas (which are given). For instance, we have ideas of the sun, of rising, and the temporality, yet the belief that the sun will rise tomorrow is a relation among these ideas.[39]

The basic function of the subject is to establish relations, which are in all cases external to their terms. Deleuze considers this the absolute fact of empiricism, Hume's as well as his own. A given object or idea does not have an inherent relation to another. For example, since resemblance is a relation, two things that resemble one another might seem to have a *property* of resemblance, but Hume would say that resemblance is merely a *relation* entirely external to the things themselves, since resemblance only arises "from the comparison that the mind makes betwixt them."[40] Hence, a relation-establishing subject is needed to create relations, since the ideas are not themselves endowed with a property which would establish an *a priori* relationship.

Empirical subjectivity is thus a dynamic process rather than a fixed identity. As Deleuze puts it, "subjectivity is essentially *practical*." To ask whether the subject is active or passive, as the history of philosophy has traditionally done in characterizing an "active" subject of rationalism and a "passive" subject of empiricism, is to raise what Bergson would have called a "false question." Deleuze explains that "the subject is an imprint, or an impression, left by the principles, that progressively turns into a machine capable of using this impression."[41] The empirical, practical subject constitutes itself on the plane of immanence, and it is recognizable in its function rather than its discrete or abstract existence. Already in *Empiricism and Subjectivity*, the subject unfolds like some rhizomatic machine. Deleuze's conclusion hints at the future directions of his thought even as it foregrounds Hume's own theory: "Philosophy must constitute itself as the theory of what we are doing, not as a theory of what there is."[42]

It may seem a bit churlish to quote the concluding remarks of Deleuze's earliest monograph as an example of his lifelong approach to the history of philosophy, but it seems to me that the very "early" Deleuze of *Empiricism and Subjectivity* is already onto something. In establishing Hume's theory of human nature, Deleuze invites us to revisit those apparently settled problems of philosophy, to see them again with fresh eyes, to think them again with intellects now freed from the categories that had shaped or limited our thoughts. Indeed, Deleuze's retrospective view of Hume in the Preface to the English Edition of his first book might serve as a model for Deleuze's nomadography: Deleuze also establishes belief and makes it superior to knowledge, understands association of ideas to be conventional, and embraces a logic of relations that are external to their terms. In his unique reconstellation of the institution, Deleuze figures forth a practical history of philosophy, allowing his own belief in his nomads (rather than the knowledge of the granite citadels of philosophy) to guide him, making associations between their ideas that are at once strikingly original and seem almost natural (as if Spinoza were really a Nietzschean all along), and establishing relations among these diverse and motley figures, and between them and himself, and between all of them and us.

In Deleuze's re-imagined history of philosophy we see something like that bizarre "subterranean *Ethics*" that Deleuze finds in Spinoza's *scholia*, "discontinuously, independently, referring to one another, violently erupting to form a zigzagging volcanic chain."[43] Deleuze's nomads are like that, sudden and bewildering eruptions of "joyful wisdom" in an apparent continuum of stable meanings, standard commentaries, settled thought. The early Deleuze, playing around behind the backs of these thinkers, discovered a novel way of doing philosophy in our era.[44]

Notes

1 G. W. F. Hegel, *Introduction to the Lectures on the History of Philosophy*, trans. T. M. Knox and A. V. Miller (Oxford: Clarendon Press, 1985), 9, 17.
2 Hegel, *Introduction*, 94.
3 Gilles Deleuze, "Letter to a Harsh Critic," in *Negotiations, 1972–1990*, trans. Martin Joughin (New York: Columbia University Press, 1995), 5–6, ellipsis in original.
4 Deleuze, "Letter to a Harsh Critic," 6.
5 Deleuze, *Difference and Repetition* [1968], trans. Paul Patton (New York: Columbia University Press, 1994); and Deleuze, *The Logic of Sense* [1969], trans. Mark Lester and Charles Stivale (New York: Columbia University Press, 1990).
6 Deleuze, *Empiricism and Subjectivity: An Essay on Hume's Theory of Human Nature* [1953], trans. Constantin V. Boundas (New York: Columbia University Press, 1991).
7 Deleuze, *Nietzsche and Philosophy* [1962], trans. Hugh Tomlinson (New York: Columbia University Press, 1983; see also Deleuze, *Nietzsche* (Paris: Presses Universitaires de France, 1965).
8 Deleuze, *Kant's Critical Philosophy* [1963], trans. Hugh Tomlinson and Barbara Habberjam (Minneapolis: University of Minnesota Press, 1984).
9 Deleuze, *Bergsonism* [1966], trans. Hugh Tomlinson and Barbara Habberjam (New York: Zone Books, 1988).
10 Deleuze, *Expressionism in Philosophy: Spinoza* [1968], trans. Martin Joughin (New York: Zone Books, 1990); and Deleuze, *Spinoza: Practical Philosophy* [1970], trans. Robert Hurley (San Francisco: City Lights, 1988).
11 Deleuze, *The Fold: Leibniz and the Baroque* [1988], trans. Tom Conley (Minneapolis: University of Minnesota Press, 1993); Deleuze, *Foucault* [1986], trans. Seán Hand (Minneapolis: University of Minnesota Press, 1988); and Deleuze, "Pericles and Verdi: The Philosophy of François Châtelet" [1988], trans. C. T. Wolfe. *The Opera Quarterly* v. 21, n. 4, 2005, 716–724.
12 Deleuze's books co-authored with Guattari include *Anti-Oedipus: Capitalism and Schizophrenia* [1972], trans. Robert Hurley, Mark Seem, and Helen R. Lane (Minneapolis: University of Minnesota Press, 1983); *Kafka: Toward a Minor Literature* [1975] trans. Dana Polan (Minneapolis: University of Minnesota Press, 1986); *A Thousand Plateaus: Capitalism and Schizophrenia* [1980], trans. Brian Massumi (Minneapolis: University of Minnesota Press, 1987); and *What Is Philosophy?* [1991], trans. Hugh Tomlinson and Graham Burchell (New York: Columbia University Press, 1994).

13 Deleuze, *Proust and Signs* [1964], trans. Richard Howard (Minneapolis: University of Minnesota Press, 2000); Deleuze, *Masochism* [1967], trans. Jean McNeil (New York: Zone Books, 1989).

14 Deleuze, *Cinema 1: The Movement-Image* [1983], trans. Hugh Tomlinson and Barbara Habberjam (Minneapolis: University of Minnesota Press, 1986); Deleuze, *Cinema 2: The Time Image* [1985], trans. Hugh Tomlinson and Robert Galeta (Minneapolis: University of Minnesota Press, 1989); and Deleuze, *Francis Bacon: The Logic of Sensation* [1981], trans. Daniel W. Smith (New York: Continuum Books, 2003).

15 Deleuze, "Nomad Thought" [1973], trans. David Allison, in *The New Nietzsche*, ed. David Allison (Cambridge: The MIT Press, 1977), 142–149; see also Deleuze and Guattari, *A Thousand Plateaus*, 351–423.

16 Deleuze, *Difference and Repetition*, 36.

17 Deleuze and Claire Parnet, *Dialogues* [1977], trans. Hugh Tomlinson and Barbara Habberjam (New York: Columbia University Press, 1987), 14–15.

18 Ibid., 13.

19 See Deleuze, "Letter to a Harsh Critic," 6; see also Deleuze, *Kant's Critical Philosophy*.

20 Immanuel Kant, *The Critique of Pure Reason*, trans. Norman Kemp Smith (London: Macmillan, 1933), 8–9.

21 Michel Tourier, *The Wind Spirit: An Autobiography*, trans. Arthur Goldhammer (Boston: Beacon Press, 1988), 127–128.

22 Ibid., 129–130.

23 Ibid., 128.

24 Gilles Deleuze and Claire Parnet. *Dialogues*, trans. Hugh Tomlinson and Barbara Habberjam (New York: Columbia University Press, 1987), 13.

25 Michael Hardt, *Gilles Deleuze: An Apprenticeship in Philosophy* (Minneapolis: University of Minnesota Press, 1993).

26 Brian Massumi, *A User's Guide to* Capitalism and Schizophrenia: *Deviations from Deleuze and Guattari* (Cambridge: The MIT Press, 1992), 2. The language here is nearly identical to that of his "Translator's Foreword: The Pleasures of Philosophy," in Gilles Deleuze and Félix Guattari, *A Thousand Plateaus*, trans. Brian Massumi (Minneapolis: University of Minnesota Press, 1987), ix–x.

27 Deleuze, "Letter to a Harsh Critic," 6.

28 Deleuze and Parnet, *Dialogues*, 16.

29 Deleuze, "Letter to a Harsh Critic," 6.

30 See Foucault, "The Ethic of Care for the Self as a Practice of Freedom," in *The Final Foucault*, ed. J. Bernauer and D. Rasmussen (Cambridge: The MIT Press, 1988), 18.

31 Deleuze, "Letter to a Harsh Critic," 6.

32 Hardt recounts, in a footnote, how Deleuze's old professor Ferdinand Alquié, after hearing a presentation by Deleuze, protested that Deleuze had failed to recognize the specificity of "properly philosophical discourse," and, visibly hurt, Deleuze responded that, while his presentation had dealt with other discourses, he followed those very rigorous methods specific to philosophical inquiry which Alquié himself had taught him. See Hardt, *Gilles Deleuze*, 124, note 3.

33 Hardt, *Gilles Deleuze*, xix.

34 Deleuze and Parnet, *Dialogues*, 15–16.

35 Ibid., vii.

36 See John Sellars, "Gilles Deleuze and the History of Philosophy," *The British Journal for the History of Philosophy* v. 15, n. 3, 2007, 551–560; see also my review of *Empiricism and Subjectivity* in *Textual Practice* 7.3 (1993), 522–525.
37 Deleuze, *Empiricism*, ix–x.
38 Ibid., 23, 114, 31.
39 Ibid., 28, 24.
40 Quoted in Deleuze, *Empiricism*, 99.
41 Ibid., 112–113.
42 Ibid., 133.
43 Deleuze, "Letter to Reda Bensmaïa, on Spinoza," in *Negotiations*, 165; see also Deleuze, *Expressionism in Philosophy: Spinoza*, 337–350; the term "subterranean *Ethics*" appears in Deleuze, *Spinoza: Practical Philosophy*, 29.
44 This essay is dedicated to my old professor, friend, and comrade Kenneth Surin.

Chapter 12

POWER TO THE EDUCATED IMAGINATION!: NORTHROP FRYE AND THE UTOPIAN IMPULSE

The celebration of a Northrop Frye centennial cannot but be bittersweet, given the circumstances surrounding the literary humanities in the twenty-first century.[1] Everywhere, it seems, the areas of scholarly inquiry that Frye cherished are under attack at colleges and universities, by politicians eager to belittle what they consider impractical or irrelevant fields of study, by corporate interests aiming to maximize one sort of profitability, and by underfunded administrations desperate to balance budgets. The discipline to which Frye devoted so much loving labor, comparative literature, has been among those hardest hit by the prevailing movements to restrict or eliminate academic programs in the humanities. The University of Toronto's 2010 decision to close the Centre for Comparative Literature, of which Frye was founding director, is perhaps symbolic of this larger pattern. Happily, that decision was reversed, at least temporarily, which may be a hopeful sign. In 2011, what Slavoj Žižek has referred to as "the year of dreaming dangerously," an apparently utopian spirit animated a number of protests against perceived social, political, and economic injustices.[2] Arguably, the resistance to the closure of comparative literature programs belongs in the same category with such movements as Occupy Wall Street or student protests in Quebec, California, and elsewhere. For, as Frye's work makes clear, if only in sometimes subtle ways, the utopian impulse animates the study of literature.

In this chapter, I want to examine this aspect of Frye's work by looking at his slender yet powerful 1964 book, *The Educated Imagination*, in the context of a critique of advanced industrial society associated with the Frankfurt School of Social Research, and particularly with the critical theory of Herbert Marcuse. A literary theorist perhaps best known for his analysis of the Bible's "great code" and a Marxist philosopher and sociologist make for admittedly strange bedfellows, and yet both thinkers call attention to the need for a literary and aesthetic education as a means of combatting the alienated, almost mechanistic, "one-dimensional" condition in which members of modern, Western societies find themselves.[3] Although both Frye and Marcuse were addressing the social and spiritual crises of the 1950s and 1960s, their work retains value today. Recent threats to programs in higher education, along with the worldwide financial crisis and the generalized anxieties that have accompanied it, have sparked spirited protests around the globe. In an earlier moment of social upheaval, the May '68 militants of Paris popularized the slogan "Power to the imagination!" In recent years, arguably, we have seen a waning of precisely this power. The postmodern condition, as Fredric Jameson has pointed out, is characterized in part by the diminution of the imagination itself, which is apparent in the inability of even the most hopeful futurists to imagine radical alternatives to the existing social and economic formations. The vocation of literature, in Frye's elegant argument, is to educate the imagination, and it makes sense that those wishing to impede the utopian impulse of the aesthetic sphere would also hope for a devaluation of comparative literature, the humanities, and liberal arts in general. Present-day struggles thus recall the earlier situation from which Frye, Marcuse, and others launched their own critiques. One hundred years after Frye's birth and more than fifty years after *The Educated Imagination*'s publication, this erstwhile "old-fashioned" critic and criticism finds new urgency and relevancy for scholars today.

In *The Educated Imagination*, Northrop Frye endeavored to explain the value of literature and literary study in the modern, scientific, and—to borrow an expression from the Frankfurt School—highly rationalized society of the early 1960s. Containing lectures originally delivered in a series of CBC Radio broadcasts in 1962, this marvelous little book was intended for a broad, non-specialist audience. This is wholly appropriate, since Frye's overall argument is that literature is not a narrow disciplinary field in which a small group of specialists debate arcane details, but a critical practice for anyone and everyone to engage in. Literary study allows one to make sense of the world by establishing new or alternative ways of imagining the world. As Frye puts it, "Literature speaks the language of the imagination, and the study of literature is supposed to train and improve the imagination."[4] In Frye's view, the function of literature is to educate the imagination, which would empower it and, in turn, lead individuals to greater fulfillment and happiness, freeing them from the crass materialism, status-seeking, and sterile technocracies of Western civilization at that time. I consider this as a fundamentally utopian vision. Indeed, although they come at it from different perspectives and with different ends, Frye's position complements that of Marcuse, perhaps the greatest utopian thinker of that day. In the writings of both thinkers, the utopian impulse behind art and literature establishes these practices in opposition to the societal status quo.

In the early 1960s, both Frye and Marcuse recognized that the aesthetic sphere was under threat in what Marcuse labeled the "one-dimensional" societies of the post-war West, not to mention the often crippling repression of literary productions elsewhere, and both expressed concern that the individual's life in such societies was becoming increasingly meaningless. For Frye and Marcuse, the imagination, nourished and instructed by literature and the arts, operated as a force that opposed the basic banality and drab thoughtlessness of the era's mainstream culture. Dated as their language sometimes sounds, with phrases like "status-symbols" or "the Establishment" occasionally jarring the ears of a reader thoroughly immersed in an unavoidable consumer culture today, Frye's and Marcuse's critiques seem to me rather timely, in this new Gilded Age of conspicuous consumption, astonishing disparities in wealth, globalization of capitalism, and the permeation of mass media into nearly all zones of everyday life.

Perhaps it seems overly optimistic to say, but the idea of imagination as a revolutionary force retains value in an era in which real alternatives to the status quo are taken to be, not just impossible, but unimaginable. In an oft-cited comment, Fredric Jameson has pointed out that "[i]t seems to be easier for us today to imagine the thoroughgoing deterioration of the earth and of nature than the breakdown of late capitalism." Less well known is Jameson's indispensable follow-up to this remark: "perhaps this is due to some weakness in our imaginations."[5] In this crucial observation lies the fate of the utopian impulse in the era of globalization, for it must be clear by now that for those in "advanced" industrialized places the technological and productive capabilities are already far beyond what the most utopian thinkers of past generations envisioned. In other words, it is not for lack of material or manpower that the vision of some radically alternative social formation seems so remote, even inconceivable; rather, according to Jameson's formulation, it is the weakness of the imagination that appears to be the greatest obstacle to any utopian project.

The predominance of a dystopian sensibility may well be a sign of the times, and Lyman Tower Sargent has suggested that "dystopia became the dominant literary form" of the twentieth century.[6] In *Scraps of the Untainted Sky*, Tom Moylan has demonstrated the degree to which "critical dystopias" might also display their own utopian impulse, that is, by highlighting the utopian text's important negative or critical function, which is to criticize implicitly or explicitly the status quo.[7] But Jameson has also argued that, with respect to both form and content, dystopias are fundamentally unrelated to utopias, and in any event the inability to imagine a more positive alternatives may be another way of merely affirming the negativity of actual existing conditions.[8] Indeed, the classic dystopias of twentieth-century literature, such as Aldous Huxley's *Brave New World* or George Orwell's *Nineteen-Eighty-Four*, were very much critiques of the present, or perhaps "near-future," rather than imaginative projections of a distant, different time. Hence, if alternatives to the present social configurations are to be envisioned, the imagination itself needs to be empowered, and the utopian impulse of Frye and Marcuse, among others, offers an example of, if not a prescription for, how the educated imagination may function as a critical tool for actual praxis in the twenty-first-century world system. This is not to say that the sufficiently well-read individual will be somehow able to design a feasible utopia. Rather, as I argue below, the individual and collective subjects with empowered imaginations may be better able to interpret, and to change, the actual world in which they live.

As Frye makes clear in *The Educated Imagination* and elsewhere, the sort of work performed by literature already projects us beyond the flaming walls of the world (to borrow a phrase from Lucretius) and into an alternate, but no doubt still quite real, realm of the imagination. "Literature belongs to the world man constructs, not to the world man sees; to his home, not his environment."[9] Even the most realistic literature is already utopian in its ability to produce alternative realities. Here I am not referring to *utopia* as a distinct genre or literary form, which is the subject of Frye's great 1965 essay "Varieties of Literary Utopias," although that study artfully demonstrates the ways that the speculative myth-making in the generic mode of utopia helps readers and writers make sense of the limits and possibilities of their own "real world."[10] But the utopian impulse to which I refer is not confined to imagined societies in other spaces or times. It is just as visible in Charles Dickens's London, Honoré de Balzac's Paris, Herman Melville's whale-ship, or William Faulkner's Yoknapatawpha County as in the more traditional utopias embodied in Thomas More's *Utopia*, Francis Bacon's *The New Atlantis*, Edward Bellamy's *Looking Backward*, or William Morris's ideal communities in *News from Nowhere*. As I have argued elsewhere, the author of a literary work projects a figurative map or spatial representation of the places, persons, and events depicted, and this literary cartography frequently figures forth what might be considered otherworldly spaces even within the seemingly real world.[11] Moreover, one could say that the elements of utopian or fantastic narrative are necessarily present in the attempt to give shape to the world through literary representation. So the utopian functions and effects of literature may reveal themselves any text. And, not surprisingly, the reader's own experience of the literary world may take on utopian dimensions not necessarily intended by the author.

The utopian impulse, in this sense, forms a sort of subterranean thread linking author to reader and text, which nevertheless emerges and becomes visible in surprising, sometimes unforeseen ways. As I have argued in *Utopia in the Age of Globalization*, utopia is not so much the depiction of an ideal place or a future state outside of the spatiotemporal limits of the present status quo as it is the attempt to map the world itself.[12] In seeing the world from this strange perspective, one discovers a reality that is in many respects *more* real, something Frye also underscores.

Fictional worlds are obviously distinct from the one in which we live. However, it is not merely that the imagination can project an alternative reality or "otherworld" that serves as a critique of the actually existing order. The empowered imagination may be all the more important in its capacity to produce an image of reality itself. As Marcuse puts it,

> The truth value of the imagination relates not only to the past but also to the future: the forms of freedom and happiness which it invokes claim to deliver the historical *reality*. In its refusal to accept as final the limitations imposed on freedom and happiness by the reality principle, in its refusal to forget what *can be*, lies the critical function of phantasy [...] Art allied itself with the revolution. Uncompromising adherence to the strict truth value of imagination comprehends reality more fully. That the propositions of the artistic imagination are untrue in terms of the actual organization of the facts belongs to the essence of their truth.[13]

Note here the reversal of the traditional priority of truth and fiction. From this rejection of the straightforwardly, scientifically factual in favor of a more comprehensive, speculative overview afforded by aesthetic productions, the educated imagination is necessarily critical, in the best sense of the word. The aesthetic dimension, which after all refers to ways of seeing, makes possible vistas that would be otherwise unavailable to the individual.

Coming at it from a somewhat different critical tradition, Frye also underscores a similar point in *The Educated Imagination*. Although he insists that works of literature maintain their independence and autonomy, remaining obstinately apart from the exigencies of the "real" world, Frye maintains that the "anything goes" realm of the imagination inoculates the careful student of literature from bigotry and closed-mindedness. For instance, to cite one of many relevant examples, Frye notes that the study of literature teaches tolerance toward others and with respect to cultural difference. "In our imagination our own beliefs are also only possibilities, but we can see the possibilities in the beliefs of others. Bigots and fanatics seldom have any use for the arts, because they're so preoccupied with their beliefs and actions that they can't see them also as possibilities."[14] The vistas and vantages made possible through a careful reading of literary texts inform our perspectives as we deal with our own reality, and through this process, they can also transform the underlying reality itself. Literature at once offers a critical distance from and a visceral engagement with the real world in which we struggle to make sense of things. Ironically, perhaps, it is the *estrangements* of literature that enable one to assess critically one's reality, not in spite of the literary world's unreality, but precisely because of it.

This sort of thinking appears especially timely, given recent events, such as the student protests in Canada, in California, and in the United Kingdom, among other places, not to mention the Occupy Wall Street movement, the demonstrations associated with the Arab Spring and its reverberations, and the protests against austerity measures throughout Europe, to name but a few among the many sites of resistance around the globe amid the events following the global financial crisis of 2008. In these we might hear distant echoes of Paris and May 1968, where one of the great slogans of the militants, scrawled as graffiti on the wall or enunciated in a political speech, was *L'imagination au pouvoir*, or "Power to the imagination!" In this utopian vision, the empowered imagination might be given free rein to create hitherto unthought social formations, as well as new personal relations, creative forms, ways of living and so on. In the heady moments of this or that protest, such utopian possibilities seem very real indeed.

From another perspective, however, such a view may seem a bit naïve. After all, is Disney not staffed by a horde of "Imagineers"? The corporate behemoth trademarked that term in 1990s, but—perhaps a sign of the corporate "babble" against which Frye posits literary speech—this ghastly portmanteau word was apparently coined by aluminum giant ALCOA and used in its advertising as far back as the early 1940s.[15] The power of the imagination, co-opted and commodified, now seems more suited to technical, industrial, and entertainment-based applications than to social revolutionary activity. A characteristic aspect of triumphant globalization is that even the individual psyche appears to have become so infused with the late capitalist mode of production and with neoliberal ideology that one's own imagination is merely so much raw material to be manufactured into commodities. Whereas Marcuse could express alarm at the efficiency with which rationalized societies absorbed, transformed, and redirected forms of revolt into products for consumption, in fact, he had barely scratched the surface of how these developments would proliferate in the coming years. It is not merely coincidental, then, that vocal leaders in the business community, while championing "efficiency" and "accountability" but also "synergy," "creative destruction," "disruptive innovation," or "strategic dynamism" (to pronounce just a few recent buzzwords), have been among the most full-throated critics of liberal education, of the humanities, and of literature in particular.[16]

The proponents of this sort of bewildering efflorescence of the latest form of capitalism find little value in the educated imagination, although they may be pleased with the more manageable "skilled" imagination, and they certainly imagine themselves as imaginative contributors to the new "realities" they wish for these skills to make possible. Tellingly, Frye already noted in *The Educated Imagination* that the study of literature also militates in favor of free speech as opposed to "the speech of the mob," which "stands for cliché, ready-made ideas and automatic babble, and it leads us inevitably from illusion to hysteria."[17] For Frye, the study of literature—which, again, meant *educating* the imagination—was itself a means for inoculating one against the disease of this degraded and false rhetoric that misunderstood the imagination as a machine for producing marketable novelties, but little else.

Frye's opposition to "the speech of the mob" should not be confused with an elitist denigration of what the Occupy Wall Street protesters called "the 99 percent." On the contrary, given the context, Frye is actually siding with the aims of the people, broadly conceived, as against those who would attempt to manipulate the people using such "automatic babble." Frye even names two of the most pernicious sources of such degraded speech: "advertisers" and "politicians at election time."[18] Using Orwell's *Nineteen-Eighty-Four* as a clear example, Frye goes on to suggest that under a totalitarian regime, "the only way to make tyranny permanent and unshakable […] is deliberately to debase our language by turning our speech into an automatic gabble."[19] But, lest he be confused with one who simply repeats the "gabble" of Cold War political rhetoric, Frye immediately notes that an anti-Communism expressed in "hysterical clichés" inevitably reproduces the state it seeks to criticize. Or, to put it in Orwell's terms, the double-speak of anti-Communists becomes just as bad as that of Big Brother's administration, and both kinds are inimical to free speech. But Frye is not merely discussing the hysteria of political "babble." By naming advertisers even before politicians in his discussion of the forces that, wittingly or otherwise, oppose free speech, Frye emphasizes the degree to which the language of commerce so frequently finds itself at odds with humanistic or humane discourse. The disruptive innovators or strategic dynamists of corporate boardrooms are undoubtedly the products as well as the producers of such degraded speech, but in their persistent appeal to a kind of "mob," Frye understands, they effectively undermine both the truth and reality.

In this matter, Frye finds another unlikely ally from the Frankfurt School, Theodor Adorno. In *Minima Moralia*, Adorno takes issue with the "ordinary language" favored by certain mid-century analytic philosophers, but he also teases out a moral and political effect of such an approach. As Adorno puts it, referring to something akin to "the speech of the mob" in Frye,

> Shoddiness that drifts with the flow of familiar speech is taken as a sign of relevance and contact: people know what they want, because they know what other people want. Regard for the object of expression, rather than for communication, is considered suspicious: anything specific, not taken from pre-existent patterns, appears inconsiderate, a symptom of eccentricity, almost of confusion. Contemporary logic, which makes so much of its clarity, has naïvely adopted this perverted notion of everyday speech. Vague expression permits the hearer to imagine whatever suits him and what he already thinks in any case. Rigorous formulation demands unambiguousness, conceptual effort, from which people are deliberately discouraged, and imposes on them in advance of any content a suspension of all received opinions, and thus a separation from oneself that the hearer violently resists. Only what they do not need to know, they consider understandable; only that which is truly alienated, the word molded by commerce, strikes them as trustworthy.[20]

Adorno is here speaking of the need for philosophy to be expressed in a language not already colonized and commodified by commercial interests, which unsurprisingly wish to appeal to "the speech of the mob" than to the considered criticism of the thoughtful reader. Here, "the mob," is in effect the product of such speech, for once its spell is broken, the "mob" dissolves into discrete thinkers once more. In Adorno, the estrangement of truly philosophical discourse, its very difference from everyday communication, makes it far more capable of approaching the truth of social life than the ostensibly more familiar, but actually more alienating, language of radio, television, and other segments of the culture industry.

In Frye, literature—particularly a multinational, multilinguistic, historically and formally varied, *comparative literature*—offers a similarly liberating estrangement from everyday experience, from the increasingly prepackaged sense of the ordinary in modern industrialized societies. In this, Frye is in the august if somewhat unexpected company of Bertolt Brecht and his *Verfremdungseffekt* and the Russian Formalists with their *ostranenie*. In all of these, the mark of an effectively literary experience is visible in its ability to estrange or defamiliarize the "real world" for the reader, viewer, or auditor. As Viktor Shklovsky put it in one well-known formulation, "[t]he technique of art is to make objects 'unfamiliar,' to make forms difficult, to increase the difficulty and length of perception because the process of perception is an aesthetic end in itself and must be prolonged."[21] This by now fairly commonplace understanding of poetic discourse, which distinguishes it from the more prosaic and informational modes of communicating, as a defamiliarization by which one can perceive and linger about the artificiality or constructedness of the work of art, is very much related to Frye's conception of literary studies as a means of educating the imagination. For once we encounter the sheer weirdness of literary language, whether in poetry or prose, we find ourselves in a contact zone between real and imagined worlds.

The British fantasist and science-fiction writer China Miéville has argued that the distinction between fantastic and realistic literature does not really hold. Rather, he has tried to make a subtler distinction between "the literature of recognition versus that of estrangement."[22] The latter might include not only works decidedly categorized the genre of fantasy, like J. R. R. Tolkien's *The Hobbit*, but also works like *Moby-Dick*, in which the events and characters are technically possible, but which is nevertheless exceedingly strange. For Miéville, both sorts of literature could do an effective job, but he finds that "there is something more powerful, ambitious, intriguing and radical" about the fiction of estrangement.

Miéville's discussion is a nuanced variation of an earlier defense of fantasy. Although he is defending the fantasy genre or mode from those very Marxist critics who would dismiss fantasy as escapist or reactionary, Miéville draws upon the Marxist critique of capitalism in making his claim that fantasy offers a better approach than even realism for getting at the truth of the "real world." After discussing Karl Marx's analysis in *Capital* of the fetishism of the commodity and the hidden social relations embedded in the commodity form, Miéville observes that "'Real' life under capitalism *is a fantasy*: 'realism,' narrowly defined, is therefore a 'realistic' depiction of 'an absurdity which is true,' but no less absurd for that. Narrow 'realism' is as partial and ideological as 'reality' itself."[23] Further, Miéville insists, the "apparent epistemological radicalism of the fantastic mode's basic predicate," namely that "the impossible is true," makes it well suited to the task of an oppositional or critical project (42–43). It should be noted, however, that Miéville quite rightly does not claim that fantasy is itself a revolutionary mode or "acts as a guide to political action."[24] The value of fantasy lies less in its politics, which could lie anywhere on the political spectrum, than in its imaginative encounter with radical alterity itself. However, as Miéville concludes, "the fantastic might be a mode peculiarly suited to and resonant with the forms of modernity. [...] Fantasy is a mode that, in constructing an internally coherent but actually impossible totality—constructed on the basis that the impossible is, for this work, *true*—mimics the 'absurdity' of capitalist modernity."[25]

Miéville's defense of fantasy or the literature of estrangement, much like Marcuse's discussion of the utopian impulse in the aesthetic sphere, aligns well with Frye's understanding of literature and literary studies as modes of educating the imagination. Like these others, Frye recognizes that literature, precisely because it provides this access to an imaginative activity beyond the crude *hic et nunc* of daily, lived experience in modern Western societies, makes possible an encounter with a world *more real* than the so-called "real world" of advertisers and politicians. In a sense, then, the worlds disclosed through literary studies are utopian after all.

Frye concludes his lectures on the educated imagination with a sort of parable about a contemporary everyman, "an intelligent man [who] has been chasing status symbols his whole life," but who suddenly discovers that this meaningless world has collapsed around him, for whatever reasons and in whatever ways. "No psychiatrist or clergyman can do him any good, because his state of mind is neither sick nor sinful."[26] Rather, it is his imagination that is impoverished. Now seeking education as a starving man seeks food, he is able to educate his imagination through a study of literature. The man realizes that what he had thought was the *only* world was really two worlds: "One is all around us, the other is a vision inside our minds, born and fostered by the imagination, yet real enough for us to try to make the world we see conform to its shape."[27] And, as Frye hastens to make clear, this is *not* a secondary world into which one might try to escape, but above all the window into a place *far more real* than the illusory society to which the man was previously limited. The world discovered by the educated imagination is emphatically not illusory, according to Frye. "It is the real world, the real form of human society hidden behind the one we see. It's the world of what humanity has done, and therefore can do, the world revealed to us in the arts and sciences."[28] With an educated imagination, such a person—and each of us, too—may at last begin to see the real world more clearly, which remains impossible while any of us can still manage to get by with weakened or inactive imaginations in a rather limited, therefore *unreal*, world that is falsely presented to us *as* the real world by those who would have us employ only the speech of the mob.

The slogan of my title, "Power to the Educated Imagination!," thus reflects a political agenda, a utopian strategy to achieve a life beyond the mind-numbing and banal consumerism affirmed on almost all sides today as our sole *raison d'être*. This is not to say that existential angst can be entirely dissipated by reading literature or that literary criticism will solve the world's material problems, of course, but that the educated imagination might offer vistas into possible alternatives to the present situation, in large part by allowing one to see the all-too-real present configuration from fresh perspectives.

The crises of the 1960s occasioned in Frye a reconsideration of an earlier moment of twentieth-century madness and, perhaps, an optative or forward-looking glance at the struggles to come. As Michael Dolzani writes in "From the Defeated: Northrop Frye and the Literary Symbol,"

> the 1969 Preface to [a new edition of] *Fearful Symmetry* notes a parallel between the crisis of World War II, to which the book was on one level a response, and a present moment in which "reactionary and radical forces alike are once more in the grip of the nihilistic psychosis that Blake described so powerfully in *Jerusalem*."[29]

But, notably, in the same paragraph from which Dolzani quotes, Frye begins by repeating two lines from Blake, about "the central Cities of the Nations,/ Where Human Thought is crush'd beneath the iron hand of Power," and Frye ends by noting that, "one of the most hopeful signs [today] is the immensely increased sense of the urgency and immediacy of what Blake had to say."[30] In other words, Frye's dismay at the existential and cultural crises of the 1960s was tempered somewhat by his conviction that literary study, here figured forth in the poetry of William Blake, might empower the imagination in ways that could enable us to overcome the "nihilistic psychosis" plaguing contemporary society. No less than destructive political ideologies, as Frye had also made clear, the venal commercialism and anti-intellectual popular culture were also mobilized against the freedoms afforded by literary studies through the production of an educated imagination. Frye understood well that, whether felt as an iron hand or as a seductive caress, certain Powers were arrayed against Human Thought.

In *An Essay on Liberation*, published the same year as Frye's preface to the new edition of *Fearful Symmetry*, Marcuse acknowledged that the limits upon the imagination might be imposed by repressive forces in society or by broader historical constraints or both, but beyond such limits, "there is also the space, both physical and mental, for building a realm of freedom which is not that of the present" and "which necessitates an historical break with the past and present."[31] Frye's own theory and criticism, as well as the incalculable influence Frye has had over others' critical and literary works, demonstrates that such a break can be descried and experienced through the study of literature. Comparative literature in particular, by extending beyond locale, region, or nation and into a proper world literature, is essential for making sense of, and imagining alternatives to, the somewhat illusory "real world" we occupy. In the purposive act of reading literature, of taking products of the imagination seriously, this utopian project is already begun.

Notes

1 An very early version of this chapter was first presented at "Educating the Imagination: A Conference in Honour of Northrop Frye on the Centenary of His Birth," at Victoria College, University of Toronto, in October 2012.
2 See Slavoj Žižek, *The Year of Dreaming Dangerously* (London: Verso, 2012).
3 See Herbert Marcuse, *One-Dimensional Man: Studies in the Ideology of Advanced Industrial Society* (Boston: Beacon Press, 1966).
4 Northrop Frye, *The Educated Imagination* (Bloomington: Indiana University Press, 1964), 134.
5 Fredric Jameson, *The Seeds of Time* (Berkeley: University of California Press, 1994), xii.
6 Lyman Tower Sargent, *Utopianism: A Very Short Introduction* (Oxford: Oxford University Press, 2010), 29.
7 See Tom Moylan, *Scraps of the Untainted Sky: Science Fiction, Utopia, Dystopia* (Boulder: Westview, 2000).
8 See Jameson, *The Seeds of Time*, 55–57.
9 Frye, *The Educated Imagination*, 27.
10 See Frye, "Varieties of Literary Utopias," *Daedalus* 94.2 (Spring 1965), 323–347.
11 See, e.g., my *Spatiality* (London: Routledge, 2013), 146–154.
12 This is the thesis of my *Utopia in the Age of Globalization: Space, Representation, and the World System* (New York: Palgrave Macmillan, 2013). For a much more sophisticated argument along the same lines, see Fredric Jameson, *Archaeologies of the Future: The Desire Called Utopia and Other Science Fictions* (London: Verso, 2005), as well as Phillip E. Wegner, *Invoking Hope: Theory and Utopia in Dark Times* (Minneapolis: University of Minnesota Press, 2020).
13 Herbert Marcuse, *Eros and Civilization* (Boston: Beacon Press, 1969), 148–149.
14 Frye, *The Educated Imagination*, 77–78.
15 See "ALCOA: The Place They Do Imagineering," *TIME* (February 16, 1942), 59.
16 To name one recent, highly publicized example, the Board of Visitors of the University of Virginia caused a nationwide outcry in 2012 when they attempted to oust the popular president of that school. Among the reported leaders of this effort were a hedge-fund manager and a real-estate developer, and, according to *The Washington Post*, the grounds for termination included the president's unwillingness to eliminate such programs German and Classics in what the Board considered a timely fashion.
17 Frye, *The Educated Imagination*, 148.
18 Ibid., 146.
19 Ibid., 147.
20 Theodor W. Adorno, *Minima Moralia: Reflections on a Damaged Life*, trans. Edmund F. N. Jephcott (London: Verso, 2005), 101, translation modified.
21 Viktor Shklovsky, "Art as Technique," *Russian Formalist Criticism: Four Essays*, eds. and trans. Lee T. Lemon and Marion J. Reis (Lincoln: University of Nebraska Press, 1965), 11.
22 Quoted in Sarah Crown, "What the Booker Prize Really Excludes," *The Guardian*, October 17, 2011: http://www.guardian.co.uk/books/booksblog/2011/oct/17/science-fiction-china-mieville.
23 China Miéville, "Editorial Introduction," *Historical Materialism* 10.4. (2002), 42.
24 Ibid., 42–43, 46.
25 Ibid., 42.

26 Frye, *The Educated Imagination*, 150.
27 Ibid., 150–151.
28 Ibid., 152.
29 Michael Dolzani, "From the Defeated: Northrop Frye and the Literary Symbol," in *Educating the Imagination: Northrop Frye, Past, Present, and Future*, eds. Alan Bewell, Neil Ten Kortenaar, Germaine Warkentin (Montreal: McGill-Queens University Press, 2015), 65.
30 Frye, *Fearful Symmetry: A Study of William Blake*, ed. Nicholas Halmi (Toronto: University of Toronto Press, 2004), 7.
31 Marcuse, *An Essay on Liberation* (Boston: Beacon Press, 1969), viii.

Chapter 13

EDWARD SAID AND MARXISM: WARS OF POSITION IN OPPOSITIONAL CRITICISM

It seems strange to put it this way, but had Edward W. Said been a Marxist, he would have been one of the most important Marxist critics of his era. In his writings and interviews, he made it clear that he was not a Marxist, and he frequently criticized both existing communism and Marxist literary criticism. And yet, as any reader of his vast and variegated corpus readily discovers, Said's thought and work is thoroughly infused with Marxist theory, critical practice, and general discourse. His most admired predecessors in literary history include a number of writers who are either self-described Marxists or sympathetic fellow travelers, and his heroes include major figures from a recognizable tradition of Western Marxism, including, notably, Karl Marx himself. Indeed, Said's writings are filled with references to a veritable who's who of twentieth-century Marxist cultural critique. And although Said never identified himself or his work as Marxist, many Marxist critics of his own generation and since, not only those engaged in postcolonial studies but also those working in other areas of literary and cultural criticism, have found his work to be valuable to their own. Said's work thus resonates with Marxism in fruitful ways, and such resonance is worth examining more closely in our present moment of neoliberalism and globalization when critics are struggling to come to terms with the state of humanistic inquiry. Said's "oppositional criticism," as he preferred to call it,[1] along with Marxist theory and criticism, remains well suited to analyzing our present situation. The elective affinities between Said's positions and Marxism suggest productive avenues for critical theory today.

This essay examines Said's anti-Marxism in the broader context of his distinctively spatial approach to literature and culture, which is tied, in large part, to his affinities toward Marxist theory. While Said does not embrace Marxism as an ideology, methodology, or epistemology, he derives much of the force of his critical investigations and discoveries from a Marxist tradition, drawing inspiration from, for example, Jean-Paul Sartre's committed aesthetics and politics, Georg Lukács's narrative theory, Antonio Gramsci's notions of hegemony and the function of intellectuals, the Frankfurt School's critique of everyday life, and Raymond Williams's cultural studies. Understanding Said's spatially oriented criticism helps to square the circle of his ambiguous relationship with Marxism and locate his quasi-Marxist theory amid his broader sense of oppositional criticism as well as his humanism and democratic criticism more generally.

Said's Quarrel with Marxism

For a critic so obviously influenced by writers associated with Marxist theory, Said has written relatively little on Marxism proper. Some might even accuse him of deliberately avoiding the topic. As Stephen Howe observes, when Said does discuss his attitude regarding Marxism, he often does so "in ways that were brief, allusive, ambivalent—and when he was more forthcoming, it was largely when directly challenged by interviewers, rather than in his own written texts."[2] Said certainly devoted no essays or books to the critique of Marxism, and he also refused to embrace Marxist criticism or theory as his own. Although Said's cultural criticism and theory owes much to that tradition, he remained somewhat ambivalent, and at times antagonistic, toward Marxism. Part of his objections, no doubt, relate to the political problems connected with what used to be called "actually existing communism"—that is, everyday life in such places as the Soviet Union, the Eastern Bloc, Cuba, China, North Korea, and Vietnam, not to mention many vaguely Stalinist regimes scattered across parts of Africa and the Middle East—but this really does not explain Said's objections to the Marxist theory of Fredric Jameson or Terry Eagleton, for instance, contemporaries whose criticism and political views Said would likely sympathize with in most cases. Nor, I think, can one simply look at the Orientalism of which Marx was, and later Marxists were, guilty as the main reason for Said's objections, because Said's secular (and later contrapuntal) approach makes room for far more objectionable figures. At first glance, Said's ambivalence toward Marxism seems to relate mostly to his vexed relationship with theory.

Said occasionally criticizes Marxists in particular and academics in general for overvaluing theory at the expense of practice. In some respects, this is Said's way of bemoaning the apolitical or at least politically disengaged or ineffective work of ivory tower intellectuals *tout court*. Said is not an opponent of the academic world, of course; he celebrates the "utopian space still provided by the university" in *Culture and Imperialism*, for example.[3] But Said decries the disciplinary rigidity and methodological narrowness he finds in the work of many of his fellow academics, and throughout his career he remained concerned that many such otherwise brilliant scholars kept themselves distant from, if not also ignorant of, the material basis for social and political theory, which is to say, the people themselves. Said is no anti-intellectual, but there is an element of E. P. Thompson's *The Poverty of Theory* in his more polemical asides; indeed, Said explicitly makes reference to this text in "Traveling Theory," a justly famous essay included in Said's *The World, the Text, and the Critic*. Just as Thompson excoriates the work of Louis Althusser and his followers, Said finds even among some very good critics a tendency toward theoretical closure that, in his view, is strictly at odds with critical consciousness. "Indeed," he writes,

> I would go so far as saying that it is the critic's job to provide resistances to theory, to open it up toward historical reality, toward society, toward human needs and interests, to point up those concrete instances drawn from everyday reality that lie outside or just beyond the interpretive area necessarily designated in advance and therefore circumscribed by any theory.[4]

Thus, the author of *Beginnings: Intention and Method*, one of the twentieth century's most profound works of literary theory, famously turns his back on theory (or at least what might now be called, in the aftermath of its heyday in academe, Theory-with-a-capital-"T"), and consequently, though almost certainly unintentionally, provides a modicum of aid and comfort to the rising tide of anti-theory sentiment within academic circles and the broader public sphere in the 1980s and after.[5]

Said is far too brilliant a critic to get caught up in mere theory-bashing, which in the United States has gone hand-in-hand with a more basic anti-intellectualism so thoroughgoing and persistent that it was noted even in the eras of Alexis de Tocqueville and Thomas Jefferson. However, in a moment that coincided with the ascent of Thatcherism and Reaganism, Said is especially hard on critics whose political sympathies ought to have made them actively resistant, but whose work seems too far removed from the exigencies of everyday life.

For example, in his 1982 essay "Opponents, Audiences, Constituencies, and Community," Said discusses Jameson's *The Political Unconscious*, a "major work of intellectual criticism" that displays "rare brilliance and learning" and makes a "remarkably complex and deeply attractive argument" regarding the priority of a political interpretation of texts and, more particularly, of Marxism as the "untranscendable horizon" (Jameson's echo of Sartre's expression) of contemporary criticism and theory.[6] Said argues that Jameson's ingenious exposition of a certain type of politics, "the politics defined by political theory from Hegel to Louis Althusser and Ernst Bloch," tends to ignore or downplay another, "the politics of struggle and power in the everyday world, which in the United States at least has been won, so to speak, by Reagan." Said thinks that this lack of attention to the second type of politics is due, in large part, to the fact that "Jameson's assumed constituency is an audience of cultural-literary critics," which "in contemporary America is premised and made possible by the separation of disciplines" into "autonomous realms of human effort."[7] Said also finds Jameson's objections to appeals to morality, something Jameson derives almost as much from Friedrich Nietzsche as from Marx, to be part of this disciplinary provincialism. Jameson argues that "ideological commitment is not first and foremost a matter of moral choice but of the taking of sides in a struggle between embattled groups."[8] Said concedes that this framing allows the category of moral choice to be "de-Platonized and historicized," but finds Jameson to be strangely naïve with respect to the roles played by moral choice and moral outrage in existent political struggles, such as those involving the dispossession of a family's land.[9]

For his own part, Jameson's position with respect to moralizing, which he views as epistemologically unproductive and ontologically false, has been consistent throughout his career and derives much of its urgency from the sort of historic political struggles Said later recognizes as requiring a contrapuntal approach. Following Nietzsche's lead (and also Sartre's, one might add), Jameson maintains that behind every ethical argument lies the traces of power relations, such that the ostensibly urgent moral or ethical arguments often mask the truly political content of such perceptions. Moreover, the dialectic itself cautions one to be skeptical of hasty judgments, especially because the logic of the dialectical reversal dictates that what might appear "bad" at a given moment or in a discrete situation can reveal itself to be altogether "good" in another time and place. In Jameson's words,

> a genuinely historical and dialectical analysis of such phenomena—particularly when it is a matter of a present of time and of history in which we ourselves exist and struggle—cannot afford the impoverished luxury of such absolute moralizing judgements: the dialectic is "beyond good and evil" in the sense of some easy taking of sides, whence the glacial and inhuman spirit of its historical vision.[10]

Being always situated (to again emphasize a Sartrean and existentialist point), our perspective is necessarily limited by the time and place in which we find ourselves at any given moment, a limitation that in turn means that our judgments about the relative goodness or badness of this or that aspect of our situation must remain somewhat provisional. That does not mean that we do not make judgments—an absurd proposition that even if possible would not be very practicable—but only that we do so from an always and already engaged, situated position. This notion actually comports well with Said's idea of oppositional criticism except for the fact that Said maintains his commitment to the moral register associated with liberal humanism. In this respect, one can liken his critique of Jameson to his eventual move away from Michel Foucault, another theorist whom Said admires but in the end cannot ultimately endorse owing to the French philosopher's theory of power, which, in Said's view, does not respond effectively to the ethical imperatives of the present.

In sum, part of Said's aversion to Marxism is its apparently bloodless abstractions in the face of real-world struggles, or in other words, its commitment to theory or to a body of theories without a concomitant engagement with the exigencies of everyday life. This is a pretty common knock on Marxism, going back to its origins. I recall a conversation with one of my former professors, the historian Lawrence Goodwyn, who asserted that Marx's *The Eighteenth Brumaire* was one of the greatest works of social theory ever written but added, "It's a little thin on people." The old theory-versus-practice divide is made a point of moral opprobrium by anti-Marxists, who argue (erroneously) that all philosophy is practically worthless and that only direct actions matter. Perhaps they would even cite Marx, in an attempt to prove the hypocrisy of Marxism, using his pithy and well-known eleventh thesis on Feuerbach: "The philosophers have only interpreted the world, in various ways; the point, however, is to change it." But even this line is not opposed to theory, as ought to be clear on the face of it and is especially vivid when considering that, in the eighth thesis of the same series, Marx advises that theory must delve into "human practice and the contemplation of this practice."[11] Marx was not opposed to theory, still less to interpretation, but he was not satisfied with *merely* doing these things. As evidenced by his entire career subsequent to writing these words, Marx maintained that although theory and interpretation are needed, they are insufficient in and of themselves, to change the world.

Despite his concern that contemporary Marxist (and other "Left") critics had ceded the moral ground of real-world politics in their pursuit of a more arcane and disciplinarily circumscribed theoretical discourse, Said was wary about anti-Marxism as well. However much disdain he may have felt for actually existing communism in the Soviet Union and other "socialist" states as well as in the deleterious effects of many self-proclaimed or Party-sponsored communist activities in Africa and the Middle East, Said certainly had no interest in red-baiting. In a 1992 interview, he repeated his by then long-held view that Marxism was "insufficient" but quickly added: "I've never indulged in anti-Marxism either. I may have been critical about certain of Marx's pronouncements, but I have never been an anti-Communist; in fact, I've denounced anti-Communism as a rhetorical and ideological ploy."[12] Following Sartre's lead, Said might prefer a policy of "anti-anticommunism," a good position to hold when faced with an unacceptable Soviet-style communism on the one hand and an almost equally abhorrent American-led anti-communism on the other. At the time, when a number of influential critics and journalists were attacking Marxists like Jameson both for being too insulated within academe and for being too radical in their views, Said's refusal to join that chorus is noteworthy, and perhaps his writings might be characterized as a kind of anti-anti-Marxism.[13] To operate under such a banner is clearly not the same thing as being a Marxist, but it also avoids the political and theoretical problems, not to mention the bad company, associated with anti-Marxism.

As this brief discussion suggests, Said's objections to Marxist criticism are largely connected to his sense that criticism, in order to function effectively, cannot be conditioned in advance by any ideological program, which would necessarily affect if not actually predetermine the results of any critical inquiry before it is even begun. In Said's view, such criticism would inevitably function as a quasi-religious discourse that removes human agency and intellect from the equation, installing instead a supra-human principle or logic that would provide answers befitting its own preconceived conceptions of the world. Said also bemoans the fact that the development of strictly defined disciplinary fields have undermined the effectiveness of criticism and even introduced their own orthodoxies, which he parodies by writing, "I'm sorry, I can't understand this—I'm a literary critic, not a sociologist."[14] For instance, Said criticizes Jameson for limiting his vision to the bailiwick of literary studies in *The Political Unconscious*, although Jameson's work, even in that book, which is devoted to the question of interpretation, certainly ranges across many disciplinary boundaries; Jameson's own range of interests seem well nigh universal, such that Colin MacCabe quips that "nothing cultural is alien to him."[15] The enhanced interdisciplinarity of cultural studies since the 1980s may have caused Said to modify this view, but one could argue that Marxism, in its insistence upon connecting the economic and the political to other spheres (including, notably, the aesthetic), was already far less guilty of disciplinary narrow-mindedness than other theoretical or critical traditions.

In addition, Said laments that, especially but not exclusively in the US, Marxism "risks becoming an academic subspecialty."[16] Considering that the United States has no truly operative socialist political presence, at least when compared with many European countries, Said finds that Marxism is largely academic, both in the literal sense that its most significant adherents and leaders are university professors rather than labor organizers or politicians and in the figurative, usually dismissive sense of not mattering in the so-called real world. As Said put it in *The World, the Text, and the Critic*, which was written amid the intellectual pathos of a moment beholden to a triumphant and hegemonic Reaganism, when the more radical or utopian prospects of the previous decades appeared to have evanesced completely, "[t]he net effect of 'doing' Marxist criticism or writing at the present time is of course to declare political preference, but it is also to put oneself outside a great many things going on in the world, so to speak, and in other kinds of criticism."[17] Without meaning to, perhaps, Said joins liberal and conservative critics in dismissing Marxism as a pseudo-religion, a merely academic exercise in theory, and an utterly irrelevant discourse.[18]

But that is certainly not Said's ultimate position with respect to the theories and practices associated with Marxism. In his very next sentence, Said avers, "I have been more influenced by Marxists than by Marxism or any other *ism*."[19] The list of names mentioned in my second paragraph above certainly testifies to this, as Said's work is infused with the ideas of earlier critics, a large number of whom viewed themselves as Marxists of one type or another, even as they often vehemently disagreed among themselves. The history of twentieth-century Marxist criticism and theory—its orthodoxies and apostasies, later developments, disputes, intrigues, refinements, adaptations, extrapolations, and so forth—is that of a robust, mostly interdisciplinary (*avant la lettre*) or multidisciplinary set of discursive practices, to borrow a Foucauldian term, in which the crisis that is modernity or postmodernity is made visible and conceptualizable. Although Said demurs understandably enough when it comes to using the label "Marxist," he recognizes the contributions of this discourse both to his work and the work he thinks we ought to be doing: "at its best, this work also teaches us how to be critical, rather than how to be good members of a school."[20]

Said's ambivalence toward Marxism reflects his reluctance to embrace any -*ism* at all, which for him necessarily implies a presupposed adherence to an ideological position that amounts to a sort of religious belief. Writing in an entirely different context, Said delivers an impassioned and persuasive argument in favor of secular criticism. By this he means both that criticism must sever its ancient connections to mysticism and to the exegesis of Scripture and that criticism should recognize its situatedness in, and its affiliations with, the world. Hence, for Said, various *grand récits* like Marxism (according to a certain understanding of it, at least) constitute a sort of "sacred narrative" that elevates and removes the object of study from the real world of human interactions and struggle, from that *irdische Welt* of Erich Auerbach's philology and from the rest of world literature. In the conclusion to *The World, the Text, and the Critic*, Said writes that such theories are similar to "religious discourse" in that "each serves as an agent of closure, shutting off human investigation, criticism, and effort in deference to the authority of the more-than-human, the supernatural, the other-worldly," whereas "secular" criticism enables "a sense of history and human production, along with a healthy skepticism about various official idols venerated by culture and by system."[21] It seems that the main thrust of Said's objection to Marxism, conceived of as a vast but coherent body of knowledge and mode of investigation, is that it may be or become a system of authority that shuts down further critical inquiry. There is no doubt that this quasi-religious status has been all too powerfully realized in various states or regimes associated with communism, although it has also been realized by most non- or anti-communist regimes as well: hence, Said's critique of Orientalism in British, French, and American political and scholarly discourse.

In an effort to eschew political labels like "Marxist" or "liberal" more generally, Said famously wrote that "[w]ere [he] to use one word consistently along with *criticism* (not as a modification but as an emphatic) it would be *oppositional*."[22] He explains that "[i]f criticism is reducible neither to a doctrine nor a political position on a particular question, and if it is to be in the world and self-aware simultaneously, then its identity is its difference from other cultural activities and from systems of thought or of method."[23] Understanding Said's aversion to systems of thought in this sense, one might also recognize how much this vision of criticism comports with Marx's and with the long line of Marxist criticism and theory that follows from it. I am thinking of the perspective of a young Marx, who in his famous 1843 letter to Arnold Ruge wrote that he was opposed to "dogmatic abstraction" and insisted that the urgent project of the present must be "a ruthless criticism of everything existing, ruthless in two senses: The criticism must not be afraid of its own conclusions, nor of conflict with the powers that be."[24] Marx's position is rooted in a sense of spatiotemporal situatedness that critics such as Sartre, Jameson, and Said also emphasize: that is, the critical consciousness of one's place in the world, of one's worldliness. This basic Marxist precept is one shared by Said, and it informs the critical practice and *Weltanschauung* of their democratic humanism as well.

Critical Consciousness as a Spatial Sense

In "Traveling Theory," his meticulously elaborated critique of contemporary literary theory, Said worries that a theory—not only Marxist theory, of course—could take on a somewhat religious role, becoming "an ideological trap" that "transfixes both its users and what it is used on," which in turn would mean that "[c]riticism would no longer be possible."[25] Said argues that, in place of theory, we should strive for what he calls "critical consciousness," which he understands in a specifically spatial way. He writes:

> No reading is ever neutral or innocent, and by the same token every text and every reader is to some extent the product of a theoretical standpoint, however implicit or unconscious such a standpoint may be. I am arguing, however, that we distinguish theory from critical consciousness by saying that the latter is a sort of spatial sense, a sort of measuring faculty for locating and situating theory, and this means that theory has to be grasped in the space and the time out of which it emerges as part of its time, working in and for it, responding to it; then, consequently, that first place can be measured against subsequent places where the theory turns up for use. The critical consciousness is the awareness of the differences between situation, awareness too of the fact that no system or theory exhausts the situation out of which it emerges or to which it is transported. And, above all, critical consciousness is awareness of the resistances to theory, reactions to it elicited by those concrete experiences or interpretations with which it is in conflict.[26]

In distinguishing critical consciousness from theory (or, again, Theory), Said argues for a more spatially oriented approach, one that pays particular attention to the situation, the site or sites of struggle, and thus also to spatial relations among various situations, places, and circumstances. Said's critique of an identifiably Marxist critical theory thus involves a spatial turn.

As I have discussed in a number of other works, including my introduction to *The Geocritical Legacies of Edward W. Said*, the concepts of, as well as practices related to, space, place, and mapping have become key elements of literary and cultural studies over the past few decades.[27] What has been called the "spatial turn" in recent critical theory has highlighted the significance of spatiality in comparative and world literature, among other areas, as the relations between geographical knowledge and cultural productions have been subject to greater scrutiny by scholars in various disciplinary fields. Geocriticism, literary cartography, and the spatial humanities more generally have introduced new approaches to and interpretations of literature, while also drawing from the spatially oriented interventions of scholars not necessarily associated with these emergent discourses. Among the most influential of these scholars, Said represents an important figure in the development of spatially oriented cultural criticism. Although it would be misleading and anachronistic to characterize him as a geocritic, Said remains a powerful precursor whose writings on a vast range of subjects offer indispensable resources for scholars interested in the relations between spatiality, representation, and cultural forms. Said's oppositional criticism connects his diverse projects in relation to a spatially inflected critical consciousness.

Said is a significant force in the development of a type of spatial cultural or literary studies. For example, he was able to connect narrative representation in a nineteenth-century novel to the most complicated conundrums of contemporary politics and extending a project like that of Williams's *The Country and the City* into a multinational approach to literature. In works such as *Orientalism* and *Culture and Imperialism*, Said directly undertakes what he refers to as a "geographical inquiry into historical experience,"[28] but even his less overtly geographical or political texts, such as *Beginnings* and *Musical Elaborations*, raise valuable questions pertaining to the relationship between space and culture. In such writings, Said persistently demonstrates the human (or, as Nietzsche would add, all-too-human) need for a sort of figurative mapping, particularly in the form of aesthetic productions, of the social, historical, and cultural spaces in which we live and struggle. From his earliest writings on Joseph Conrad and literary theory to his monumental studies of Orientalism and postcolonial criticism, Said always paid attention to the spatial and geographical registers of literary art, history, and representation.

The significance of both spatiality and geography is apparent, though understated, even in Said's first book, *Joseph Conrad and the Fiction of Autobiography*. Originally written as his Ph.D. dissertation at Harvard and first published by Harvard University Press in 1966, Said's study subtly assesses the spatial form as well as the geographical and historical content of Conrad's letters and short fiction. For example, Said notes that "[w]riting and life were, for [Conrad], like journeys without maps, struggles to win over and then claim unknown ground. [...] As the physical and moral geography of Europe changed, he changed too."[29] Whether speaking more or less metaphorically about *l'espace littéraire* or focusing attention on the all-too-real geography of territorial conquest, Said's entire body of work is infused with a keen sense of the spatial.

Said is perhaps best known for his contributions to postcolonial studies, which as an interdisciplinary field has been at the forefront of geocritical or spatial literary theory. Postcolonial critics like José Rabasa and Ricardo Padrón have provided significant deconstructive readings of geographical discourses surrounding New World colonization, and geographers such as J. B. Harley and Derek Gregory have demonstrated how cartographic practices frequently served imperialist programs, whether or not the cartographers involved were aware of it.³⁰ In *How to Lie with Maps*, Mark Monmonier shows how even the mathematical projections used in mapmaking came to serve ideological purposes, often in ways that supported colonial practices. Speaking of the Mercator projection, a map projection that distorts the represented areas of space by aggrandizing those located further from the equator, Monmonier writes that "[t]he English especially liked the way the Mercator flattered the British Empire with a central meridian through Greenwich and prominent far-flung colonies like Australia, Canada, and South Africa."³¹ Said makes clear the ways that both literary and scientific productions in the eighteenth and nineteenth centuries abetted the spread and consolidation of imperialism.

In *Orientalism*, Said shows how "imaginative geography" represents different spaces and types of space according to the rather arbitrary distinctions made by individuals or groups. He observes that the

> practice of designating in one's mind a familiar space which is "ours" and an unfamiliar space which is "theirs" is a way of making geographical distinctions that can be quite arbitrary. [...] It is enough for "us" to set up these boundaries in our own minds; "they" become "they" accordingly, and both their territory and their mentality are designated as different from "ours."³²

Drawing on Gaston Bachelard's arguments in *The Poetics of Space*, Said notes that "space acquires emotional and even rational sense by a kind of poetic process, whereby the vacant and anonymous reaches of distance are converted into meaning for us here."³³ Just as the "country" and the "city" emerged, in different ways, as models for organizing the domestic spaces of Great Britain and, eventually, the world, the ancient dichotomy of "our land—barbarian land" translates into a basic structure with which to organize the spaces of one's imaginative geography.³⁴ For Said, this lies at the heart of the Orientalism that develops in and alongside European culture, especially during the nineteenth and early twentieth centuries.

In *Culture and Imperialism*, Said takes as his starting point the notion that "none of us is completely free from the struggle over geography," a struggle that is not only about imperial armies and direct conquest, but also "about ideas, about forms, about images and imaginings."³⁵ Indeed, narrative is as much the contested territory that Said wishes to explore as are the earth's physical spaces. He writes: "The main battle in imperialism is over land, of course; but when it came to who owned the land, who had the right to settle and work on it, who kept it going, who won it back, and who now plans its future—these issues were reflected, contested, and even for a time decided in narrative."³⁶ Clearly, material interests such as the profit motive and the geopolitical balance of power inspired the expansion of colonial empires, but Said rightly emphasizes the cultural aspects of imperialism (which itself is distinct from, though obviously related to, colonialism) that "allowed decent men and women to accept the notion that distant territories and their native peoples *should* be subjugated" and "these decent people could think of the *imperium* as a protracted, almost metaphysical obligation to rule subordinate, inferior, or less advanced peoples."³⁷ In his examination of the topic in *Geographical Imaginations*, Gregory alludes to this ideological aspect of the imperialist project as "dispossession by othering," whereby an identifiable "they" can be deemed unfit to govern themselves, which in turn allows the colonizers to undertake a humanitarian "civilizing mission."³⁸ Once a kind of *mission civilisatrice* is accepted, taken for granted even, it becomes the duty of those in the metropolitan center to look out for or take care of their colonized populations on the periphery. Both cartography and narrative played significant roles in establishing these cultural attitudes.

Said points out that the so-called age of empire coincided neatly with "the period in which the novel form and the new historical narrative become preeminent," but he insists that "most cultural historians, and certainly all literary scholars, have failed to remark the *geographical* notation, the theoretical mapping and charting of territories that underlies Western fiction, historical writing, and philosophical discourse of the time."³⁹ A proper analysis of this historical coincidence would require greater attention to the spatiality of empire, to the geographical and cartographical aspects of the imperial mission and its multifarious effects. An example of the type of work Said has in mind can be found in Paul Carter's magnificent *The Road to Botany Bay*, an extended essay on what Carter calls "spatial history" that explores the polyvalent uses of myth, history, geography, and mapping in the colonization of Australia.⁴⁰

Such narrative representation is not limited to the great realist tradition of the nineteenth-century novel, historiography, and ethnography. In his "Note on Modernism" in *Culture and Imperialism*, Said suggests that the new aesthetic forms reflect a growing apprehension of the irony of imperialism, of the ways in which the presence of the peripheral "other" comes to be felt in the metropolitan centers. This sentiment is enunciated by Marlow in Conrad's *Heart of Darkness* (1899) when, regarding England from the Thames River, he observes that "this also [...] has been one of the dark places on the earth," thus suggesting the degree to which Europe's supposed superiority is contingent and ephemeral.⁴¹ The greater social complexity undergirded by a multinational colonial network called for new narrative forms, and the modernist novel emerged in response. "To deal with this [complexity]," writes Said, "a new encyclopedic form became necessary." The features of the modernist novel include "a circularity of structure, inclusive and open at the same time" (as, for example, in the stream-of-consciousness narrative technique deployed in James Joyce's *Ulysses*), whose "novelty [is] based on a reformulation of old, even outdated fragments drawn self-consciously from disparate locations, sources, and cultures."[42] In Said's view, the formal structures and literary techniques of the modernist novel, in many cases irrespective of the content of the individual texts, can be seen as ways of making sense of the spatial and cultural transformations attendant on the age of imperialism.

Writing of the same historical situation from an explicitly Marxist perspective, Jameson argues that the age of imperialism or monopoly capitalism brought about a schism between "truth" and "experience," wherein, for instance, the material conditions for the possibility of an individual's lived experience in a metropolitan center are actually to be found in the far-flung colonial elsewhere. As Jameson puts it,

> [a]t this point the phenomenological experience of the individual subject—traditionally, the supreme raw material for the work of art—becomes limited to a tiny corner of the social world, a fixed-camera view of a certain section of London or the countryside or wherever. But the truth of that experience no longer coincides with the place in which it takes place. The truth of that limited daily experience of London lies, rather, in India or Jamaica or Hong Kong; it is bound up with the whole colonial system of the British Empire that determines the very quality of the individual's subjective life. Yet those structural coordinates are no longer accessible to immediate lived experience and are not even conceptualizable for most people.[43]

For Jameson, the stylistic innovations of literary modernism were attempts to deal with this existential condition, effectively operating as strategies of containment that repressed the historical and political content of the novels. However, for Said this aesthetic of modernism was a reaction to the impending breakdown of the imperial system, as the artist attempted to hold an imaginary reality together that was no longer feasible in the real world. Said concludes that "[s]patiality becomes, ironically, the characteristic of an aesthetic rather than of political domination, as more and more regions—from India to Africa to the Caribbean—challenge the classical empires and their cultures."[44] The spatiotemporal transformations of the world system in the early-to-mid-twentieth century thus find representational counterparts in the aesthetic and formal innovations within modernist literary practices.

The spatial turn in the humanities and social sciences, motivated in part by the work of Marxists and postcolonial critics, has placed greater emphasis in recent years on literary geography, literary cartography, and geocriticism, enabling critical interventions into these fields and suggesting new possibilities for them. Said's wide-ranging literary criticism, cultural history, and political activism have been and remain extremely influential with respect to such important developments.

Conclusion

In an essay that very much appears to be an acknowledgment of influence (and bearing the deceptively broad title "History, Literature, and Geography"), Said discusses three critics whose analyses of literature, culture, and society helped to shape his own: Auerbach, Lukács, and Gramsci. The latter, in particular, may be credited with helping to focus Said's thinking on matters of space and geography. As Said writes, Gramsci is "the producer of a certain type of critical consciousness, which I believe is geographical and spatial in its fundamental coordinates."[45] (463). In Gramsci's "unity" of theory and practice, Said asserts,

> all ideas, all texts, all writings are imbedded in actual geographical situations that make them possible, and that in turn make them extend institutionally and temporally. History therefore derives from a discontinuous geography. [...]
>
> Connected to all this, then, we must remember that most of Gramsci's terminology—hegemony, social territory, ensembles of relationship, intellectuals, civil and political society, emergent and traditional classes, territories, regions, domains, historical blocks—is what I would call a critical and geographical rather than encyclopedic or totalizing nominative or systematic terminology. [...] The basic social contest for Gramsci is the one over hegemony, that is, the control of essentially heterogenous, discontinuous, non-identical, and *unequal* geographies of human habitation and effort.[46]

For Said, part of the appeal of Gramsci's work is its insistence, as with Sartre's work, that "politics and power and collectivity are always involved when culture, ideas, and texts are to be studied and/or analyzed. More important, this also applies to the writing of texts—such as his own, which are always *situated*."[47]

For all his implicit or explicit criticism of a certain Hegelian or totalizing Marxism, Said here again participates in a vibrant Marxist tradition.

For example, Jameson notes that a core feature of the dialectic is its unflagging commitment to the "logic of the situation," as opposed to logic of individual consciousness or abstract notions like "society." He contends that "[t]he emphasis on the logic of the situation, the constant changeability of the situation, its primacy and the way in which it allows certain things to be possible and others not: that would lead to a kind of thinking that I would call dialectical."[48] From this position, Jameson's exploratory elaboration of a dialectical criticism at the end of *Marxism and Form* is intimately related to his later work on the political unconscious, cognitive mapping, and utopia, and this once more demonstrates its essentially Sartrean heritage, a heritage that Said himself shares. And, although the phrase itself is not yet in his mind, Jameson's reflections on the "new modernism" of the 1960s, distinct from its *fin-de-siècle* predecessor, suggest the degree to which the concept of the postmodern was already insinuating itself into his criticism as early as 1971 or before.[49] In such a postmodern situation, the project of dialectical criticism is all the more needed, since only that project heroically attempts to square the circle of, and give form to, both lived experience and the social totality, which is impossible from the limited perspective of various specialized disciplines. As Jameson observes, "[t]he works of culture come to us as signs of an all-but-forgotten code, as symptoms of diseases no longer even recognized as such, as fragments of a totality we have long since lost the organs to see." Today, Jameson asserts, everything "cries out for commentary, for interpretation, for decipherment, for diagnosis"—in other words, for the traditional duties of literary criticism.[50] Marxist criticism is uniquely suited to this situation, not only because it does a better job than those other, more specialized or local varieties of criticism, but also because it always and already contains their concerns within its own.

As Jameson makes clear, building on the work of others in the Marxist tradition, the logic of the situation and the Sartrean insistence upon our fundamental situatedness, historically and geographically, are not fundamentally at odds with some more global conception of the totality. In other words, Marxism does not, strictly speaking, impose some abstract structure upon the particularities of concrete situations but rather attempts to identify and to make connections between seemingly separate and discrete phenomena, which are themselves often held apart conceptually in such a way as to exert the hegemony of a particular group over another, as when the artifacts of culture and held to be outside the realm of social or political struggles. In many respects, the Marxist approach to culture and society is similar to Said's.[51] In his emphasis on the spatiality of critical consciousness, he joins with Marxism in the ruthless criticism of all that exists, perhaps even against his own instincts.

Notes

1. Edward W. Said, *The World, the Text, and the Critic* (Cambridge: Harvard University Press, 1983), 29.
2. Stephen Howe, "Edward Said and Marxism: Anxieties of Influence," *Cultural Critique* 67 (Fall 2007), 50. This article provides a superb overview of Said's critical relationship with Marxist theory and criticism.
3. Said, *Culture and Imperialism* (Knopf, 1993), xxvi. Given the heavy-handed ideological assaults on higher education and the academic world more generally, far worse today than in 1993, it is well worth quoting Said's comment in full: "In its writing [the writing of *Culture and Imperialism*] I have availed myself of the utopian space still provided by the university, which I believe must remain a place where such vital issues are investigated, discussed, reflected on. For it to become a site where social and political issues are actually either imposed or resolved would be to remove the university's function and turn it into an adjunct to whatever political party is in power" (xxvi).
4. Said, *The World, the Text, and the Critic*, 242.
5. See, e.g., Stephen Knapp and Walter Benn Michaels, "Against Theory," *Critical Inquiry* 8.4 (Summer 1982), 723–742; republished in W. J. T. Mitchell ed., *Against Theory: Literary Studies and the New Pragmatism* (Chicago: University of Chicago Press, 1985).
6. Said, "Opponents, Audiences, Constituencies, and Community," *Critical Inquiry* 9.1 (1982), 13.
7. Ibid., 13, 14.
8. Fredric Jameson, *The Political Unconscious: Narrative as a Socially Symbolic Act* (Ithaca: Cornell University Press, 1981), 290.
9. Said, "Opponents, Audiences," 14.
10. Jameson, *Postmodernism, or, the Cultural Logic of Late Capitalism* (Durham: Duke University Press, 1991), 62.
11. Karl Marc, "Theses on Feuerbach," trans. W. Lough, in *The Marx-Engels Reader*, ed. Robert C. Tucker (New York: W.W. Norton, 1972), 109.
12. Said, "Interview," in *Edward Said: A Critical Reader*, ed. Michael Sprinker (Oxford: Blackwell, 1992), 259–260.
13. This period, roughly the early 1980s through the mid-1990s, witnessed the emergence of anti-Left critique of higher education by such figures as former director of the National Endowment of the Humanities and President Reagan's Secretary of Education William J. Bennett, whose 1984 government report *To Reclaim a Legacy*, criticizing canon reform and multiculturalism, became national news. In 1987, Allan Bloom's *The Closing of the American Mind: How Higher Education Has Failed Democracy and Impoverished the Souls of Today's Students* and E. D. Hirsch's *Cultural Literacy* became bestsellers. These texts were followed in rapid succession by even more venal, politically charged Jeremiads such as Charles J. Sykes's *ProfScam*, Roger Kimball's *Tenured Radicals*, and the later-to-be-convicted-felon Dinesh D'Souza's *Illiberal Education*. With the continuing publication of similarly outraged diatribes against university professors and higher education over the past thirty years, one could argue that this genre, launched in the mid-1980s, has never gone out of style.
14. Said, "Opponents, Audiences," 13.
15. Colin MacCabe, "Preface," in Fredric Jameson, *The Geopolitical Aesthetic: Cinema and Space in the World System* (Bloomington and London: Indiana University Press and the British Film Institute, 1992), ix.

16 Said, *The World, the Text, and the Critic*, 28.
17 Ibid., 29.
18 Harry Harootunian points out a potential contradiction in the way that Said's work valorizes the literature, music, and art of a European tradition while also arguing for the elimination of cultural and geographical divisions on the order of "East" and "West." See Harootunian, "Conjectural Traces: Said's 'Inventory'," *Critical Inquiry* 31.2 (Winter 2005), 431–442.
19 Said, *The World, the Text, and the Critic*, 29.
20 Ibid.
21 Said, *The World, the Text, and the Critic*, 290.
22 Said, *The World, the Text, and the Critic*, 29. In "Criticism between Opposition and Counterpoint," Jonathan Arac observes that Said's shift toward a "contrapuntal" approach to criticism in *Culture and Imperialism* is a dramatic revision of his earlier "oppositional" view. See Arac, "Criticism between Opposition and Counterpoint," *boundary 2* 25.2 (Summer 1998), 55–69.
23 Said, *The World, the Text, and the Critic*, 29.
24 Marx, "For a Ruthless Criticism of Everything Existing," trans. Ronald Rogowski, in *The Marx-Engels Reader*, ed. Robert C. Tucker (New York: W.W. Norton, 1972), 8.
25 Said, *The World, the Text, and the Critic*, 241.
26 Ibid., 241–242.
27 See, e.g., my "Introduction: The World, the Text, and the Geocritic," in *The Geocritical Legacies of Edward W. Said: Spatiality, Critical Humanism, and Comparative Literature*, ed. Robert T. Tally Jr. (New York: Palgrave, 2015), 1–16.
28 Said, *Culture and Imperialism*, 7.
29 Said, *Joseph Conrad and the Fiction of Autobiography* (New York: Columbia University Press, 2008), 63.
30 See José Rabasa, *Inventing America: Spanish Historiography and the Formation of Eurocentrism* (Norman: University of Oklahoma Press, 1993); Ricardo Padrón, *The Spacious Word: Cartography, Literature, and Empire in Early Modern Spain* (Chicago: University of Chicago Press, 2004); Derek Gregory, *Geographical Imaginations* (Oxford: Blackwell, 1994); and J. B. Harley, *The New Nature of Maps: Essays in the History of Cartography*, ed. Paul Laxon (Baltimorre: Johns Hopkins University Press, 2001).
31 Mark Monmonier, *How to Lie with Maps* (Chicago: University of Chicago Press, 1991), 96.
32 Said, *Orientalism* (New York: Vintage, 1978), 54.
33 Ibid., 55. See also Gaston Bachelard, *The Poetics of Space*, trans. Maria Jolas (Boston: Beacon Press, 1969).
34 Said, *Orientalism*, 54.
35 Said, *Culture and Imperialism*, 7.
36 Ibid., xii–xiii.
37 Ibid., 7; emphasis in original.
38 Gregory, *Geographical Imaginations*, 179.
39 Said, *Culture and Imperialism*, 58; emphasis in original.
40 Paul Carter, *The Road to Botany Bay: An Exploration of Landscape and History* (Minneapolis: University of Minnesota Press, 2010).
41 Joseph Conrad, *Heart of Darkness and the Secret Sharer* (New York: Bantam, 1981), 6.
42 Said, *Culture and Imperialism*, 189.
43 Jameson, *Postmodernism*, 411.
44 Said, *Culture and Imperialism*, 190.

45 Said, "History, Literature, and Geography," *Reflections on Exile and Other Essays* (Cambridge: Harvard University Press, 2000), 463.
46 Ibid., 466–467, emphasis in original.
47 Ibid., 465–466, emphasis in original.
48 Jameson, "Interview with Xudong Zhang," *Jameson on Jameson: Conversations on Cultural Marxism*, ed. Ian Buchanan (Durham: Duke University Press, 2007), 174.
49 Jameson, *Marxism and Form: Twentieth-Century Dialectical Theories of Literature* (Princeton: Princeton University Press, 1971), 413–414.
50 Ibid., 416.
51 But see Vivek Chibber, "Orientalism and Its Afterlives," *Catalyst* 4.3 (2020): https://catalyst-journal.com/vol4/no3/orientalism-and-its-afterlives.

Chapter 14

AN AMERICAN BAKHTIN: JONATHAN ARAC, OR, THE VOCATION OF THE CRITIC

In his Preface to *Impure Worlds: The Institution of Literature in the Age of the Novel* (2011), Jonathan Arac reflects upon his more than forty-year career as a literary scholar, critic, and historian, tying his own multifaceted project to the inspiring figures of Walter Benjamin and Edward Said, "two exiles, the Jew and the Arab," whose critical thinking had fueled Arac's own work. Arac refers especially to his personal experience, first as a university student, then as a professor, but in naming these two thinkers—two radically different, yet somehow mutually resonating cultural critics—Arac also registers the degree to which mixed, hybrid, or indeed "impure" strains of critical inquiry contribute to his own distinctive work. As Arac puts it, the phrase *impure worlds* "names a zone of inquiry and resource that has shaped my thought for a long time."[1] Indeed, one might go so far as to say that "purity," in literature, culture, and society, is inimical to criticism, in as much as literature, a social institution, necessarily reflects and gives form to the heterogeneous elements that make up social experience in a distinct time and place. Benjamin's kaleidoscopic analysis of the Paris arcades and Said's contrapuntal, secular criticism offer examples of this critical vocation in practice.[2] So does Arac's new literary history of the age of the novel, an era in which that form's heteroglossia and multi-formalism, as Mikhail Bakhtin explored so evocatively, approximates the transformative diversity of the societies and cultures in which it is produced.[3]

With Arac, this commitment to "impurity" underwrites a methodological imperative as well, as he has consistently sought to trouble disciplinary distinctions, making connections between previously separate phenomena and finding hidden affiliations among apparently unrelated writers and texts. It would be difficult to characterize Arac's body of work, given the sort of professional, disciplinary, or subdisciplinary labels available to us. To be sure, Arac is an Americanist, particularly with respect to nineteenth-century

American literature, and he has written influential articles and books on Herman Melville, Nathaniel Hawthorne, Mark Twain, and others. His book-length study of narrative forms in the nineteenth-century United States, which appeared in the monumental *Cambridge History of American Literature* project edited by Sacvan Bercovitch and was later made available in bookform in 2005 as *The Emergence of American Literary Narrative, 1820–1860*, confirms his status as one of the most prominent scholars of this period, place, and genre.[4] Arac's magnificent study of Twain's *Adventures of Huckleberry Finn*, as I will discuss at greater length below, is a powerful enquiry into the cultural value of a literary masterpiece in the twentieth century, as well as a sobering reflection on the role of literary criticism in national political discourse.[5] In such works he has produced innovative readings and alternative histories of well-known texts, but he has also called into question the premises, methods, and practices of American literary studies as a whole, making Arac at once a leading Americanist and a leading critic of American Studies. Arac's as yet forthcoming book, *Against Americanistics*, will undoubtedly serve as a critique of the all-too-national disciplinary field which imagines American literature by and for Americans, without paying sufficient attention to comparative, international, transnational, and postnational cultural practices. In "messing with American exceptionalism," as he has promised, Arac's revisionary approach opens up the literature of the United States to a more properly comparative literature, which may finally release the writers and texts under consideration from their long-term indentured servitude to a nationalist cultural program.[6]

Although Arac is an unquestionably influential scholar of American literature, he is also a scholar of British romanticism and Victorian literature, as well as the periods or genres of realism and modernism. Arac has, through a number of essays, made significant contributions to the study of William Wordsworth, Samuel Taylor Coleridge, Charles Dickens, and Thomas Carlyle, not to mention George Eliot and later writers. Were he inclined to remain in that particular geopolitical and literary historical zone, Arac would likely be right at home studying the literature and culture of the U.K., yet he was always a proponent of examining transnational literary relations, well before such an approach achieved its current levels of respectability. The very title of his first monograph, *Commissioned Spirits: The Shaping of Social Motion in Dickens, Carlyle, Melville, and Hawthorne* (1979), indicates not only Arac's transatlantic frame of reference, but also the degree to which he was willing to call into question traditional distinctions between nonfiction and fiction, novel and romance, or, more generally, artistic practice and social representation.[7] Moreover, while his academic background lies in these Anglophone traditions, Arac has throughout his career engaged productively with other languages and literatures, as evidenced by his marvelous essays on Goethe, Flaubert, and Baudelaire, among many others. Arac's commitment to a comparative literary approach has meant that, even when his focus has been on a particular U.S. or British text, he recognizes the profoundly resonant circulation of aesthetical, cultural, social, and political energies that make possible production, and consumption, of any distinct work of literary art.

In addition to his expertise in national or transnational literatures, Arac ought to be considered as a prominent literary theorist in his own right, even if he does not easily fit into this or that "school" of thought. The field served by what Vincent Leitch has called "Theory Incorporated,"[8] which thrives on its use of prefabricated marketing labels and reductive, bullet-point-friendly summaries, does not offer much space for considering a wide-ranging and innovative critic as Arac, whose fluency with the trendiest, cutting-edge theories of the day has always been enriched by a deep knowledge of critical traditions extending back, seemingly, to the origins of literary studies itself. In his career, Arac has proved adept at bringing Marxist, Freudian, structuralist, and poststructuralist thought to bear on his interpretations, but he has shown equal facility in considering the immense and current value of such "old-fashioned" thinkers as I. A. Richards, R. P. Blackmur, or M. H. Abrams, not to mention D. H. Lawrence, Hippolyte Taine, Matthew Arnold, or the Schlegel brothers. Given his attention to the form, Arac must certainly be viewed as an important historian and theorist of the novel, and his recent forays into debates over world literature have demonstrated the degree to which what he has called "the age of the novel" is a global affair. Among some readers, Arac may be best known for his edited or co-edited volumes, such as *The Yale Critics: Deconstruction in America* (1983), *Postmodernism and Politics* (1986), *After Foucault* (1988), or *The Consequences of Theory* (1990), all of which proved influential in those heady days when "high theory" drew such attention, for better or worse, in literature programs.[9] In that epoch, Arac imbibed much of vital substance of the theory boom—particularly through the work of Benjamin, Said, Jacques Derrida, Michel Foucault, and Fredric Jameson—without relinquishing the most valuable work of past and present, include such critics as F. O. Matthiessen, Northrop Frye, Frank Kermode, or Walter Jackson Bate, who cannot but have been considered *passé* by the then *au courant* students of criticism and theory.[10]

With his ecumenical approach to various "schools" of criticism, Arac's own scholarship has managed to preserve well-nigh forgotten critical traditions, while open-mindedly considering recent or new interventions into the field, and also keeping a weather eye out for potentially productive future forms or ideas. In fact, without losing any respect for his meticulous and sensitive readings of poetry and fiction, one might argue that Arac is best thought of as a critic or historian of literary criticism, someone with an immense knowledge of and appreciation for the methods, theories, and practices of literary studies in general. Few if any scholars working in the humanities today have his comprehensive grasp of the field of literary studies, broadly conceived, and Arac has an uncompromising vision of the critic's vocation today, while maintaining such generosity of spirit in assessing the various ways that such a vocation might express itself in practice.

And yet, as much ground as this glancing survey seems to cover, the various areas of specialization or emphasis listed in these foregoing paragraphs still do not register fully the sense of Arac's almost catholic, yet critical approach to modern literary and cultural studies.[11] The fact is that Arac has been at once a sort of generalist literary intellectual, whose interests have carried him into disparate fields of academic research and teaching, and an intensely focused, meticulous scholar who is not likely to stray into a new discursive territory before becoming thoroughly informed about its history, geography, and culture in advance. The result is that Arac has always seemed to be a kind of throwback, an academic intellectual of the F. R. Leavis or William Empson type, but who also shared the commitment of such public intellectuals as Edmund Wilson or Lionel Trilling, for whom the history and theory of literary culture, broadly conceived, was utterly integral to the reading of individual texts. At the same time, Arac has maintained a fairly "cutting edge" approach to criticism, which has colored his apparently traditional methods with a radical tinge that makes his readers aware of entirely new ways of seeing the texts and contexts under consideration.

Arac's equanimity sometimes belies his passion, as he can be at his most strikingly adversarial in those moments when he seems to be serenely observing this or that fascinating detail. Thus did his dual reading of *The Scarlet Letter*'s "Custom House" introduction and the historical circumstances of the Compromise of 1850 not only offer insight into Hawthorne and his world, but also called into question the assumptions and methods of American literary studies as practiced for more than 40 years.[12] Similarly, and more recently, his modest suggestion that Franco Moretti's wildly innovative program of "distant reading" would entail an "Anglo-Globalism" far more culturally imperialistic than previous, less "worldly" methods immediately gave pause, and it remains a sobering thought for those engaged in the study of world literature today.[13] As generous and open-minded as his critical approach remains, Arac has never shied away from conflicts when it comes to matters of personal, social, political, and professional conviction. Accordingly, a deeply polemical strain runs throughout his work. Arac is ever ready to find kernels of value in unlikely sources, but he does not suffer fools gladly when it comes to critical practice.

Perhaps this is because an intensely personal, yet also social, political, and professional, sensibility pervades Arac's work. Although Arac has not importuned his readers with undue autobiographical detail, he has followed the lead of his old teacher, Harry Levin,[14] in allowing for some personal anecdote or explanation to creep into his writing, thereby demonstrating an honesty and engagement with criticism wholly consistent with his vision of the critic's vocation. Particularly in his introductions and increasingly in journal articles, Arac discloses a self-reflective and retrospective cast of mind, by which he connects his personal experience, motives, and goals to the larger practice of literary criticism, theory, and history. These indulgences, if I may call them that, are easily forgiven, since Arac has himself lived (and read) through the radical transformations of the profession since the 1960s. Moreover, his eyewitness testimony comports well with the theory he espouses, since he has always maintained that the critic, no matter the periods or genres or themes that occupy his or her attention, is *situated* in a particular time and place. The critic, however versed in history and theory, cannot rise above the rooftops to take a God's-eye view of the scene, but always operates *in mediis rebus*, as Kermode famously noted.[15] Criticism, like literature, is a social institution, and the critic operates within the social, as well as historical and political, milieu.

Arac's first book, *Commissioned Spirits*, takes as its *Ansatzpunkt* the development of a new literary technique or formal possibility in the nineteenth-century novel, as seen especially in Dickens's *Bleak House* and Melville's *Moby-Dick*, works which attempted to represent the social totality of their day. This "totalized organization" was the made possible by literary *overview*—and, while Arac does not overload his carefully formal and historical argument with an abundance of citations, the influence of Foucault (especially *The Birth of the Clinic* and *Discipline and Punish*) is apparent—by which these authors were able to "reveal and transform through their powers of knowledge and vision the brute circumstances of the changing world in which they and their readers lived."[16] In his analysis, Arac deftly maneuvers between meticulously formal (even "close") readings and a broader historical survey, tying such major events and movements as the French Revolution, romanticism, urbanization, and industrialization to aesthetic forms by looking at the way that these writers, "commissioned spirits" in an apt phrase from Wordsworth, struggled to represent and to shape what Arac refers to as social motion. The almost bewildering mobility, indeed, chaos, of these mid-nineteenth-century societies, symbolized in part by the transformative technology of the railroad, "fostered a wish for a clarifying overview."[17] Arac draws out the means by which Dickens, Carlyle, Melville, and Hawthorne register the profound effects of these revolutionary shifts in social energies.

Particularly memorable to me is the way Arac takes specific passages that then demonstrate the connection of minute detail to a social totality. For instance, in his reading of "The Line" from *Moby-Dick*, which begins with a description of a discrete thing, but eventually circumscribes and encompasses all, physically and metaphysically, Arac shows how "[m]etaphor and metonymy interact to form a whole, a synecdochic cosmos of interlinked parts."[18] In this manner, Arac reveals a powerful new way of imaginatively ordering social space, but he does not condemn this apparently panoptic power as an evil. Rather, in his conclusion, Arac encourages us "to explore what the potentials of this literary and social form were and are, to try to recover what we have lost of them, and to bring to fruition the best possibilities of the systems of knowledge and power that still encompass us."[19]

Embedded in Arac's method and argument is a vision of a new literary history, one that relies neither upon a narrow view of literary tradition or a sense of individual geniuses (or a succession of them, as with accounts of "influence").[20] In order to achieve this new literary historical practice, Arac and other like-minded scholars availed themselves of the innovative forms of critical theory that were becoming so influential in literary studies during this time, but Arac also grounded his inquiries in a historical practice that frequently seemed at odds with the semiotic or deconstructive practices of a Roland Barthes, Paul de Man, or Derrida. In *Critical Genealogies: Historical Situations for Postmodern Literary Studies* (1989), this makes for a striking and invigorating combination. Arac there offers a history of literary criticism, one that links the rich traditions of British romanticism to the most cutting edge poststructuralist theory on that moment, but Arac's presentation is also an enactment of a kind of literary criticism and history that makes connections between previously separated or ignored cultural phenomena. Using different kinds of theory—for instance, the romantic aesthetics of Wordsworth's *The Prelude* or Coleridge's *Biographia Literaria*, or the writings of Matthew Arnold, and later F. O. Matthiessen, Frank Kermode, Harold Bloom, and Geoffrey Hartman, but also Benjamin, de Man, and Jameson, among many others—Arac tries to lay a foundation for a new approach to writing literary history. Speaking of the professional vocation of literary criticism, as well as of the current intellectual climate more generally, Arac says that this study "aims to excavate the past that is necessary to account for how got here and the past that is useful for conceiving alternatives to our present condition," an elegant if provisional definition of the genealogical project envisioned by Nietzsche or Foucault.[21] Thus, in a manner far more fundamental and with more lasting repercussions than the simplistic old argument about the invasion of literary studies by certain fashionable (mostly French) philosophies, Arac demonstrates the vital connections between the formal analysis of literary texts, the social contexts out of which these texts arise, and the practice of literary criticism as a whole. Arac's attempt to lay the foundations of a new literary history in *Critical Genealogies* is also, therefore, evidence of a new way of doing criticism itself.

At around this time Arac had already begun researching what would become his book-length contribution to Bercovitch's monumental and revisionary *Cambridge History of American Literature* project. Comprising eight large volumes, the *Cambridge History* registered the profound changes in American literary and historical studies in the decades following Robert Spiller's 1948 *Literary History of the United States*, and Bercovitch enlisted an impressive array of leading scholars to essentially rewrite this history.[22] Bearing the deceptively simple title "Narrative Forms," Arac's contribution appeared in 1995, in the volume devoted to U.S. prose writing produced between 1820 and 1865; "Narrative Forms" was republished by Harvard University Press as *The Emergence of American Literary Narrative, 1820–1860*.

The stand-alone book's title gives away part of the underlying argument of Arac's project, for Arac takes as his point of departure the emergence, around 1850, of literary works that will be almost universally recognized in the twentieth century as "literary," in the now more specialized sense referring to works of written art that evince the creativity, originality, and aesthetic power of the authors. Arac is thinking especially of *The Scarlet Letter* (1850) and *Moby-Dick* (1851), books that by the mid-twentieth century had become "hypercanonized" in American literary studies.[23] Looking back, these works could be distinguished from other popular and influential narratives that did not come to be seen as *literary*, whether because on their too-timely topicality, their limited regional appeal, the narrowness of their themes, or some other such reason. Rather than telling a straightforwardly chronological story à la V. L. Parrington's 1927 *Main Currents in American Thought*, Arac adopts a generic approach, although the genres he identifies are not the usual suspects (e.g., romance, history, autobiography, etc.). Arac contrasts literary narrative with *national* narrative, a form that takes shape in the writings of James Fenimore Cooper and George Bancroft, culminating in Stowe's *Uncle Tom's Cabin*, works that attempt to represent and give form to a distinctively national culture. The dominant form during the period Arac looks at, national narratives receded from view after the Civil War, as literary writing came to be more valued, although the themes of national narrative remain audible today, in mainstream political discourse, for instance. "National narrative was part of the process by which the nation was attempting to form itself and not merely a reflection of an accomplished fact, yet it defined the ground against which the other major narrative types would stand out."[24] Arac also considers two other types, *local* and *personal* narratives, whose more limited geographical and psychological frames of reference distinguished them from both national and literary narratives; as such, they might be viewed as rival forms, even though it is clear that these genres can overlap in interesting ways, visible in what Jameson has called "generic discontinuities."[25] In examining a wide range of writers from this era, including those well known to English majors (Irving, Hawthorne, Poe, Melville, Douglass, Thoreau, and Twain), others not so familiar (Bancroft, Thorpe, Parkman, Dana, Longstreet, Henry Adams), and some who are not even American (Coleridge, Goethe, Scott, Balzac, Tocqueville), Arac manages to change the way one sees nineteenth-century U.S. literature, broadly conceived, while also more subtly intervening in current critical discussions in the 1990s, including the then-heated canon debates. Specifically, his genealogical study of antebellum prose addressed questions of what "counts" as literature, why it matters, and what are the functions of literature in society at large.

Not surprisingly, what might be considered Arac's most overtly political work, *Huckleberry Finn as Idol and Target: The Function of Criticism in Our Time* (1997), emerged from this literary historical project. As Arac relates, his interest in the subject of the use and abuse of Twain's masterpiece also stems from his concerns as both a scholar and a citizen, and he mentions not only his scholarly research but his membership in the ACLU in presenting his case. In this book, Arac takes on the controversy over the teaching of *Huckleberry Finn* in high schools (even junior high schools) that erupted in the early 1980s, garnering national attention around the novel's 1985 centennial celebrations, and continuing into the present. The most inflammatory issue, of course, involved the use of a single racist term, one that appears more than two hundred times in Twain's novel and which, as Arac pointedly obverses, was "banned from CNN and *USA Today*" during the coverage of the O. J. Simpson trial,[26] but at stake in the controversy was the value of literature and criticism in the culture more generally. Arac's study is exemplary of his methodical, even-handed, and yet thoroughly *engaged* approach to literary criticism, as Arac blends meticulous historical research, sensitive close reading, and acute political analysis in addressing the question of why this late nineteenth-century masterpiece had managed to become a site of battle in the late twentieth-century culture wars.

Crucial to this analysis are the related phenomena of what Arac names "hypercanonization" and "the nationalization of literary narrative." After all, *Huckleberry Finn* is not just any nineteenth-century novel, but arguably the *most* canonical of the works produced in the United States. As Arac shows, this hypercanonization only occurred sometime after 1930, and it really crystallized when Lionel Trilling, in a remarkably influential essay that also served as an introduction to a college textbook edition of the novel, named Huck and Jim "a community of saints," thus enlisting Twain's picaresque romance in the service of postwar liberalism.[27] Using the terms of "Narrative Forms," Arac notes that Twain's ingeniously wrought, manifestly artistic, and densely allusive *literary narrative* had become, for mid-century readers, a *national narrative* tasked with speaking deep truths about the nation's foundational sin: that is, slavery, but transmuted into the then-contemporary civil rights struggles and extended toward racial bigotry in general. At this point, Twain's novel became required reading more for its salutary lessons in civics than for its intrinsic literary value.[28] Following from this academic hypercanonization, a mainstream or popular cultural idolization of the text placed *Huckleberry Finn* beyond critique. During the 1980s, in Op-Ed pieces and other media, journalists saw fit to excoriate parents, students, and educators for questioning the propriety of teaching *Huckleberry Finn*, which, as Arac observes with irony, led to mostly white authorities attacking mostly Black parents and students for being too ignorant—the racism or, at least, the racially tinged paternalism in these formulations is difficult to miss—to understand that they are the beneficiaries of a book that repeats the *N-word* on virtually every page. But, asks Arac, "Why must the book be rescued from African American parents and students for their own good?"[29]

Arac's analysis directly addressed the contemporary debate, including Shelly Fisher Fishkin's provocative theory that Huck himself was Black (and, therefore, presumably, incapable of being a bigot, which also somehow exonerates Twain from any charges of racism),[30] but his argument demonstrates the flexibility of his sense of a "new literary history" by deftly considering, almost simultaneously, three other distinctive periods: the antebellum era in which the events of *Huckleberry Finn* are set, the late nineteenth-century America in which the novel was written and initially received, and the mid-twentieth century in which it became hypercanonized. By carefully tracking down the facts from each of these epochs, as well as scrupulously investigating Twain's own writings and the scholarship on his work, Arac is able to discredit many of the idolaters' arguments—including the specious and dismissive "That's just how everybody talked back then" canard—with respect to both historical and literary matters. Arac convincingly demonstrates that Twain and his contemporaries did not view the novel as a political allegory, and readers in the 1880s would hardly have been impressed by anti-slavery arguments twenty years after abolition, and they would not have recognized any anti-racist argument, even if the novel were to make one (for the record, it does not). Twain himself probably would not have recognized in his own work the morality that later readers would not only find there, but would insist was the very point of the novel.

For example, take a moment in the story made famous by twentieth-century critics as a sign of *Huckleberry Finn*'s inherently moral and political correctness: Huck's decision to "go to Hell." In a memorable scene, Huck debates whether he should turn in the runaway slave Jim to his owners, which he had been told was the moral thing to do, or risk damnation for neglecting to do so and thus committing a sin. Famously, he decides, "All right, then, I'll go to Hell." Many readers have cited this as a brave renunciation of a widely held but morally wrong beliefs, but Huck's decision would have been universally ratified by contemporary readers, as by twentieth-century readers, as an uncontroversially appropriate choice. The facts that Huck had already indicated his personal preference for Hell over Heaven and that Jim was already a free man (unbeknownst to himself and Huck) are also worth noting. The liberal embrace of *Huckleberry Finn* as a national narrative is thus revealed to be, at once, a sort of wish-fulfillment that assuages guilty consciences and a weapon against those who argue that more, much more remains to be done in order to atone for these sins in the present. As Arac puts it,

> This is what the idolatry adds up to. Liberal white American opinion identifies with the wonderful boy Huck. Even though his society was racist, he was not, and so "we" are not. For African Americans to challenge this view is to challenge "us" just where "we" feel ourselves most intimately virtuous, and it is also to challenge Mark Twain, and thereby the America he "quintessentially" represents. I find this structure pernicious.[31]

By looking into the long history of *Huckleberry Finn*, Arac shows how the notion that Twain's masterpiece was somehow a denunciation of racism only appeared around 1950, and to now deny that *Huckleberry Finn* is a fundamentally anti-racist narrative "is not to oppose struggles against racism, but it is to try to take that argument beyond the stage of 1950."[32] The academic hypercanonization and journalistic idolatry, with its nationalization of a literary narrative, has endorsed the unwelcome proposition that an imaginary solution to the real problem of racial inequality, made available to American students through the teaching of this exemplary novel, can actually serve as a meaningful substitute for the political action required to realize the ideal of racial equality in the United States.[33]

As the subtitle of Arac's study indicates, the ultimate question concerns not how or whether to use a particular cultural artifact but, rather, the functions of criticism in our time. Unmistakably discernible just beneath the mass of scholarly research and elegant prose is Arac's smoldering anger that literary criticism itself has been so effectively employed to support "pernicious" structures of power and knowledge that have caused real social harm, despite whatever good intentions lay at the sources. The vocation of the critic is, in some senses, sacred, but Arac has no interest in imagining some critical priesthood. Indeed, part of his critique of "Americanistics"— the appreciative, even celebratory, study of America by Americans and for Americans—is surely the degree to which it has formed an almost religious image of its object of inquiry. To borrow from Said, one of Arac's former teachers and sources of intellectual inspiration, this sort of scholarship effectively closes off pathways for critical inquiry, which require a "secular criticism." Speaking of Orientalism, with its notions of "the" West and "the" Orient, but I think it would apply to other disciplinary formations, including various kinds of literary studies, Said asserts:

> To say of such grand ideas and their discourse that they have something in common with religious discourse is to say that each serves as an agent of closure, shutting off human investigation, criticism, and effort in deference to the authority of the more-than-human, the supernatural, the other-worldly. [...] [W]hat a secular attitude enables—a sense of history and human production, along with a healthy skepticism about various official idols venerated by culture and by system—is diminished, if not eliminated, by appeals to what cannot be thought and explained, except by consensus and appeals to authority.[34]

Arac's commitment to impurity, as well as his aversion to idols, derives from a similar concern for the human, the hybrid, and the heteroglossic.

Famously, the literary form best suited to represent or embody this sort of heterogeneous, human experience is the novel, and Bakhtin is among the more influential theorists and historians of the novel *as* a polyphonic, heteroglossic, and multiformal form. Long before he had read Bakhtin, Arac says, he was drawn to "the big, complicated, messy worlds" imagined by Dickens and Melville in the nineteenth century, or by Thomas Pynchon and Doris Lessing in the twentieth.[35] Bakhtin discovered such productive messiness in Sterne, Cervantes, Rabelais, and even earlier writers, but Arac has been particularly interested in what he has recently referred to as "the age of the novel." In *Impure Worlds*, Arac mentions the period "from Balzac and Dickens to the deaths of Joyce and Woolf, a century in which the Western novel seems to dominate cultural accomplishment."[36] Arac's literary history has disclosed that, "[t]he age that invented world literature [i.e., Goethe's] has long seemed to posterity as the age of the novel," and [h]ardly had *literature* come to replace *poetry* as the operative term than literature came to mean novels."[37] Arac has suggested that, in the United States at least, this age of the novel is over, as more dominant forms have taken its erstwhile central place.[38] But if the age of the novel, as Arac sees it, is past, its legacies and reverberations are not. The critic who is professionally attuned to the form's intrinsic impurities and social possibilities, which exert their power even after their "age" has ended, is thus capable of making sense of the ways these representational forms give shape to the world, which itself has become all the more complicated and unrepresentable. As Jameson observed,

> no society has ever been quite so mystified in quite so many ways as our own, saturated as it is with messages and information, the very vehicles of mystification (language, as Talleyrand put it, having been given us in order to conceal our thoughts). If everything were transparent, then no ideology would be possible, and no domination either: evidently that is not our case.[39]

The critic, trained in close reading, interpretation, and comparative literature, is perhaps best equipped to undertake the task of understanding such a society, the first step toward imagining alternatives.

Regarding my title, I am not really sure that Arac should be thought of as an American Bakhtin, although I think Arac, with his nuanced criticism, theory, and history of the novel and of modern literature in general, deserves to be considered in the company of this Russian forebear. I borrow the allusion from Marshall Brown, who in his back-cover endorsement of *Impure Worlds* identified Arac as "a Bakhtin for the twenty-first century." The breadth of his interests, the acumen of his analysis, and the forcefulness of his conclusions would certainly make Arac a worthy successor to Bakhtin and his illustrious generation of critics. Like Bakhtin, but also somewhat like Benjamin and Said, Arac's work is not easy to categorize, and he has never been credited or burdened with such labels as Marxist, deconstructionist, new historicist, or psychoanalytic critic, even when he frequently avails himself of useful insights of these "schools." Without limiting himself to this or that methodological or political position, Arac has consistently demonstrated the effectiveness of a blended approach to criticism, theory, and history. Additionally, Arac's thoroughgoing commitment to the critical exigencies of his own time and place, as well as his insistence on taking into careful consideration other times and places, animates all of his work, in the classroom as in his writings.

I have not spoken of Arac the teacher, although I first encountered his perceptive mind and generous spirit in the university classroom, but it almost goes without saying—but, as Foucault apparently joked,[40] it goes better *with* saying—that Arac's approach to criticism comports especially well with a pedagogy designed to include all manner of students, to support their variegated interests, and to guide them as they explore complicated, impure worlds. Arac's teaching and writing have influenced virtually all of my own, which is likely the case for all of his former students.[41] As quite probably the United States' leading critic and historian of literary criticism, Arac has educated generations of literary critics and historians in the richly diverse materials of that field, while always paying close attention to both the aesthetic and social value of literature. His example alone offers an education in the vocation of the critic today, and his thoroughly historical and astutely political body of work is richly suggestive of future directions in criticism.

Notes

1 Jonathan Arac, *Impure Worlds: The Institution of Literature in the Age of the Novel* (New York: Fordham University Press, 2011), vii.
2 See, e.g., Walter Benjamin, *The Arcades Project*, trans. Howard Eiland and Kevin McLaughlin (Cambridge: Harvard University Press, 1999); Edward W. Said, *Culture and Imperialism* (New York: Knopf, 1993).
3 See Mikhail Bakhtin, "Discourse in the Novel," in *The Dialogic Imagination: Four Essays*, trans. Carol Emerson and Michael Holquist (Austin: University of Texas Press, 1981).
4 See Arac, "Narrative Forms," in Sacvan Bercovitch, ed., *The Cambridge History of American Literature, Vol. 2: Prose Writing, 1820–1865* (Cambridge: Cambridge University Press, 1995), 605–777; republished, with a new bibliographic essay, as Arac, *The Emergence of American Literary Narrative, 1820–1860* (Cambridge: Harvard University Press, 2005).
5 Arac, *Huckleberry Finn as Idol and Target: The Functions of Criticism in Our Time* (Madison: University of Wisconsin Press, 1997).
6 Arac, *Impure Worlds*, viii; Arac mentions that *Against Americanistics* was to be published in 2011, but the project has apparently been scrapped or postponed; as of October 2022, it has not appeared.
7 See Arac's "Preface to the Morningside Edition," in *Commissioned Spirits: The Shaping of Social Motion in Dickens, Carlyle, Melville, and Hawthorne* (New York: Columbia University Press, 1989), ix.
8 See Vincent B. Leitch, *Literary Criticism in the 21st Century: Theory Renaissance* (London: Bloomsbury, 2014), 151–152.
9 Arac's edited collections of essays on literary and critical theory include *The Yale Critics: Deconstruction in America*, co-edited with Wlad Godzich and Wallace Martin (Minneapolis: University of Minnesota Press, 1983); *Postmodernism and Politics* (Minneapolis: University of Minnesota Press, 1986); *After Foucault: Humanistic Knowledge, Postmodern Challenges* (New Brunswick: Rutgers University Press, 1988); *Consequences of Theory*, co-edited with Barbara Johnson (Baltimore: Johns Hopkins University Press, 1990). Arac has also co-edited, with Harriet Ritvo, *Macropolitics of Nineteenth-Century Literature: Nationalism, Exoticism, Imperialism* (Durham: Duke University Press, 1991); and, with Ronald A. T. Judy, *Ralph Ellison: The Next Fifty Years*, a special issue of *boundary 2* 30.2 (2003).

10 Arac once told me a story of trying to induce graduate students in the early 1980s to read Jean-Paul Sartre, whom the students thought had been rendered *passé* by Derrida and Foucault; Arac said that he was able to convince them of Sartre's relevance by pointing out the French thinker's influence on Said and Jameson.
11 Not that Arac's approach is "undiscriminating," but he has praised Northrop Frye's aversion to "negative evaluation" and insisted that the critic's purview not be limited to a handful of approved texts. See Arac, "The Social Vision of Frye's Criticism: The Scandal of Undiscriminating Catholicity," *The University of Toronto Quarterly* 81.1 (Winter 2012), 163–173.
12 See Arac, "The Politics of *The Scarlet Letter*," in Sacvan Bercovitch and Myra Jehlen, eds., *Ideology and Classic American Literature* (Cambridge: Cambridge University Press, 1986), 247–266.
13 See Arac, "Anglo-Globalism," *New Left Review* 16 (July–August 2002), 35–45.
14 In *The Power of Blackness*, Harry Levin, who was Arac's dissertation director at Harvard, begins by accounting for his unlikely entry into formal American Studies in writing that study of Hawthorne, Poe, and Melville, noting that "[t]o begin a book with a personal word is, as I have learned from Hawthorne, rather an act of diffidence than of presumption." See Levin, *The Power of Blackness* (Athens: The Ohio University Press, 1989 [orig. 1958]), v–xii.
15 Frank Kermode, *The Sense of an Ending: Studies in the Theory of Fiction* (Oxford: Oxford University Press, 1967), 7.
16 Arac, *Commissioned Spirits*, xvii.
17 Ibid., 3.
18 Ibid., 35.
19 Ibid., 190.
20 Arac, "Preface to the Morningside Edition," *Commissioned Spirits*, ix.
21 Arac, *Critical Genealogies: Historical Situations for Postmodern Literary Studies* (New York: Columbia University Press, 1989), 2.
22 Bercovitch himself was himself arguably the leading Americanist of his generation, and the other contributors to the *Cambridge History* form, albeit with a few notable omissions, a veritable "Who's who" list of major scholars of American literature. In addition to Arac, contributors include Myra Jehlen, Emory Elliott, David S. Shields, Robert A. Ferguson, Michael T. Gilmore, Michael D. Bell, Eric Sundquist, Barbara L. Packer, Richard H. Brodhead, Nancy Bentley, Walter Benn Michaels, Susan L. Mizruchi, Neal Dolan, Barbara Packer, Shira Wolosky, Andrew Dubois, Frank Lentricchia, Irene Ramalho Santos, William Cain, Jonathan Fortescue, David Minter, Rafia Zafar, Werner Sollors, Christopher Bigsby, Morris Dickstein, John Burt, Wendy Steiner, Cyrus R. K. Patell, Robert von Hallberg, Evan Carton, and Gerald Graff.
23 Arac coined the term "hypercanonization" in "Nationalism, Hypercanonization, and *Huckleberry Finn*," *boundary 2* 19.1 (1992), which was reprinted in Donald E. Pease, ed., *National Identities and Post-Americanist Narratives* (Durham: Duke University Press, 1994) and later became a chapter in Arac's *Huckleberry Finn as Idol and Target*.
24 Arac, *The Emergence of American Literary Narrative, 1820–1860* (Cambridge: Harvard University Press, 2005), 3.
25 See, e.g., Jameson, *The Political Unconscious: Narrative as a Socially Symbolic Act* (Ithaca: Cornell University Press, 1981), 144.
26 Arac, *Huckleberry Finn as Idol and Target*, 24.

27 See Trilling, *The Liberal Imagination: Essays on Literature and Society* (Garden City, NY: Doubleday, 1953), 104, 106.
28 See Arac, "Why Does No One Care about the Aesthetic Value of *Huckleberry Finn*?," *New Literary History* 30.4 (Autumn 1999), 769–784.
29 Arac, *Huckleberry Finn as Idol and Target*, 10.
30 See Shelley Fisher Fishkin, *Was Huck Black?: Mark Twain and African-American Voices* (Oxford: Oxford University Press, 1993).
31 Arac, *Huckleberry Finn as Idol and Target*, 13.
32 Ibid., 15.
33 Ibid., 217–218.
34 Edward W. Said, *The World, the Text, and the Critic* (Cambridge: Harvard University Press, 1983), 290.
35 Arac, *Impure Worlds*, vii–viii.
36 Ibid., x.
37 Arac, "Literary History in a Global Age," *New Literary History* 39.3 (Summer 2008), 757.
38 See Arac, "What Kind of History Does the Theory of the Novel Require?," *NOVEL: A Forum on Fiction* 42.2 (2009), 190–195.
39 Jameson, *The Political Unconscious*, 60–61.
40 D. A. Miller cites Foucault's quip in *The Novel and the Police* (Berkeley: University of California Press, 1988), viii.
41 But see my tribute to Arac's teaching, written on the occasion of his retirement from the University of Pittsburgh: "On Jonathan Arac," *The Fifth Floor* 21 (Fall/Winter 2020), https://www.english.pitt.edu/jonathan-arac.

Chapter 15

BATHSHEBA'S STOMACH: *POIESIS* AND CRITICISM IN PAUL A. BOVÉ'S *LOVE'S SHADOW*

Love's Shadow, by Paul A. Bové, is at once a monumental study and an enigma.[1] In modeling the sort of criticism that Bové would like to see, *Love's Shadow* also becomes impossible to discuss in the sort of critical terms Bové wishes us to abjure or abandon. *Love's Shadow* in its entirety is an essay, but also one that is made up of essays, which makes it rather recursive (not to say repetitive). This in turn makes the experience of reading and rereading it a bit like wading into the ocean, fighting through, jumping atop, diving beneath, or body-surfing on wave after wave, each one different, yet each partaking of the same substance and spirit. I would characterize that experience as exhilarating, as the diversity of forms and subjects proliferate—cultural theory, philosophy, drama, poetry (including lengthy, detailed discussions of individual poems), visual art (the chapter on Rembrandt is a *tour de force*), and so forth—while the focus on *poiesis* and criticism remains constant throughout. In its own form, *Love's Shadow* is difficult to summarize, and even more difficult to subject to critique, since its arguments remain slightly ungraspable, like those waves at the beach. To speak of this book as if it were a treatise, for example, would be to deny its essential character, but to understand and to criticize it, a reader often falls back on old habits, which would mean eliding the poetic aspects of *Love's Shadow* while highlighting its putatively philosophical ones. *Love's Shadow* is not a philosophical work, but ultimately a poetic one.

This is not to say that Bové does not make an argument. Indeed, his is a provocative and at times polemical argument aimed at key figures in literary and cultural criticism, naming names and, at the same time, as speaking critically to the field of criticism *tout court*. Bové argues that literary criticism has been under the pervasive sway of a fundamentally life-denying melancholy, which he associates primarily with the work and influence of Walter Benjamin. From that perspective, as Bové recounts, all human history is fundamentally a ruin; its "experiential mode is allegory, reduced especially in the American academy to the redundancy of allegoresis, the reading of all materials as allegories" (ix). Utopia, which Bové connects to messianism, as the secularized but still quite religious form of redemption, displaces salvation from the human world, and thus it too deals in death and destruction. Bové singles out Fredric Jameson, himself a Benjaminian critic who has long advocated for both allegory and utopia, as the chief antagonist to his argument, and Bové invokes Jameson's own success—measured largely by his having won so many professional prizes in his lifetime—as evidence of the almost insuperable hegemony of *allegoresis* in contemporary literary and cultural studies. This characterization of the work of Benjamin and of Jameson will likely be controversial, and as I discuss below, I am not convinced, even as I recognize the urgency and value of Bové's critique of the institutionalized profession of academic criticism.

Whether intended as such or not, *Love's Shadow* strikes me as a sequel to Bové's 2008 book, *Poetry against Torture: Criticism, History, and the Human*.[2] Only, in *Love's Shadow*, melancholy, *allegoresis*, and perhaps even Fredric Jameson have taken the place of torture. As Bové had then said, "poesis is the counterpoint to torture" and "there are deep civilizational and species implications in the choice of power for torture over and against poesis as the unique human quality able to make history according to humanity's best potential for subject creation."[3] In arguing for poetry *contra* torture, Bové also decried the bad faith and poor practices of academic literary criticism, specifically the "quietism of certain kinds of professionalization and 'specialization'," but there he rightly identified Stanley Fish, who unlike Jameson has unapologetically and indeed enthusiastically embraced the crassest vision of literary studies as merely one profession among others and who has gleefully celebrated the "free market" as a model for criticism.[4] Jameson is certainly not Fish. Nevertheless, in many respects, Bové's defense of *poesis* (or *poiesis*) and critique of academic critical practices in *Poetry against Torture* are taken up and elaborated further in *Love's Shadow*.

However, in *Love's Shadow*, Bové himself preemptively disavows the sort of reading I am doing here, committed as it is to the author-function and older sense of intellectual continuity, by announcing his own startling epiphany, a road-to-Damascus moment in which all that he had previously thought about criticism suddenly changed: "Visiting Rembrandt in the Louvre, I realized the relative poverty of even the best academic criticism and accepted the primacy of art and criticism over the professionalized shibboleths of neoliberal university practice" (xi). Bové recounts that he "walked into the Louvre having spent one morning rereading Walter Benjamin's notebooks of 1940," and standing before "an even more moving work, *Bethsabée au bain tenant la letter de David*, a work of a far greater imagination than Benjamin's" (284), Bové experiences his epiphany (not the term he would use, I'm sure); according to Bové, this is "the story of the book's beginning." The opposition Rembrandt *versus* Benjamin, in other words, stands in a sort of symbolic relationship to *poiesis versus allegoresis* and to criticism as it ought to be practiced *versus* its debased, cynical form in contemporary American literary studies. That he marks this occasion for us so vividly, juxtaposing Benjamin's Angel of History with Rembrandt's Bathsheba, means that we are probably not supposed to see his earlier work in the light of this one or vice versa, but nevertheless, the critique of "professional" criticism remains a constant.

The polemic which runs throughout *Love's Shadow* is directed at what Bové takes to be the dominant mode of academic criticism in the past fifty years or more, one that privileges *allegoresis* over *poiesis* and "analysis" over "criticism," as Bové defines these terms. Bové takes Jameson as the cautionary example, symptomatic of a more pervasive trend. As he puts it on the very first page of *Love's Shadow*, "Jameson's commitment to allegory and the willingness of the university literary profession to award him all the honors offered by the Modern Language Association and far more [...] marks the generalized absorption of a scholastic opinion within the guardian institutions of culture and society" (ix), and Bové returns to this theme repeatedly, in greater or lesser detail, throughout the book's remaining nine chapters. Thus, for instance, in the last chapter Bové argues that "academic critics" make and compound their mistakes when they "not only argue a priori that no work is accessible except through one or more already authorized and sometimes invisible codes of apperception but also makes the study of these codes the sole object of their attention, drawing intelligence away from the delightful study of imitation" (335). Some attentive readers will detect the reference to Jameson, and perhaps even to his famous line from *Marxism and Form*: "The works of culture come to us as signs in an all-but-forgotten code, as symptoms of diseases no longer even recognized as such, as fragments of a totality we have long since lost the organs to see."[5] Yet Jameson's own readings of such texts hardly seem to involve the "the arrogance behind melancholy, behind the monotonous dissatisfaction with finitude and technical dominance," as Bové puts it (375).[6]

Traditionally, the critique of allegory is not aimed at readers, but rather at writers who insist upon imposing a restrictive and preordained "real" meaning upon those texts, thereby limiting their readers' own imaginative acts of interpretation. Hence, for example, John Bunyan's *Pilgrim's Progress*, with its crudely one-to-one system of Christian symbols and corresponding meanings, became the default *bête noir* for Romantic critiques of allegory in the nineteenth century. To cite a more modern writer, J.R.R. Tolkien, in rejecting the view that there is any putative allegorical significance in *The Lord of the Rings*, stated that "I cordially dislike allegory in all its manifestations, and always have done so since I grew old and wary enough to detect its presence. [...] I think that many confuse 'applicability' with 'allegory'; but the one resides in the freedom of the reader, and the other in the purposed domination of the author."[7] Interestingly enough, Bové's critique of *allegoresis* targets the reader who would dominate the work of art and the artist through a hermeneutic act of transcoding, which may be closer to what Tolkien means more innocently by referring to the ways readers finds works of art to have meanings be applicable to their own historical, cultural, and social situation.

Moreover, the work of *poiesis* already involves some element of *allegoresis*, such that the two modes cannot be entirely set in opposition to one another or even separated for long. In that Aristotelian sense, in which *poiesis* is tied to imitation (*mimēsis*), the making of a work of art is already at some level the making of something *different*; that is, difference is inherent to the poetic project. And in a way, we might recognize that this "speaking differently"— that is, drawing on the Greek *allos* (different) and *agoreuein* (speaking openly)— is allegorical. The figurative, the metaphorical, the symbolic, and thus broadly speaking the allegorical seem to me to be fundamental aspects of poetry or the work of art. In our critical appreciation and, indeed, *love* for the work of art, it seems to me that we recognize its formal and semantic richness, which would include its various potential levels of polysemy. Of course, Bové knows all this far better than I do. In fact, he opens the concluding chapter with a discussion of Aristotle's *Poetics*, so I confess I remain somewhat confused by his hostility to *allegoresis* in *Love's Shadow*. At times, it seems to be based on a sense of the critic's attitude toward the work of art, rather than any explicit methodology, but Bové's chapter on Adorno, in which Adorno becomes the exemplary critic as opposed to those who work Bové decries, is enough to distinguish Bové from the proponents of surfacing reading or postcritique of recent years.[8]

Most crucial for Bové, I think, is that criticism remain attuned to *poiesis* at a fundamental level which would preclude the critic's attempt to impose one previously formulated views on the work of art under consideration. In some ways, this may be akin to Edward Said's objection to "criticism modified in advance" (e.g., by such discourses as Marxism or psychoanalysis), which would entail some sort of pre-ordained reading of the text regardless of the particular text to be read.[9] But the real problem Bové has with the sort of criticism he opposes is its professionalization, which does return him to a theme upon which he has devoted decades to sounding out. Professional criticism, including perhaps especially its institutionalization within academic disciplines and the vast systems of higher education, necessarily involves *power*, or what Bové refers to as "authoritative ways of speaking, the regularized discourses and disciplines at home in the academy" (375). That Bové himself has spent most of his life ensconced within this system is not itself an objection, for this position of privilege is also potentially the best vantage from which to bear witness to these phenomena. As the editor of *boundary 2* for over thirty years, with nearly twenty years' experience with the journal before that, Bové has seen more professional academic literary criticism and theory than most, to be sure. A true "outsider," if such a thing were possible, would be incapable of seeing any of this with much clarity. (This is yet another thing that separates Bové's arguments from those of the various anti-academic mudslingers of the popular media, for instance, as well as from those claiming to value the "lay" reader over and against the work of critics.) As early as *Intellectuals in Power* (1986),[10] and really before that too, Bové observed the degree to which critical humanism was bound up within systems of power, institutional hierarchies, and modes of legitimation (and delegitimation, of course) that gave the lie to the older image of the disinterested intellectual. The exigencies of life in the "profession" of literary criticism, Bové seems to argue, makes it virtually impossible for the critic to do otherwise than succumb to "the given and enabling habits of mind" formed in such institutional settings (335).[11]

Bové sees the true critic as an amateur, which is to say, a lover. Criticism would not only serve and illuminate that *poiesis* that affirms the human in its finitude and presence, but it is itself a *poiesis*, at least when done right, through the humble, searching, and form of the essay: "The essay is a form of *poiesis*," writes Bové, whereas "[t]he academic thesis and research article in the institutions of official culture are its antagonist. The capacities inherent in the essay form are elements of being human, the fate of which poses (and helps answer) the question of what the human is, and how it is to be human. *Poiesis* and essay manifest and enact the human" (374–375). *Love's Shadow* not only advocates for this throughout, but *models* it as well, for Bové's own readings—of Adorno, Wallace Stevens, Rembrandt, and Shakespeare, among many others—demonstrate the sort of critical *poiesis* or poetic criticism he champions.

In my view, this is no better exemplified than in the chapter devoted to Rembrandt's *Bathsheba*, the encounter with which Bové had identified as the *locus classicus* of his own personal and poetic transformation as a critic. *Love's Shadow* includes a black-and-white image of it, but I am sure that in order to truly appreciate it as a poetic critic would, we, like the author, should spend some patient and attentive time with the painting in person. (Citing a comment by Van Gogh, Bové notes that the notorious *flâneur* Charles Baudelaire failed to understand Rembrandt because he was "in a hurry," thus spending insufficient time "standing in front of the painting" [288].)

A sign of the care with which Bové himself attended to this painting's details may be found in one of my favorite paragraphs of that chapter and of *Love's Shadow*, which I admittedly quote out of context:

> Bathsheba's stomach may be lovingly painted, but it is not a realistic representation of any woman's stomach. The nude achieves its realism effectively by tricks of proportion, place, and shadow that separate this body from any anatomically or biologically existing body. The twisted left arm, in a posture that the human body cannot assume, tells the story of art's unfaithfulness to the given. It stresses the imagination's desire to achieve the goal of its own intelligence, which is importantly independent of the given. The human, in the Abrahamic stories, might be secondary, but Bathsheba is not. The craft of the stomach, of the body itself, as the vehicle for innerness or experience has value in its texture, not only in its formal design. Rembrandt's impasto combined with the rough traces of brush strokes to create the thigh and hip, as they are. His technique created the bodies marked by their physicality and position as well as by traces of experience, motion and emotion, on their flesh and bones. If there is love, it exists as Genet's goodness exists, because of art. (325)

Such a paragraph makes me wish I, too, could stand before the *Bathsheba* at the Louvre for hours on end. As Bové says, "[t]he painting is a gift to the species from its own existence as the venue for *poiesis*" (326).

Bové's language in this section amounts to poetry itself, as if the critic here has been transported by the powers of love—"Imagination as love," to be more precise—into an almost ecstatic state. "Where is love, then? It is in the immediate creation, which *poiesis* dwelling in the master of the imagination puts on offer as a mystery of the human, shadowed by the darkness of its own complex emergence, the burden of its own imagination and its remains" (326). But lest the reader imagine that such lofty sentiments incline us toward the divine, Bové will also insist that this power is "something human that lives in the species," and he observes that "the human can create the world as the dream of its own desires, fully aware that the secular finitude precludes perfection or escape from its own limited but loving nature" (326). For Bové, *poiesis* and criticism are transformative powers that celebrate the human existence, without denigrating it through nostalgia (which elegiacally demeans the present by elevating the past) or messianism (which degrades the present by positing a future as salvation from it). Nor do these powers merely reinforce the *status quo*, however, since creativity and the imagination are the very core of *poiesis* and criticism.

Throughout my readings of *Love's Shadow*, I kept finding myself reminded of Nietzsche, and indeed, I would characterize Bové's sense of criticism as a kind of *fröhlich Wissenschaft*, a *gaya scienza* or joyful wisdom, which is perhaps not too surprising, for Walter Kaufmann, in his Translator's Introduction to Nietzsche's book, has pointed out that the term "gay science" (from the fourteenth-century Provençal *gai saber*) literally referred to "the art of poetry."[12] Bové's ideas and arguments in *Love's Shadow* strike me as profoundly Nietzschean, perhaps even as modified by Gilles Deleuze's revelatory reading of the great philologist as the philosopher of affirmation and of creative thinking, the embodiment of a "nomad thought" that eludes any static (and statist) institutional encumbrances. Like Bové's poetics, Nietzsche's *amor fati*, which he had said was the basic core of his own thought,[13] eschews historical nostalgia and messianic hope, affirming existence without capitulating to the given *per se*. Surprisingly, Bové hardly cites Nietzsche at all; the index shows Nietzsche's name appears only five times in the whole book, and in each case, it is only *en passant*. Yet Nietzsche in his anti-Platonism and his anti-Christianity was the philosopher of the *gut*, thus like Rembrandt with Bathsheba's stomach more attuned to the physical substance of the human body and its transformative potential as art.

In the end, I cannot say that I am completely convinced by Bové's main arguments. I still see room for *poiesis* and *allegoresis* to fruitfully coexist, as they seem to do so elegantly and powerfully in Dante, and I believe that the critical task can involve an analytical and evaluative function that nevertheless maintains always its proper respect for the work of art and for the poet. But I agree in spirit with Bové's joyful wisdom, his commitment to *poiesis* and to criticism. *Love's Shadow*, notwithstanding my focus on that which Bove abjures, remains a book of "Yea-saying" (as Nietzsche would put it), an affirmation of the creative, imaginative, and critical in an era in which thus things are terribly lacking. If I may borrow and adapt another line from Nietzsche, this time in a late letter to Peter Gast from 1889, I would say "Sing me a new song: the world is transfigured and all the heavens are filled with joy."[14] *Love's Shadow* is such a song, dedicated to us all, and for that, I am grateful.

Notes

1 Paul A. Bové, *Love's Shadow* (Cambridge: Harvard University Press, 2021); hereinafter cited parenthetically in the text.
2 Indeed, as I recently heard Donald E. Pease assert, those two books along with *A More Conservative Place: Intellectual Culture in the Bush Era* (2013) could be thought of as a trilogy, even as they are formally quite different; *Poetry against Torture* is based on a single series of lectures, whereas *A More Conservative Place* collects articles written over a period of nearly two decades, and *Love's Shadow* is, as I say, an almost unclassifiable work.

3 Bové, *Poetry against Torture: Criticism, History, and the Human* (Hong Kong University Press, 2008), xv.
4 See, e.g., my review Gary A. Olson's *Stanley Fish, America's Enfant Terrible: An Authorized Biography*: Tally, "Keeping Up with the Fishes," *American Book Review* 39.2–3 (2018), 15–16.
5 Fredric Jameson, *Marxism and Form: Twentieth-Century Dialectical Theories of Literature* (Princeton: Princeton University Press, 1971), 416.
6 As chance would have it, Jameson published a book on Benjamin just two months prior to the publication of *Love's Shadow*, and at least part of Jameson's reading involves recuperating the critic from that pervasive sense of melancholy and ruin. See Jameson, *The Benjamin Files* (London: Verso, 2020).
7 J. R. R. Tolkien, "Foreword," *The Fellowship of the Ring* (New York: Del Ray, 2012), x–xi.
8 See, e.g., my *For a Ruthless Critique of All That Exists: Literature in an Age of Capitalist Realism* (Winchester: Zer0 Books, 2022).
9 See Edward W. Said, *The World, the Text, and the Critic* (Cambridge: Harvard University Press, 1983), 28. I think it is fair to say that Said remains a tutelary spirit and exemplar for Bové in *Love's Shadow*.
10 Bové, *Intellectuals in Power: A Genealogy of Critical Humanism* (New York: Columbia University Press, 1986).
11 Anecdotally, I recall Bové citing Said, who had complained about *la machine derridienne*, which operated with such force in the early 1980s; by that, Said meant the enabling institutions that allowed so many critics to churn out predictable deconstructions of this or that text, thereby making names for themselves and appearing in prominent academic journals, but without necessarily contributing much to the understanding of the texts or authors under consideration. Undoubtedly there is a degree to which critical practice, academic or otherwise, succumbs to "fashion" in this manner—but then, so do the publishing industries, editorial policies, grant reviewers, funding bodies, and so on, which makes the problem far more pervasive than would be the case were this the willful acts of feckless literary critics. Moreover, amid whatever "bad" work was being produced by scholars who could be accused of chasing trends, much of value was also created, not the least of which could be found among Bové's own critical writings from the 1980s.
12 Walter Kaufmann, "Translator's Introduction," to Friedrich Nietzsche, *The Gay Science* (New York: Vintage, 1974), 5–6.
13 See Nietzsche, *The Gay Science*, §276.
14 Nietzsche, *The Portable Nietzsche*, ed. and trans. Walter Kaufmann (New York: Viking, 1968), 685.

Conclusion

AN ANAGOGICAL EDUCATION

It sometimes seems that a perennial task of laborers in the vineyard of the liberal arts is to defend that labor, that vineyard, and those arts. That liberal education is under attack on various fronts is as indubitable as it is now tiresome, and in the media covering the state of higher education we see almost daily apologias, jeremiads, and polemics aimed at sounding the increasingly apocalyptic alarm. Literature students hear it a lot, of course, as they frequently deal with jokes or jibes, or sometimes earnest warnings, about the uselessness or impracticality of their field of study. Even within universities, we sometimes find ourselves on the defensive from those whom Terry Eagleton has referred to as "hard-faced philistines and crass purveyors of utility."[1] Under such circumstances, the idea of the critical genius seems utterly foreign or laughably nostalgic, and yet, the need for this sort of genius, here understood as a guide or spirit of inspiration, has perhaps never been greater.

As a scholar and critic working in the literary humanities, I do not think we need to adopt a defensive posture against such threats; nor do we need to argue for the usefulness of literature, at least not in any instrumental form. That all too easily plays into the enemies' hands, inviting those who do not appreciate what the humanities are all about to use "metrics" and "data" to characterize our "outcomes" and demonstrate our "productivity." This is, in more ways than one, quite literally beneath us as teachers, students, and lovers of literature. I want to speak of the vocation of the critic, which is the fundamental role of literary scholars, at least for the last hundred years or so. I am aware that we do much more in our language and literature departments today: rhetoric and composition, technical communication, creative writing, film and media studies, to name a few, and even within literary studies, activities include literary history, biography, and theory, along with analysis and evaluation. And yet criticism remains the cornerstone, and all students of literature are, in one way or another, guided by a spirit of critical genius.

In speaking of the "vocation" of criticism, I am well aware of the religious connotations of a "calling," even if I must emphatically emphasize criticism's *worldly* value. In many of its most powerful forms, literary criticism draws upon foundations in what we tend to think of as religious studies, whether understood in relation to textual exegesis, hermeneutics, ethics, or more speculative, theoretical visions. That is, the analysis, interpretation, and evaluation of literary and other texts, even in a purely secular context, may partake of aspects of religious scholarship. Indeed, the vocation of criticism, in the good old Weberian sense, involves a similar project of demystification, while also respecting the wealth of spiritual substance proper to literature, as may be seen in critics as different as Northrop Frye, Fredric Jameson, and Paul de Man. Drawing on the medieval conception of *anagoge*, I want to argue that the vocation of criticism today involves the patient, meticulous engagement with a given text that we know as "close reading," yes, but with the view toward a certain ascent that is the aim and effect of literary studies, or, more generally, a liberal arts education. This ascent is not that of the pilgrim's progress into the celestial spheres or the bold careerist's climb up some corporate ladder. Rather, it is the elevation of a mind now equipped to apprehend, interpret, and perhaps even transform the worldly world (*irdische Welt*) today.

In a well-known formulation, Dante distinguishes between the four levels of meaning in his letter to Can Grande della Scalla, which Dante wrote partly in order to explain what is going on in his *Commedia*. As Dante explains:

> For me be able to present what I am going to say, you must know that the sense of this work is not simple, rather it may be called polysemantic, that is, of many senses; the first sense is that which comes from the letter, the second is that of that which is signified by the letter. And the first is called the *literal*, the second *allegorical* or *moral* or *anagogical*. Which method of treatment, that it may be clearer, can be considered through these words: [Dante here quotes from Psalms] "When Israel went out of Egypt, the house of Jacob from a barbarous people, Judea was made his sanctuary, Israel his dominion" (Douay-Rheims, Ps. 113.1-2). If we look at it from the letter alone it means to us the exit of the Children of Israel from Egypt at the time of Moses; if from allegory, it means for us our redemption done by Christ; if from the moral sense, it means to us the conversion of the soul from the struggle and misery of sin to the status of grace; if from the anagogical, it means the leave taking of the blessed soul from the slavery of this corruption to the freedom of eternal glory. And though these mystical senses are called by various names, in general all can be called allegorical, because they are different from the literal or the historical. Now, allegory comes from Greek *alleon*, which in Latin means "other" or "different."[2]

A significant part of this argument involves the medieval attempt to absorb the Old Testament's message into a Christian narrative, something Dante himself does so brilliantly, while also adding Greco-Roman mythology to the ensemble, in the *Commedia*. Dante obviously wishes to emphasize the religious import of these allegorical senses, but he also underscores the degree to which *alterity* or *difference* is crucial to the interpretation of the work.

This *commitment to difference* is, in some respects, essential to the practice of criticism itself, while also informing literature and the liberal arts more generally. Although neither criticism nor the liberal arts is opposed to empirical research, it is also the case that at their core lies a deep-seated belief that one cannot simply trust the evidence of one's eyes, that one cannot stop at the merely literal interpretation. (And, yes, it is worth remembering that even a literal reading is still an interpretation.) However, in a certain calculating, more-or-less social scientific, nominally utilitarian, but nakedly commercial approach to higher education, the alterity of criticism and of the liberal arts is viewed with suspicion if not denounced entirely.

I do not think that mere pragmatism is to blame. Rather, it is probably a sort of American optimism, a duty to "be positive," that so threatens the arts and sciences of alterity. In these fields, imagining alternatives to the reality that presents itself to us is part of the job, so we also cannot help but notice when things look bad or go wrong with that reality. Fantastic visions can show us entirely different worlds, but the even most mimetically exacting forms of realism can be shown to produce other meanings, perhaps allegorical, moral, or anagogical ones. But this is partly because we can look beyond the merely apparent, rise above the scene, and achieve some critical distance. This is the critical genius at work, and such genius frequently reveals itself through our own reading, teaching, and learning. Dante has Virgil and Beatrice to guide him, just as we have our own guiding spirits, Dante among them, in literature.

In Canto XXII of *Paradiso*, for instance, Dante looks down from the fixed stars and sees the planet earth in the distance. In John Ciardi's translation:

> With my eyes I returned through every one
> of the seven spheres below, and saw this globe of ours
> to be such that I smiled, so mean did it appear.

From that vast, critical distance, the "real" world appeared quite different. Dante's point, of course, is similar to that of Hugo of St. Victor, the medieval theologian who warned against having too great a love for one's earthly home, and taught that we should view the entire world as a foreign land: *mundus totus exilium est*. But Erich Auerbach, in his marvelous essay on the philology of world literature, noted that this principle is actually well suited to one who would have a proper love *for* the world, since freeing ourselves from the limitations of the familiar, the homely, and readily apparent will actually make it possible to *know* and therefore to *love* the world all the better.[3] Critics such as Auerbach necessarily embody that critical genius that makes an educated imagination possible.

In practice, at least, this is what works like Dante's *Commedia* do: they provide us with a powerfully imaginative vision of an alternative world that, one hopes, will serve us in our own self-development. As Frye insisted back in the 1960s, in direct opposition to the "one-dimensional society" of his day, the purpose of literature as a field of study is to educate the imagination. Only with an educated imagination can one conceive of alternatives to the status quo. More, in fact: only with an educated imagination can one properly understand the status quo *as it is*, since the critical distance afforded by the imagination's distinctive vantage is a *sine qua non* for making sense of reality. The figurative overview afforded by the imagination's projection of an alternate vision literally makes possible understanding. Again, this is the role of critical genius, in elevating us, altering our perspective by estranging the world, and enabling a sense of productive alterity that can best serve us in this epoch of increasingly restrictive conformity.

Hence, perversely, the anagogical education produced through a study of the liberal arts, an education vociferously disparaged by the pragmatically minded reformers of higher education today, is in some senses *more* practical than the instrumental, supposedly jobs-oriented fields so favored by politicians, reformers, and "disruptors" of the traditional university. I am not even talking about my poor comrades in the S.T.E.M. fields; it is clear that most of the work being done in science and math in the United States is not valued at all, and the only technology and engineering that gets celebrated is that which can be seen to turn a quick buck. The anagogical aspects of S.T.E.M., which also involve the work of the imagination—it is hardly accidental, after all, that Dante compares the highest reaches of the Empyrean to the contemplations of a mathematician over a difficult problem—do not seem to be celebrated by the mass media in our time, and whatever Dantean aspects are recognized are usually intended to indicate only what is infernal.

Yet the liberal arts never excluded science, in that sense; rather, they are and remain the arts and sciences required of a free person (that's what "liberal" meant, after all), who by now must be understood, at least in part, as a person with an educated imagination. The vocation of criticism today must then be connected to this climb, to rise above the debased education that can only prepare one to serve, and to imagine alternatives available to those who may, one day, become truly free. In fact, this can be accomplished only if we are all free, which is why criticism itself, properly conceived, cannot help but be, in a sense, revolutionary: the "ruthless criticism of all that exists," to use the words of a young Karl Marx: "ruthless both in the sense of not being afraid of the results it arrives at and in the sense of being just as little afraid of conflict with the powers that be."[4] An anagogical education in the liberal arts and sciences, committed to the educated imagination and fortified with the spirit of critique, would be a significant step in the right direction.

Notes

1. Terry Eagleton, "The Slow Death of the University," *The Chronicle of Higher Education*, April 6, 2015: https://www.chronicle.com/article/the-slow-death-of-the-university/.
2. Dante, "Letter to Can Grande della Scalla," trans. James Hollander. Available online: https://faculty.georgetown.edu/jod/cangrande.english.html.
3. Erich Auerbach, "Philology and *Weltliteratur*," trans. M. and E. W. Said, *Centennial Review* 13.1 (1969), 17.
4. Karl Marx, "Letters from the *Franco-German Yearbooks*," trans. Rodney Livingstone, in *Early Writings* (New York: Vintage, 1975), 207. See also my *For a Ruthless Critique of All That Exists: Literature in an Age of Capitalist Realism* (Winchester: Zer0 Books, 2022).

ACKNOWLEDGMENTS

The Critical Situation: Vexed Perspectives in Postmodern Literary Studies comprises a number of revised versions of essays written over about a fifteen-year period, but the pedagogical, collegial, and critical influences on the thoughts contained in them go back much further. It would be impossible to list all the teachers, students, colleagues, and friends who have contributed to this work and who have done so in incalculable ways, but I hope that my gratitude is tacitly understood. Many of the ideas and arguments to be found in these papers were first presented at academic conferences and as invited talks, and I want to acknowledge the organizers, participants, and audiences, all of whom contribute to the broader culture of scholarly exchange that makes criticism possible. I would like to thank Jeffrey Di Leo, editor of the *symplokē Studies in Theory* series, as well as the editors at Anthem Press, for their help and encouragement. Colleagues at Texas State University have been supportive, and my students there provide an unlimited reservoir of inspiration. I am especially grateful to Reiko Graham for her love and support, and also to Windy Britches, Steve French, and Nigel Tuffnail for keeping things lively around here.

This book is dedicated to Youngmin Kim, Distinguished Research Professor Emeritus at Dongguk University, Korea, and the Jack Ma Chair Professor at the College of International Studies, Hangzhou Normal University, China, who has been an indefatigable proponent of comparative literary studies and scholarly exchange for many years. I am grateful to him for all he does.

Earlier versions of these chapters first appeared in the following publications, and I want to thank again the editors, referees, publishers, and readers for their valuable feedback and support.

Chapter 1. "Swerve, Trope, Peripety: Turning Points in Criticism and Theory," *Journal of English Language and Literature* 64.1 (March 2018), 25–37.

Chapter 2. "The Aesthetics of Distance: Space, Ideology, and Critique in the Study of World Literature," *Journal of English Language and Literature* 66.1 (2020), 563–586.

Chapter 3. "World Literature and Its Discontents." *Journal of English Language and Literature* 60.3 (2014): 401–419.

Chapter 4. "Worlding Spatiality Studies." *Bloomsbury Handbook on World Theory*, eds. Jeffrey Di Leo and Christian Moraru (New York: Bloomsbury, 2021), 417–426.

Chapter 5. "In the File Drawer Labeled 'Science Fiction': Genre after the Age of the Novel," *Journal of English Language and Literature* 63.2 (2017): 201–217.

Chapter 6. "'Believing in America': The Politics of American Studies in a Post-National Era," *The Americanist* XXIII (2006): 69–81.

Chapter 7. "'Some men ride on such space': Charles Olson's *Call Me Ishmael*, the Melville Revival, and the American Baroque," *49th Parallel: An Interdisciplinary Journal of North American Studies* 31 (Spring 2013): 1–31.

Chapter 8. "The Southern Phoenix Triumphant: Richard Weaver, or, the Origins of Contemporary U.S. Conservatism," *b2o: An Online Journal* of the *boundary 2* editorial group (March 30, 2017): available at http://www.boundary2.org/2017/03/robert-t-tally-jr-the-southern-phoenix-triumphant-richard-weaver-or-the-origins-of-contemporary-u-s-conservatism/.

Chapter 9. "Bleeping Mark Twain?: Censorship, *Huckleberry Finn*, and the Functions of Literature," *Teaching American Literature: A Journal of Theory and Practice* 6.1 (Spring 2013), 97–108.

Chapter 10. "I am the Mainstream Media (and So Can You!)" in *The Stewart/Colbert Effect: Essays on the Real Impact of Fake News*, ed. Amar Amarasingam (Jefferson, NC: McFarland, 2011), 149–163.

Chapter 11. "Nomadography: The 'Early' Deleuze and the History of Philosophy," *Journal of Philosophy: A Cross-Disciplinary Inquiry* 5.11: *Gilles Deleuze*, ed. Daniel Smith (Winter 2010), 15–24.

Chapter 12. "Power to the Educated Imagination!: Northrop Frye and the Utopian Impulse," in *Educating the Imagination: Northrop Frye, Past, Present, and Future*, eds. Alan Bewell, Neil Ten Kortenaar, Germaine Warkentin (Montreal: McGill-Queens University Press, 2015), 83–95.

Chapter 13. "Said, Marxism, and Spatiality: Wars of Position in Oppositional Criticism," *ariel: A Review of International English Literature* 51.1 (2020), 81–103.

Chapter 14. "An American Bakhtin: Jonathan Arac, or, the Vocation of the Critic in the Age of the Novel," *symplokē* 23.1–2 (2015), 407–420.

Chapter 15. "Bathsheba's Stomach; or, *Poiesis* and Criticism in Paul A. Bové's *Love's Shadow*," *symplokē* 29.1–2 (2021), 563–570.

Language included in the Conclusion appeared as "An Anagogical Education," *American Book Review* 38.3 (March/April 2017), 6–7.

INDEX

Abrams, M. H. 229
Adams, Douglas 78
Adams, Henry 132, 234
Adorno, Theodor W. 52, 58n34, 143n16, 129, 201, 202, 206n20, 246, 247
Adorno, Theodor W. 6, 14, 24
Allen, Woody 166
Alquié, Ferdinand 192n32
Althusser, Louis 211, 212
Anderson, Benedict 5, 48, 57n18, 75
Anderson, Perry 120n6
Anker, Elizabeth S. 39n4
Apter, Emily 39n3, 42, 52, 53, 56n1, 58n31, 58n37
Aquinas, Thomas 184
Arac, Jonathan 2, 6, 73–77, 84, 114, 151, 152, 155, 227–229, 257
Arac, Jonathan 7n3, 85n5, 85n7
Arias, Santa 69n2
Aristotle 18, 19, 23n20, 184, 246
Arnold, Matthew 229, 232
Atwater, Lee 137
Atwood, Margaret 79
Auerbach, Erich 13, 44, 51, 52, 55, 57n28, 58n30, 58n31, 216, 222, 253, 254, 255n3
Augé, Marc 67
Aykroyd, Dan 165

Babbitt, Irving 127
Bachelard, Gaston 219, 225n33
Bacon, Francis 182, 192n14, 198
Bakhtin, Mikhail 227, 237, 238, 239n3
Balzac, Honoré de 45, 198, 234, 237

Bancroft, George 94, 233, 234
Barthes, Roland 232
Bate, Walter Jackson 229
Baudelaire, Charles 229, 247
Baudrillard, Jean 160, 162, 163, 176n9, 176n11
Beaver, Harold 153
Beck, Glenn 172
Beckett, Samuel 50
Bee, Samantha 174
Beecroft, Alexander 43, 56n5
Bellamy, Edward 198
Benjamin, Walter 29, 115, 122n42, 227, 229, 232, 238, 239n2, 243–245, 250n6
Bennett, William J. 224n13
Bentham, Jeremy 35
Bercovitch, Sacvan 99, 101, 102n5, 103n6, 103n8, 103n9, 103n17, 154, 157n15, 228, 233, 239n4, 240n12, 240n22
Bergson, Henri 182, 183, 185–187, 190
Berkeley, George 184, 188
Blackmur, R. P. 229
Blake, William 205, 207n30
Bloch, Ernst 212
Bloom, Allan 224n13
Bloom, Harold 232
Blum, Hester 4, 12, 22n1, 67, 70n24
Borges, Jorge Luis 41, 55, 58n43, 163
Bourdieu, Pierre 43
Bové, Paul A. 6, 139, 142n5, 145n49, 243–249, 249n1, 250n3, 250n9, 250n11
Brecht, Bertolt 202

Brodhead, Richard H. 121n10
Brokaw, Tom 165
Brooks, Cleanth 127, 133, 144n33
Brooks, Mel 78
Brooks, Van Wyck 95, 106, 110, 111
Broughton, J. Melville 123
Brouillette, Sarah 26, 39n6, 57n21
Brown, Marshall 12, 22n2, 238
Brown, Robert B. 153, 1156n12
Buchanan, Ian 226n48, 257
Buell, Lawrence 43, 56n3, 120n2
Bunyan, John 245
Burckhardt Jacob 114
Burgis, Ben 176n7
Burke, Kenneth 17, 2n16
Bush, George H. W. 137
Bush, George W. 139, 168–171
Butler, Octavia 77

Carlin, George 155
Carlin, George 157n16
Carlyle, Thomas 228, 231, 239n7
Carroll, Siobhan 67, 70n22
Carter, Jimmy 140
Carter, Paul 220, 225n40
Casanova, Pascale 42, 76, 56n3
Cash, W. J. 140, 141, 143n26, 143n28, 144n28, 145n51
Certeau, Michel de 31
Cervantes, Miguel de 143n25, 237
Chase, Richard 111
Châtelet, François 182, 191n11
Cheah, Pheng 39n3, 69n1
Chesterton, G. K. 83, 86n22
Chibber, Vivek 226n51
Christie, Agatha 157n19
Clinton, Bill 140, 145n50, 167, 168, 171, 173
Colbert, Stephen 160–174, 175n5, 175n7
Coleridge, Samuel Taylor 228, 232, 234
Conrad, Joseph 50, 218, 220, 225n29
Cooper, James Fenimore 94, 150, 233
Cosgrove, Denis 60, 69n3
Creeley, Robert 108, 120n5
Crews, Frederick 98, 103n19

Cronkite, Walter 165
Cuomo, Mario 140
Curtin, Jane 165

D'Haen, Theo 56n6
D'Souza, Dinesh 224n13
Damrosch, David 39n3, 43, 56, 56n4, 57n7, 58n45
Dana, Richard Henry 150, 234
Dante 6, 81, 116, 118, 252–254
Dante 122n47, 225n2
Davidson, Donald 127, 142n7
de Man, Paul 232, 252
Debord, Guy 162, 176n10
Deleuze, Gilles 6, 14, 15, 22n8, 22n9, 22n10, 29, 60, 69n5, 181–191, 191n3, 249
DeLillo, Don 79
Dent, Harry 134
Derrida, Jacques 185, 229, 232, 240n10
Descartes, René 183–185
Di Leo, Jeffrey R. 70n10
Díaz, Junot 79
Dickens, Charles 83, 86n22, 198, 228, 231, 237, 239n7
Dimock, Wai Chee 43, 63, 56n3, 70n13
Doctorow, E. L. 77
Dolzani, Michael 205, 207n29
Donne, John 50
Douglass, Frederick 94, 152, 234

Eagleton, Terry 27, 48, 50, 57n17, 57n23, 74, 85n8, 210, 225n1, 251
Eco, Umberto 160, 163, 175n6
Elden, Stuart 67, 70n23
Elias, Amy J. 63, 64, 70n11
Eliot, George 228
Eliot, T. S. 49, 85n14
Emerson, Ralph Waldo 94, 103n10, 138
Empson, William 230
Engels, Friedrich 36, 40n28, 45–47, 54, 57n10, 57n12, 57n14, 65, 70n18

INDEX

Faulkner, William 198
Felski, Rita 3, 7n5, 7n6, 37, 39n3, 40n29, 257
Feuerbach, Ludwig 213, 224n11
Fichte, Johann Gottlieb 184
Fiedler, Leslie 150, 156n6
Fish, Stanley 244, 250n3
Flaubert, Gustave 229
Focillon, Henri 107, 116, 117, 120n4, 122n44
Foucault, Michel 27, 29, 35, 37, 45, 40n10, 40n27, 57n11, 60, 69n4, 182, 185, 187, 191n11, 192n30, 213, 229, 231, 232, 238
Freud, Sigmund 19, 43, 112
Freud, Sigmund 121n27
Frye, Northrop 6, 34, 84, 195–205, 229, 252, 254
Frye, Northrop 86n25, 206n1, 206n4, 206n9, 206n10, 206n14, 206n17
Fukuyama, Francis 53, 58n36

Gast, Peter 249
Genovese, Eugene D. 144n36
Giddens, Anthony 60
Goethe, Johann Wolfgang von 12, 26, 32, 33, 40n18, 42–45, 49, 53, 229, 234, 237
Golding, William 149, 156n4
Goodwyn, Lawrence 213
Gore, Al 124
Graff, Gerald 2
Graham, Frank Porter 123, 133, 142n1
Gramsci, Antonio 29, 144n36, 210, 222
Gray, Jonathan 170, 177n23
Greenblatt, Stephen 15, 16, Derek 218, 220
Gregory, Derek 218, 220, 225n30
Gribben, Alan 148–151, 153, 154, 1565n2
Guattari, Félix 60, 69n5, 182, 191n12, 192n26

Habermas, Jürgen 100, 104n30
Hannity, Sean 168

Hardt, Michael 185, 186, 192n25, 192n32, 192n33
Harley, J. B. 218, 225n30
Harootunian, Harry 225n18
Hartman, Geoffrey 232
Harvey, David 29, 60, 61, 69n7, 122n49
Hawthorne, Nathaniel 47, 80, 81, 85n19, 94, 108, 120n1, 122n31, 144n33, 239n7, 240n14, 228, 230, 231, 234
Hegel, G. W. F. 11, 47, 53, 181, 183, 184, 191n1, 212
Helms, Jesse 123, 124
Hemingway, Ernest 49
Hirsch, E. D. 224n13
Hoggart, Richard 89, 95, 114
Homer 116–118
Horkheimer, Max 52, 58n34, 129, 143n16
Howe, Stephen 210, 224n2
Hume, David 181–183, 185–190, 191n6
Hume, Kathryn 82, 85n20
Huxley, Aldous 198

Irving, Washington 94, 234
Ishiguro, Kazuo 72, 80

Jackson, Jesse 140
James, C. L. R. 47, 50, 55, 94, 102, 104n32, 112, 117, 121n25, 122n46
Jameson, Fredric 1, 2, 17, 7n4, 18, 20, 23n19, 25, 27, 29, 31, 34, 37, 38, 39n1, 39n7, 40n30, 40n32, 54, 58n41, 60, 61, 68, 69, 69n6, 73, 78, 83, 84, 86n25, 196, 197, 206n5, 206n12, 210–214, 216, 221, 223, 224n8, 224n10, 224n15, 225n43, 226n48, 226n49, 229, 232, 234, 238, 240n10, 240n25, 241n39, 244, 245, 250n5, 252, 250n6, 257
Jefferson, Thomas 15, 211
Jehlen, Myra 98

Jones, Alex S. 176n14
Jones, Jeffrey P. 159, 168, 170, 175n3, 177n20, 177n23, 177n24
Joyce, James 49, 50, 221, 237
Juvan, Marko 58n6

Kafka, Franz 6, 182, 191n12
Kant, Immanuel 182–185, 188, 191n8, 192n19
Kaufmann, Walter 249, 250n12, 250n14
Kennedy, Ted 140
Kermode, Frank 21, 22n3, 229, 231, 232, 240n15
Kerouac, Jack 77
Kilborn, Craig 161, 165–167
Kim, Youngmin 39n5
Kimball, Roger 224n13
Kimble, E. W. 153
Kinkle, Jeff 69
Kirwan, Albert D. 145n46
Konuk, Kader 57n25

Labov, William 31
Lacan, Jacques 82
Lafargue, Paul 48, 57n10
Lamis, Alexander P. 145n45
Lawrence, D. H. 43, 50, 56n3, 93, 120n2, 121n14, 229
Le Guin, Ursula 79, 80, 85n18
Leavis, F. R. 230
Lefebvre, Henri 29, 60
Leibniz, Gottfried Wilhelm 182, 184, 191n11
Leitch, Vincent 229, 239n8
Lentricchia, Frank 61
Leonard, James S. 152, 156n10
Lessing, Doris 237
Letterman, David 175n5
Levin, Harry 114, 122n31, 231
Lewis, R. W. B. 93, 96, 103n15
Leyda, Jay 122n43
Limbaugh, Rush 168
Liming, Sheila 3, 7n5, 257
Linde, Charlotte 31
Longstreet, Augustus Baldwin 234

López, Ian Haney 142n1
Luce, Henry 5, 114, 122n36
Lucretius 14, 15, 22n6, 181, 183, 198
Lukács, Georg 210, 222
Lumet, Sidney 160

MacCabe, Colin 61, 70n9, 214, 224n15
Mailer, Norman 153
Malebranche, Nicolas 184
Mantel, Hilary 79
Marcuse, Herbert 6, 195–200, 204, 205, 206n3, 206n13, 207n31
Martel, Yann 79
Martin, George R. R. 83
Marx, Karl 26, 36, 40n28, 44–47, 49, 51, 52, 54, 55, 57n10, 57n12, 57n15, 65, 203, 209, 210, 212–214, 216, 255
Marx, Leo 89, 90, 92–94, 96, 101, 102n1, 103n7, 103n16, 114, 122n35
Massumi, Brian 186, 192n26
Matthiessen, F. O. 94, 103n10, 106, 109, 111–114, 120n1, 121n26, 121n29, 122n33, 229, 232
Maud, Ralph 121n9
McCarthy, Cormac 72, 79
McClennen, Sophia A. 176n15
McLaughlin, Thomas 61
McMurtry, Larry 79
Melville, Herman 5, 43, 49, 54, 55, 58n41, 94, 102, 105–114, 116–120, 120n1, 121n7, 121n8, 121n12, 121n14, 121n17, 122n31, 122n46, 122n49, 150, 198, 228, 231, 234, 237, 239n7, 240n14
Mencken, H. L. 144n19
Michaels, Walter Benn 98, 121n29
Michelet, Jules 114
Miéville, China 82, 83, 203, 204, 206n23
Miller, D. A. 241n40
Miller, Perry 96, 103n15, 106, 111, 153
Milton, John 119
Mitchell, W. J. T. 224n5
Moi, Toril 37, 40n29

Monmonier, Mark 219, 225n31
Moore, Lorrie 151, 155, 156n8
Moraru, Christian 63, 64, 66, 70n11
More, Paul Elmer 127
More, Thomas 59, 65, 198
Moretti, Franco 27, 29–34, 40n15, 40n17, 40n18, 40n22, 42, 44, 49, 54, 57n22, 75, 230
Morris, William 198
Morrison, Toni 79
Moses, Michael Valdez 58n35
Moylan, Tom 197, 206n7
Mumford, Lewis 93, 106, 110
Murakami, Haruki 79

Nabokov, Vladimir 50
Nealon, Jeffrey 2, 7n4, 257
Nietzsche, Friedrich 27, 42, 181–183, 185–188, 191n7, 192n15, 212, 218, 232, 249, 250n15, 250n14
Nixon, Richard M. 125, 134
Noah, Trevor 169, 174, 175n1, 176n8
North, Joseph 2

O'Reilly, Bill 168, 171, 175n5
Obama, Barack 136
Ohmae, Kenichi 39n6
Oliver, John 174
Olson, Charles 5, 105–113, 115–120, 120n1, 120n3, 121n9, 121n14, 121n28, 122n45, 122n49
Olson, Gary A. 250n4
Orwell, George 35, 77, 151, 198, 201

Padrón, Ricardo 218, 225n30
Paik, Peter Y. 38, 40n31
Parkman, Francis 234
Parnet, Claire 192n17
Parrington, V. L. 93, 95, 233
Pattee, Fred Lewis 110, 111, 121n24
Pease, Donald E. 95, 98, 99, 103n14, 103n18, 103n20, 103n23, 104n24, 113, 120n2, 121n29, 122n33, 122n48, 240n23, 249n2

Plato 184, 185
Poe, Edgar Allan 94, 103n10, 113, 122n31, 152, 234, 240n14
Pratchett, Terry 77, 78, 85n15
Prawer, S. S. 45, 47, 57n15
Prendergast, Christopher 43, 56n3
Proust, Marcel 6, 182, 192n13
Pynchon, Thomas 72, 79, 237

Quayson, Ato 70n17

Rabasa, José 218, 225n30
Rabelais, François 237
Radner, Gilda 161
Ransom, John Crowe 127
Rather, Dan 161, 165
Reagan, Ronald 137, 145n50, 212, 224n13
Rembrandt 243, 244, 247–249
Renker, Elizabeth 95, 103n13
Richards, I. A. 229
Robbins, Bruce 7n2, 40n14, 40n33, 257
Rowe, John Carlos 103n18, 120n2
Rowling, J. K. 72, 149
Rushdie, Salman 53

Sacher-Masoch, Leopold von 182
Said, Edward W. 6, 13, 22n5, 27, 29, 39n9, 44, 51, 52, 54, 55, 101, 102, 209–223, 227, 229, 237, 238, 246
Sanford, Terry 124
Sargent, Lyman Tower 197, 206n6
Sartre, Jean-Paul 1, 18, 49, 210–212, 214, 216, 222
Sassen, Saskia 64, 70n16
Saussy, Huan 43, 56n3
Schelling, Friedrich Wilhelm Joseph von 184
Schlegel, August Wilhelm 229
Schlegel, Friedrich 229
Scholes, Robert 48, 50, 57n16
Scotchie, Joseph 128, 142n8
Scott, Robert 7n6, 257
Scott, Walter 234
Sellars, John 193n36

Shakespeare, William 85n14, 105, 106,
    112, 114, 120n1, 129
Shamir, Milette 99, 104n25
Shippey, Tom 84
Shklovsky, Viktor 202, 206n21
Shumway, David 48, 49, 57n19, 99, 100,
    104n27, 108, 109, 111, 121n11,
    121n15
Simpson, O. J. 234
Smith, Henry Nash 96, 103n15, 111
Smith, Willis 123, 124, 137, 143n18,
    145n46
Smithberg, Madeleine 175n1
Soja, Edward 25, 29, 39n2, 60, 61
Sophocles 19, 23n21
Spanos, William V. 109, 110, 112,
    121n18
Spark, Clare L. 109, 112, 121n17
Spiller, Robert 233
Spinoza, Baruch 181–187, 190, 191,
    191n10, 193n43
Spivak, Gayatri Chakravorty 43, 56n3,
    62, 63, 66, 70n12
Steinberg, Philip E. 67, 70n23
Steiner, George 50, 57n24
Sterne, Lawrence 237
Stewart, Jon 157n16, 159, 161–169, 171–3,
    175n1, 175n4, 175n7
Stowe, Harriet Beecher 94, 110, 233
Surin, Surin 193n44
Swift, Jonathan 78
Sykes, Charles J. 224n13

Taine, Hippolyte 229
Tally, J. O. 124
Tally, Lura S. 124
Tenney, Thomas Asa 152, 156n10
Thomas, Clarence 172
Thompson, E. P. 211
Thompson, Ethan 170
Thoreau, Henry David 94, 138, 234
Thoreau, Henry David 145n47
Thorne, Christian 54, 58n38, 65,
    66, 70n19
Thorpe, Thomas Bangs 234

Thrift, Nigel 61, 40n11, 69n8
Thurmond, Strom 137
Tocqueville, Alexis de 211, 234
Tolkien, J. R. R. 77, 81, 83, 84, 86n23,
    126, 129, 203, 245, 246, 250n7
Tompkins, Jane 98
Toscano, Alberto 69
Tournier, Michel 184, 186, 192n21
Trilling, Lionel 147, 153, 156n1, 230,
    234, 241n27
Trump, Donald 142n2
Turner, Arlin 144n33
Turner, Frederick Jackson 95, 112, 119
Twain, Mark 5, 147–156, 156n2, 228,
    234–236

Underwood, Ted 40n21

Van Doren, Carl 106, 110, 111, 116,
    121n19
Van Gogh, Vincent 247
Vonnegut, Kurt 71–73, 77, 79, 84, 85n1

Wallace, George 125
Wallerstein, Immanuel 54
Walters, Barbara 161
Warf, Barney 69n2
Warren, Robert Penn 127
Watt, Ian 74
Weaver, Raymond 106, 108–111,
    121n13
Weaver, Richard M. 125–141, 142n3,
    143n24, 143n28, 144n36, 145n41,
    145n47, 145n53
Weaver, Richard 5, 52, 58n34
Weber, Max 6
Wellek, René 115, 122n38
Westphal, Bertrand 29, 40n12
White, Hayden 16, 17, 18, 22n13
Whitman, Walt 94, 130n10, 106, 114,
    121n26
Williams, Raymond 29, 46, 61, 74,
    85n6, 133, 144n32, 210, 218
Wilson, Edmund 230
Winstead, Lizz 175n1

Wölfflin, Heinrich 115, 199n39
Woodward, C. Vann 153
Woolf, Virginia 237
Wordsworth, William 228, 231, 232

Yanacek, Hannah 61, 70n9

Zeigler, James 112, 117, 121n28
Zhang, Longxi 56n6
Zhang, Xudong 226n48, 257
Žižek, Slavoj 176n9, 195

www.ingramcontent.com/pod-product-compliance
Lightning Source LLC
Chambersburg PA
CBHW021138230426
43667CB00005B/173